AGRICULTURE AND ECONOMIC GROWTH IN AN OPEN ECONOMY: THE CASE OF ARGENTINA

Domingo Cavallo
Yair Mundlak

Research Report 36
International Food Policy Research Institute
December 1982

Library of Congress Cataloging in Publication Data
Cavallo, Domingo, 1946-
Agriculture and economic growth in an open economy—the case of Argentina.

(Research report ; 36)
Bibliography: p. 160.
1. Agriculture—Economic aspects—Argentina. 2. Argentina—Economic conditions—1945- . I. Mundlak, Yair, 1927- . II. Title. III. Series: Research report (International Food Policy Research Institute) ; 36.
HD1862.C35 1982 388.1′0982 82-23288
ISBN 0-89629-037-9

CONTENTS

TABLES

ILLUSTRATIONS

FOREWORD

It is increasingly obvious that the progress of agricultural development is important to the total processes of development. It is becoming equally obvious that policies often thought of as extraneous to agriculture affect agriculture profoundly. These circumstances raise concerns. To be more precise, decisions from finance ministries, planning ministries, and central banks, among others, about exchange rates, taxation, credit, and other policies have major, even overwhelming, effects on agriculture. In this report Yair Mundlak and Domingo Cavallo provide a model that makes it possible to explore the effects and the interaction of agriculture with other sectors of the economy. They then apply this model to a large body of data, providing a case study of Argentina. The research is a cooperative effort between the International Food Policy Research Institute (IFPRI) and the Instituto de Estudios Económicos Sobre la Realidad Argentina y Latino Americana (IEERAL) of the Fundación Mediterránea. Both institutes bring a wealth of related research and commitment to this subject.

Yair Mundlak's earlier work on this topic, *Intersectoral Factor Mobility and Agricultural Growth* (Research Report 6, March 1979) was awarded the American Agricultural Economics Association award for quality of research discovery. That work provided the basic background for the present study. Similar research is being actively pursued in collaboration with the Universidad Católica in Chile, and other work is under consideration. In addition, IFPRI has begun a major set of field studies that looks at specific aspects of the relation between agricultural growth and employment expansion. These aspects include factor shares, income distribution, consumption effects, and employment multipliers. This micro work will relate to the macro work and culminate in a full set of recommendations for increasing the efficiency of development and development policies, particularly with respect to the agricultural sector.

Similarly, the Fundación Mediterránea has published most of Domingo Cavallo's research on the working of the Argentine economy and his contributions to the discussions on economic policymaking in Argentina. Fundación Mediterránea has several studies under way examining development and stabilization issues in Argentina and Latin America.

IFPRI and the Fundación Mediterránea are delighted at the opportunity to combine our respective experience and resources on this important question. We believe this research is valuable in its own right and provides a necessary base for a number of extensions to specific policy questions, which we plan as a next step.

John W. Mellor
Director, IFPRI

Carlos A. Givogri
Acting Director,
IEERAL—Fundación Mediterránea

December 1982

ACKNOWLEDGMENTS

The burden of translating ideas into numerical results was shouldered faithfully by Rafael Conejero of the Fundación Mediterránea and Dwight Peterson of IFPRI. In revising the manuscript, we benefited from the comments of Victor Elías, Lucio Reca, Ammar Siamwalla, and several anonymous reviewers. The report was edited by Phyllis Skillman and James Voorhees with the assistance of Uday Mohan.

1

SUMMARY

It is well known that agriculture's share of output shrinks in the process of economic growth. A major reason for this is that the income elasticities for food are small. However, this explanation is only true for a closed economy. For an open economy that does not significantly affect world prices, the capacity of the domestic market does not limit the expansion of agricultural output. Thus, lack of development cannot be attributed to a lack of demand. Nevertheless, there are countries producing primary agricultural commodities for the international market that have shown little growth over a long period of time. A good example is Argentina, whose per capita agricultural output in the seventies was less than before World War II. This creeping growth occurred while agriculture elsewhere underwent the green revolution and many countries changed their agricultural production dramatically.

Why has agriculture grown so slowly in a country with so much potential and a history of economic vigor? It cannot be the physical environment: Argentina's agricultural conditions are excellent. It cannot be a random occurrence because it has lasted so long. It can only be attributed to the economic environment and policies of the country. This assertion should be evaluated against the historical record.

The data indicate that the average rate of growth of agricultural production for the period 1940-72 in Argentina was 1.4 percent per year. During the same period, the output of the rest of the economy (nonagriculture) grew 3.7 percent per year, agricultural labor declined by 0.4 percent, and nonagricultural labor increased by 2.3 percent, indicating a migration of labor out of agriculture. Meanwhile, capital stock grew 3.0 percent per year in nonagriculture and 3.7 percent in agriculture. By aggregating the rates of change of the inputs weighted by their factor shares, the average annual rate of growth of the total factor is obtained—2.5 percent in nonagriculture and 0.8 percent in agriculture. As a result, the residual obtained as the difference between rates of growth of output and total factor was 1.2 percent for nonagriculture and 0.6 percent for agriculture. These aggregate calculations show that agriculture was losing resources to nonagriculture and that its productivity grew more weakly.

The intersectoral factor allocation is explained by the different rates of factor remunerations. Agricultural wages were less than half nonagricultural wages, and this gap did not close during the period. The ex post return on capital showed a similar pattern; the average for the period as a whole was 7.8 percent for agriculture and 14.5 percent for nonagriculture, and the gap between the two tended to increase. The stronger increase in agricultural capital stock can be attributed to capital using technical change and to special programs of agricultural credit. In spite of this, however, agriculture remained less profitable than nonagriculture. It is postulated that low profits were also the reason for the weakness of the increase of agricultural productivity. In other words, it is postulated that the production function is not a pure physical relationship; it also depends on the economic environment. Consequently, factor productivities can be explained by economic variables.

Why was the profitability of agriculture so low? Quite simply, the prices received by farmers for their products were low relative to the prices they paid for their inputs. These prices were very different from the international prices. Agricultural prices were kept down using several institutional instruments. These took the form of taxes and tariffs, quantitative restrictions like quotas or bans, price controls, and credit rationing. A relatively low real exchange rate, that is, high prices of nontraded nonagricultural goods relative to traded goods, was maintained by way of price control regimes affecting mainly agriculture and manufacturing combined with fixed nominal exchange rates, high government expenditures oriented mainly toward nontraded goods, taxation schemes that provided more loopholes or possibilities of evasion for services than manufacturing, and similar devices.

Analytically, these instruments represented two policies: first, to put an implicit tax on agricultural exports; and second, to maintain a low real exchange rate. Conversely, the prices of nonagricultural traded goods, though reduced by the low real exchange rate, were kept high through implicit tariff protection. The result of the implicit tax was to extract, on average for the period 1940-73, 50 percent of agricultural output evaluated at factor cost. Obviously, there were wide variations. Taxes on agriculture were highest during the Second World War and immediately thereafter when foreign terms of trade favored agriculture. These taxes were reduced significantly after 1950 when foreign terms of trade became less favorable, but they still took 30 percent of agricultural output in the period 1950-73.

This extraction, of course, forced funds to flow out of agriculture, but it seems that the low profitability of agriculture made part of the flow voluntary. The average rate of savings generated by agricultural income for the period was 50 percent, whereas investment in agriculture was much smaller. As a consequence, the voluntary flow of funds out of agriculture averaged 30.6 percent of the factor cost of agricultural output. This indicates that investment opportunities in agriculture were perceived as poor.

On the other hand, nonagriculture was heavily protected. If resource productivity depends on profitability, then one would expect a more vigorous increase in factor productivity in that sector than in agriculture. Indeed the analysis indicates that the growth of productivity for the two sectors differed, reflecting the economic forces involved.

This study presents a framework for analyzing the development of the Argentine economy, particularly agriculture, and applies it to the period 1940-72. This analysis can be looked at from several angles. It can be viewed as a case study of the Argentine experience. But any case study, properly conducted, has general implications. It can also be viewed as a study of sectoral growth and development where the factors affecting growth are identified and quantified. The empirical results can then be compared with other cases to verify or modify the hypotheses about growth and development. This task, however, is not as simple as it may appear, for there is no quick method for dealing with these issues in the detail they require. This study extends the framework used in an earlier study for a closed economy to an analysis of an open economy. Thus, it is also a study of how to analyze sectoral growth. Finally, by its nature it is an empirical study, estimating various economic relationships using past data and suggesting new approaches for similar analyses, particularly of production.

Some readers may be interested only in the Argentine experience and others only in subtle methodological issues. However, in this study the Argentine experience is not evaluated independently of the analytical framework. It is this feature that distinguishes the approach and the results of this study from other studies.

The framework formulated reconstructs the Argentine experience. The economy is divided into two sectors, agriculture and nonagriculture. The latter, all parts of the economy other than agriculture, implicitly includes traded and nontraded goods and a government that collects indirect taxes and spends them on nonagriculture for public consumption. The intersectoral resource allocation, technology, and output of each sector at any one time are given. The utilization of output is determined by the demand for its components. The demand for final consumption is determined by relative prices and permanent consumption. Three functions determine the demand for investment goods: an overall investment function, a function that allocates investment between sectors, and a function that assigns the origin of agricultural investment. Indirect taxes collected from exports, imports, and domestic transactions are all spent on nonagricultural consumption. Agricultural exports and nonagricultural imports are treated as residuals. Tax policy and foreign prices determine the real rate of exchange and the domestic product and factor prices. These, in turn, determine productivity and intersectoral resource allocation.

An important objective in formulating the model is to confront it with the data to determine its relevance. Consequently, equations are estimated for consumption, demand, investment, investment allocation, labor migration, cultivated land, and the real exchange rate. These equations are used to simulate the past performance of the economy. The exogenous variables are foreign prices, rates of indirect taxes, population, depreciation rates, unemployment rates, share of agriculture in total credit, and a monetary variable measuring the excess supply of domestic credit.

The model, consisting of a small number of behavioral equations suggested by basic economic theory, successfully reproduces the main patterns of Argentine growth, including the postwar decline in agricultural production and the slow recovery in the 1960s. It accurately describes the postwar boom in nonagricultural output, the decline during the early 1950s, and the rapid growth of nonagriculture in the following decades. And, although the government intervened extensively by setting wages and prices, the main trends of factor prices are satisfactorily captured. Thus, government policies were successful only in dampening the cyclical variations of real wages and augmenting the variability of the returns to capital.

The keys to this simple explanation lie in the formulation of resource allocation and of changes in productivity. In explaining the response of the economy to economic forces, it is essential to take the current state of the economy into account explicitly. In dealing with economic dynamics it is not meaningful to start with a concept of long-term equilibrium and infer from it the present movements of the economy. On the contrary, such movements are largely determined by the state of the economy. Whether or not the economy will eventually reach the long-term equilibrium point presently perceived depends largely on the economic signals that develop.

The foregoing discussion suggests that alternative policies had to be considered by Argentine policymakers. The first alternative, referred to as trade liberalization, involves the elimination of the implicit tax on agriculture and the implicit tariff on nonagricultural imports. The effect of such policies on the system of equations and parameters in this study is evaluated using the historical values of the exogenous variables and thereby generating a growth path that can be compared to the path fitted to the data. The comparison shows that the hypothetical trade liberalization, accompanied by the same fiscal and monetary policies that were actually applied, led to a decline in the real exchange rate, thereby reducing the prices of agricultural products and diluting the effect of tax reduction on agricultural prices. This reduction in the real exchange rate and the elimination of the implicit tariff on imports reduced incentives to the traded component of nonagriculture, whose productivity, according to the empirical results, grew more than the productivity of the nontraded component. As a consequence, per capita output of nonagriculture decreases more than the corresponding increase in agriculture and the performance of the economy under this alternative policy would have been worse than it actually was.

The second alternative is to try to prevent the real exchange rate from falling in response to trade liberalization. Trade liberalization is then accompanied by a policy referred to as exchange rate management. This implies fiscal and monetary policies that aim at keeping the real exchange rate about 20 percent above the rate realized under trade liberalization alone. This is compatible with the historical rate. As a result, the price of nontraded goods was kept low relative to the price of traded goods.

This combination of trade liberalization and exchange rate management produces impressive increases, of between 30-40 percent in 20 years, in both agricultural and nonagricultural per capita output. Furthermore, it shows that it is the combination of trade liberalization and exchange rate management and not simply the latter that produces these impressive results.

The combined policy of trade liberalization and exchange rate management causes the price of food to increase more than nonagricultural wages or simply causes the food wage to decline. Food wages were a target of policy, primarily during the Perón government. The policy was to keep food wages high to protect the standard of living of the urban workers. This consideration suggests an examination of an alternative policy where a food subsidy is introduced to prevent the food wage from declining as a result of trade liberalization and real exchange rate management. This alternative results in an increase of about 25 percent in the overall per capita growth of the economy.

Trade liberalization and exchange rate management create incentives to agriculture unrealized in the period 1940-73. For that matter, it is suggested that under such an improved economic environment for agriculture the improvement in productivity will exceed the estimated response based on the sample. A simulation taking this hypothesis into account shows that the quantitative impact of such a possible outcome is rather substantial. That enhances the scope for growth following trade liberalization with exchange rate management.

Another way to encourage growth is to invest some of the indirect taxes used by the government instead of spending them. If 20 percent of the taxes collected were invested, they would expand production significantly. This would increase the amount of inputs required and consequently call for increased foreign savings. Therefore this policy could be complemented with trade liberalization, which has an opposite effect on foreign saving.

The dependence of the economy on world prices is examined by evaluating exogenous changes in the foreign terms of trade of agriculture relative to nonagriculture. If the real exchange rate were isolated from such changes and maintained at about what it was historically, the response of the economy would be as expected. The overall performance of the economy is directly related to the terms of trade. An improvement in the terms of trade leads to growth in the per capita output of both sectors. The extent of that growth depends strongly on domestic policies. The exercises show how an improvement in the terms of trade tends to be more than neutralized when a fall in the real exchange rate is induced and how an active domestic macro policy is called for to take full advantage of the improved terms of trade. On the other hand, it is shown that a deterioration of the terms of trade has less depressing effects than if a compensatory increase in the real exchange rate, such as the one shown by the exchange rate equation, did not occur.

The model is used to evaluate all of these alternatives. The outcomes of the evaluations are alternative growth paths of the economy for the period 1950-71. They are complete in that they produce all the endogenous variables of the system.

There is no easy way to present the results. To concentrate on the substance, the discussion of the supporting empirical analysis is postponed to the last three chapters. After an introductory chapter that provides an historical framework, the structure of the model is described. The model is then fitted to the data, using the results of the empirical analysis discussed in the last three chapters.

Chapters 3-6 can be read without studying the methodology and detailed analysis in Chapters 7-9, but to do that requires taking a few results on faith. The basic data on which the study is based appear in the appendixes.

2

A BRIEF HISTORICAL DESCRIPTION

During the last three decades of the nineteenth century and the first three decades of the twentieth, Argentina's economy grew rapidly. The basis of this growth was crop production and cattle raising for export. Manufacturing and services developed as population and income increased. From time to time, when financial crises or wars interrupted imports, the production of import substitutes was encouraged.

Between 1869 and 1929 the population grew by 3.2 percent a year, exports by 5.5 percent, imports by 4.6 percent, and cultivated land by 6.5 percent. Transportation facilities, developed by foreign investors attracted by the favorable conditions created by the government, helped to integrate the production of the pampas with expanding world markets. The railroad system increased from 503 kilometers in the mid-1860s to 38,000 kilometers in 1930. Figures in national accounts are not available for the whole period, but the indicators available suggest that the economy was growing at a cumulative rate of about 5 percent a year.[1]

This period of rapid growth was temporarily interrupted by financial crises in 1875-76, 1890-91, and during World War I. But though these crises affected the flow of foreign capital and drastically reduced investment, each one was followed by a period of renewed growth.[2]

The Great Depression of the 1930s and the interruption of world trade that followed severely affected Argentine economic performance and changed the prevailing thinking. The first reaction of the government was to intervene in agricultural markets to diminish the harmful effects the disruption in foreign trade had on farm income. The persistence of the decline and the new disruption associated with World War II finally led to a policy of industrialization emphasizing manufacturing oriented toward import substitution. Such a development strategy was in accordance with the ideology that has been dominant since then.

The political aspects of this ideology were manifested by the development of the Peronist movement, which became powerful during the 1940s. After a decade of declining real wages and deteriorating living conditions for the working class, the movement, backed by the trade unions, adopted as its main goal the redistribution of income in favor of workers, especially urban workers. The most natural way to shift the income and economic power of landowners to urban workers and the trade unions was to change the structure of production from land-intensive agriculture to the more labor-intensive manufacturing industries and urban services. This important political shift is described by Mallon and Sourrouille:

> At the time the Argentina pampas was opened up to the world trade boom in the latter part of the last century, agricultural property was so concentrated that a relatively small elite was able to appropriate most of the benefits of agricultural expansion. The cattle barons and the so-called agro-exportador oligarchy, who virtually monopolized political power up to World War I and continued to exercise considerable influence in later years, were closely identified with foreign trading and financial interests and with antiprotectionist, antinationalist and antipopular policies. After national populism came to power under the leadership of Perón in

[1] See Carlos F. Diaz Alejandro, *Essays on the Economic History of the Argentine Republic* (New Haven, Conn.: Yale University Press, 1970).

[2] See Aldo Ferrer, *La Economía Argentina: Las Etapas de su Desarrollo y Problemas Actuales* (Mexico: Fondo de Cultura Económica, 1963).

1943, the pendulum of policy swung violently in the opposite direction and never again returned to its initial position.[3]

The economic ideology of Argentina developed from a strong belief that the terms of international trade were deteriorating; consequently, the country should reduce its dependence on exports of primary products. The main instruments used to execute this development strategy were exchange controls, tariffs, prohibitions, other restrictions on imports, taxes on agricultural exports and, since the early 1960s, subsidies for nonagricultural exports. Other instruments used were multiple exchange rates, selective credit policies and other forms of direct intervention by the government in setting wages and prices, and the allocation of expenditures through the growing government budget.

The model developed and estimated in this report is designed to trace the effects of the main economic policies that were followed, especially those of trade restrictions, exchange rate management, and domestic taxation. The study concentrates on the evaluation of the effects of those policies on resource allocation, technical change, factor prices, and the rates of growth of the whole economy and of two sectors, agriculture and nonagriculture, which includes all parts of the economy except agriculture. The analysis begins with World War II. To assist readers who are not familiar with the history of the Argentine economy, a brief summary of the main political and economic events that have taken place since the early forties is provided.

Main Political and Economic Events Since the Second World War

The association of the main political events and changes in economic policies with the actual performance of the economy can be seen in Table 1, which presents annual rates of growth between designated five-year periods.

By the end of the 1930s, the Argentine economy had not completely recovered from the Great Depression, though some of its effects were reduced. This period of slow growth contrasted sharply with the rapid growth of previous decades.

World War II interrupted the slow recovery of the world markets. Foreign trade was severely restricted. At the same time, domestic political changes were taking place. These were the first indications of changes in the country's dominant political and economic ideology, although their effects on factor prices were not yet evident. Nor did they immediately affect the growth of the economy and resource allocation; they did, however, lead to major changes in long-term trends. Between the periods1935-39 and 1940-44 overall GDP grew at an annual rate of 2.8 percent, with agriculture growing by 2.6 percent a year and nonagriculture by 2.9 percent. Substantial changes took place in economic policies, especially after the change of government in 1943. The terms of trade for agricultural goods in foreign markets provoked by the war deteriorated an average of 3.7 percent a year between 1935 and 1944. The terms of trade for those goods in the domestic market declined about three times as much, with an average decrease of 9.2 percent a year. At the same time, the real exchange rate was decreasing at an annual rate of 1.1 percent. Agricultural goods were becoming cheaper in relation to both imported and nontraded goods.

The regime that emerged from the military coup of 1943 continued after the unrestricted general elections of 1945 that made Perón the undisputed leader. He dominated the next decade. As World War II ended, he faced unusual conditions. Argentina had accumulated large foreign reserves and its economic structure was not damaged by the war. While world

[3]Richard D. Mallon and Juan V. Sourrouille, *Economic Policymaking in a Conflict Society* (Cambridge, Mass.: Harvard University Press, 1975).

Table 1—Indicators for the Argentine economy, 1900-74

Variable	1900-04 to 1925-29	1925-29 to 1930-34	1930-34 to 1935-39	1935-39 to 1940-44	1940-44 to 1945-49	1945-49 to 1950-54	1950-54 to 1955-59	1955-59 to 1960-64	1960-64 to 1964-69	1964-69 to 1970-74
X	4.6	0.4	3.3	2.8	4.4	1.6	4.0	3.0	4.8	5.6
X_1	3.5	0.0	2.6	2.6	−0.2	0.4	2.5	1.3	2.6	1.0
X_2	5.0	0.5	3.5	2.9	5.9	1.9	4.3	3.3	5.2	6.4
I	4.6	−7.7	4.1	0.9	18.4	3.8	2.7	6.0	3.8	6.8
X^e	3.4	−1.3	0.0	−1.4	3.0	−9.1	10.5	4.4	2.6	6.7
X^m	3.6	−9.5	3.4	−5.3	10.2	−3.2	13.0	2.9	−2.1	8.0
N	2.8	2.5	1.7	1.8	1.8	2.3	2.0	1.7	1.5	1.4
L_2	...	...	...	5.5	6.4	3.4	1.2	0.7	1.9	2.7
K_1	...	...	...	−4.2	−0.5	0.7	4.4	6.7	5.9	7.5
K_2	...	...	...	0.5	0.5	3.4	3.0	3.8	4.1	6.1
w_1	...	...	...	−3.2	−1.5	5.4	−0.2	−1.3	5.6	4.5
w_2	...	...	...	−1.8	1.0	1.9	0.1	0.4	4.6	3.1
p_A	...	...	...	0.3	2.4	−1.2	5.1	5.0	3.7	5.2
p_1/p_2^{nd}	...	...	...	−9.2	5.9	6.0	−0.9	1.0	−0.7	1.7
p_1^f/p_2^f	...	...	...	−3.7	11.0	−8.8	−3.7	1.6	−0.3	4.6
REp^f	...	...	...	−1.1	−8.2	−12.6	25.4	0.2	−4.5	1.1
s_f	...	...	−271	−411	−308	23	107	63	−181	−180

Notes: All variables except foreign savings (s_f) are average annual rates of growth between two five-year periods. Foreign savings are in millions of 1960 pesos. All indexes with the subscript 1 are for agriculture; all indexes with the subscript 2 are for nonagriculture. Lack of a sectoral index implies a total for the economy. X is GDP at factor cost, I is investment, X^e is exports, X^m is imports, N is population, L is labor force, K is stock of capital, w is real wages, p_A is the price of land. p_1/p_2^{nd} is the terms of trade of agriculture relative to imported goods prevailing domestically. p_1^f/p_2^f is the same measure for the foreign market. REp^f is the real exchange rate inflated by p^f where p^f is the weighted average of p_1^f and p_2^f and the weights are the shares of exports and imports of the two sectors in total trade.

trends that evolved from the Great Depression and the war that encouraged countries to close their economies were beginning to reverse, Argentina adopted still stronger policies of import substitution and expansion of urban services. These policies, aimed at closing the economy, were in sharp contrast to the revival and expansion of world trade that occurred during the1950s and 1960s. Between 1940-44 and 1945-49, the upward swing of the Perónist cycle, real GDP grew at an average annual rate of 4.4 percent. Agricultural production actually decreased at a rate of 0.2 percent a year and the bulk of the growth took place in nonagriculture, which expanded 5.9 percent a year. The capital stock in agriculture continued to decline, as it had in the previous period, whereas capital in nonagriculture grew. Urban wages rose 1 percent a year while agricultural wages declined, and labor migrated to the cities.[4]

The bias against agriculture continued, although some relief came from changing trends in foreign markets. Foreign terms of trade improved by 11 percent a year. However, this change was only partly transmitted to the domestic market, where the average increase amounted to 5.9 percent a year. Perón used the increase in foreign agricultural prices to improve the profitability of the production and nontraded goods and services, mostly the latter. This was done by reducing the real exchange rate, which declined at an annual average rate of 8.2 percent.

By 1950 the Perónist boom was over, and the country faced difficult problems. The stagnation of agriculture and the increase in domestic consumption seriously affected traditional exports. Between the periods 1945-49 and 1950-54 exports declined an average of 9 percent a year. Indeed, this phenomenon was augmented by the drought of 1951/52 and the deterioration of foreign terms of trade. Imports were also reduced but only by 3.5 percent a year. As a consequence, a balance-of-payments problem signaled the need for a change in policies. While foreign terms of trade decreased 8.8 percent a year, the domestic terms improved by 6 percent a year. This made agricultural goods more expensive. But to keep real wages high, the government continued to hold down the real exchange rate, thereby reducing the prices of exportables and importables in terms of domestic goods. The real exchange rate declined at an average rate of 12.6 percent a year. Urban real wages increased at an average rate of 2 percent a year, whereas agricultural wages increased 5.4 percent a year, reflecting the scarcity of labor in rural areas resulting from past migration.

During this period, overall GDP grew an average of only 1.6 percent a year, agriculture was still stagnant, growing only 0.4 percent a year, and nonagriculture grew 1.9 percent a year. These figures indicate that a reversal of the trend was taking place.

Although Perón was forced by events to introduce changes in his early policies, especially for agriculture, it was only after a military coup took him out of office in 1955 that substantial changes in economic policy were made. The new military government restored incentives to farmers and accelerated the accumulation of capital in agriculture. The real exchange rate increased at an average rate of 25 percent a year. Simultaneously, foreign terms of trade for agriculture deteriorated 3.7 percent a year, but the domestic terms of trade declined by only 1 percent a year. In other words, although the domestic prices of agricultural goods were more or less constant in relation to the price of imports, they increased significantly for nontraded goods. These policies caused agriculture to become more profitable, as the 5.1 percent a year increase in the price of land shows. The stock of capital in agriculture rose 4.4 percent a year compared to a 3 percent increase in the stock of capital in nonagriculture. The rate of growth of the economy averaged 4 percent a year, with agriculture growing at a rate of 2.5 percent and nonagriculture at a rate of 4.3 percent.

---

[4]Lucio Reca has pointed out that the outflow of labor from agriculture in the period 1940–55 included a large number of skilled workers, which meant a loss of human capital.

In 1958 the new constitutional government emphasized capital accumulation to accelerate economic growth and adopted this as a national goal. No important changes were introduced into agricultural policies. The attempts to develop the basic sectors of the economy were successful at first and attracted foreign investors. The new policies brought the economy close to self-sufficiency in petroleum production, which in later years proved to be an important contribution to Argentine economic development. By 1962, however, the economy had entered into a deep recession as a consequence of a balance-of-payments crisis. The president was ousted from office by a military coup in that year.

In 1963 the new constitutional government addressed its policies to recovery. Its sectoral economic policies followed the trends begun after 1955. The real price of land increased an average of 5 percent a year between the periods 1955-59 and 1960-64. The stock of capital in agriculture increased by 6.7 percent a year and in nonagriculture by 3.8 percent. Overall GDP grew an average of 3 percent a year, with agriculture growing 1.3 percent and nonagriculture, 3.3 percent. Real wages remained almost constant, as they had in the previous period.

In mid-1966 a military coup again replaced the constitutional government. The new authorities implemented an economic program aimed at fighting inflation and increasing the efficiency of the economy. The attempt to stabilize prices harmed agriculture. The real exchange rate for exports deteriorated an average of 4 percent a year between 1960-64 and 1965-69. In addition, the domestic prices of agricultural products decreased an average of 1.4 percent a year relative to imported goods, twice as fast as prices fell in world markets. But there was still fair growth in agriculture, 2.6 percent a year. In 1968 and 1969 the stock of cattle was drastically reduced because low prices for beef were expected.[5] The economy as a whole grew 4.8 percent per year and nonagriculture grew 5.2 percent per year. Urban real wages also increased 4.6 percent. From 1970 to the beginning of 1973 the regime focused its attention on the transition of the government to political parties. Anti-inflationary targets were abandoned, and agricultural policy was aimed at improving the terms of trade. The domestic terms of trade increased 6.4 percent a year, whereas the foreign terms of trade improved by 1.7 percent a year. The real exchange rate also increased 1 percent a year. The economy grew an average of 5.6 percent a year, though agriculture grew only 1 percent a year. The low rate of growth reflects the drop in beef production that followed the liquidation of stocks in 1968/69.

Questions to be Addressed

This brief description of political events, changes in economic policy, and the performance of the economy suggests interrelations that seem to be supported by the aggregate data in Table 1. But there are figures that do not fit easily into such a simple interaction of observed facts. Even when facts seem to be clearly related, the causality, the strength of the relationship, and the speed of adjustment to changes are not obvious. The analytical framework developed in this research tries to organize the available information to provide more precise answers to questions that are suggested by this brief description of historical events.

It is apparent from Table 1 that the structure of the economy has changed significantly during the last 40 years, and these changes seem to be related to changes in economic policies and foreign events. But what were the main channels enabling economic policies to affect resource allocation and sectoral growth and how long did the adjustment process take?

---

[5]Juan Carlos De Pablo, *Politica Antiinflacionaria en la Argentina 1967–1970* (Buenos Aires: Amorrortu Editores, 1972).

The purpose of the postwar policies was to shift the distribution of income in favor of wages. How were factor prices affected by the shifts in economic policies, especially trade restrictions and exchange rate policies? How did these effects change and how were they related to technical change? How were technical change and changes in productivity in general affected by economic policies?

The economic policies followed after World War II have been justified on the grounds that the domestic economy needed to be protected from the deterioration in foreign terms of trade. How important was such a deterioration and how could it have been offset by domestic policies? These and related questions are discussed in what follows.

3

THE STRUCTURE OF THE MODEL

This model is based on a closed-economy model used for Japan,[6] but it contains the modifications and extensions required for dealing with an open economy. In addition, it allows for indirect domestic taxes and for taxes and tariffs on foreign trade. It may be simpler to present the model in stages, starting with a simplified version. In spite of its simplicity, this version contains the core of the model. Subsequent versions add details that are necessary to confront the model with the data.

The Economy at Time t, First Representation

The economy is assumed to consist of agriculture (sector 1) and nonagriculture (sector 2). At any time t the technology and the resource allocation between the two sectors are predetermined. Consequently, outputs are also predetermined. The economic problem in the short run is to distribute the outputs of the two sectors among the outlets they can go to. The number of outlets and the sources of supply depend on the level of aggregation. Here it is assumed that agriculture is a net exporter and that nonagriculture is a net importer. Accordingly, there are three outlets for the agricultural product, final consumption ($X_1^{c,s}$), investment (X_1^{i}), and export (X_1^{e}).[7] Government consumption is not taken into account explicitly. There are two sources of supply for nonagricultural products, production (X_2) and import (X_2^{m}), and they are used for consumption ($X_2^{c,s}$) and investment (X_2^{i}). The identities are written using lowercase letters to denote per capita values:

$$x_1(t) = x_1^{c,s}(t) + x_1^{i}(t) + x_1^{e}(t), \tag{3.1}$$

and

$$x_2(t) + x_2^{m}(t) = x_2^{c,s}(t) + x_2^{i}(t). \tag{3.2}$$

All variables are functions of time as indicated above. However, in the remaining discussion, the dependence of the variables on time will not be explicitly indicated unless it becomes necessary to avoid ambiguity.

Outputs are predetermined, but each of the other components in equations (3.1) and (3.2) must be determined.

Composition of Final Consumption

The equilibrium conditions to be imposed below require that the quantity demanded ($x_j^{c,d}$) be equal to the quantity supplied ($x_j^{c,s}$). The quantities demanded are determined by the

---

[6]Yair Mundlak, *Intersectoral Factor Mobility and Agricultural Growth,* Research Report 6 (Washington, D.C.: International Food Policy Research Institute, 1979).

[7]Quantities of outputs and their components are denoted by Xs. Value terms are denoted by other letters and, where possible, notations are used that are common in the literature.

demand equations. The demand for final consumption is given in equations (3.3) and (3.4). Let c represent per capita consumption and p the price ratio of output of sector 1 in terms of output of sector 2, then

$$x_1^{c,d} = D_1(p,c), \tag{3.3}$$

and

$$x_2^{c,d} = D_2(p,c), \tag{3.4}$$

It is assumed that the income elasticities are positive, the price elasticities are negative, and that for any $p > 0$ and $c > 0$ there is positive demand for the products of both sectors.

Consumption and Domestic Savings

Per capita consumption is determined by the consumption function,

$$c = c(y^p), \tag{3.5}$$

where y^p is the vector of permanent incomes by their sources. The sources of income can be defined by factors and sectors, as discussed in Chapter 8. What is important for the present discussion is that permanent income is determined by present income and past income. Per capita income is given by

$$y = px_1 + x_2.$$

Because all variables on the right-hand side of this equation are predetermined in t, so is per capita income. Consequently, per capita consumption, as given in equation (3.5), is also predetermined. With per capita consumption determined, demand equations determine $x_j^{c,d}$. The equilibrium conditions are imposed,

$$x_j^{c,d} = x_j^{c,s} = x_j^c, \tag{3.6}$$

and per capita consumption is written as

$$c = px_1^c + x_2^c.$$

Note that by determining x_j^c, equations (3.1) and (3.2) can be rewritten as

$$x_1^i + x_1^e = x_1 - x_1^c, \tag{3.7}$$

and

$$x_2^i - x_2^m = x_2 - x_2^c, \tag{3.8}$$

where the right-hand side is predetermined. There are several ways to solve for the remaining variables, x_j^i, x_1^e, and x_2^m.

Autonomous Investment

Assuming for the time being that investment is determined by variables that are all predetermined at time t, the investment function is denoted by

$$i = i(\ ). \tag{3.9}$$

The allocation of total investment to the two sectors is postulated to depend upon the expected differential rates of return in the two sectors. This dependence is expressed by

$$i_1 = \theta(\ )\, i, \tag{3.10}$$

and

$$i_2 = [1 - \theta(\cdot)]\, i, \tag{3.11}$$

where $\theta(\ )$ is a function that assumes values between zero and one. The specification of $\theta(\cdot)$ is discussed with the empirical estimation in Chapter 8. What is relevant for the present discussion is that θ is specified by variables that are predetermined in time t.

In order to relate the sectoral investments to demand for sectoral outputs, note that investment in agriculture consists of products of agriculture, such as livestock and land improvement, and products of nonagriculture, such as machines. The investment in nonagriculture is assumed to originate solely in nonagriculture. Consequently, the production of investment goods by nonagriculture is determined by the demand for such goods generated in that sector and by the demand of agriculture. This assumption can now be expressed as

$$x_1^i = \lambda(\ )\, i_1/p, \tag{3.12}$$

and

$$x_2^i = [1 - \lambda(\ )]\, i_1 + i_2. \tag{3.13}$$

The allocation of agricultural investment to the two sectors is represented by the function $\lambda(\ )$, which takes on values between zero and one.[8] This function is also discussed in Chapter 8.

Combining equations (3.10) to (3.13),

$$x_1^i = a\, i/p, \tag{3.14}$$

and

$$x_2^i = (1 - a)\, i, \tag{3.15}$$

where a is the product of the two functions, $a = \lambda\theta$.

[8]When livestock constitutes an important component of investment it is possible to have in some years negative values for x_2^i and hence for λ. However, in order to avoid too many details at this stage, this possibility is ignored here.

Consequently, x_1^i and x_2^i are determined by i. Then for any given i, imports and exports are residuals:

$$x_1^e = x_1 - x_1^c(\ \ ) - x_1^i(\ \ ), \tag{3.16}$$

and

$$- x_2^m = x_2 - x_2^c(\ \ ) - x_2^i(\ \ ). \tag{3.17}$$

Having determined the quantities of exports and imports, foreign savings (s_f) are determined:

$$s_f = x_2^m - p\, x_1^e. \tag{3.18}$$

Note that foreign savings are determined so that they generate the equality of saving and investment. This can be seen by simply substituting equations (3.16) and (3.17) in equation (3.18) to obtain $- s_f = y\text{-}c\text{-}i$. But y-c is domestic saving, to be denoted as s_d, so

$$i = s_f + s_d \equiv s. \tag{3.19}$$

A number of features help to simplify the structure of the system. Sectoral outputs are predetermined in any given year t. Consequently, contemporary income is predetermined. So is permanent income, which depends on present and past values. Consumption is determined by permanent income. Demand for individual commodities is determined by consumption and relative prices, all of which are given. Investment is determined by variables that are predetermined at t. And the production of investment goods is related to overall investment.

This system has a simple recursive structure that determines the amount of foreign trade of the two commodities in terms of the variables, which are predetermined at time t. The structure of the system is shown by the flow chart of Figure 1. The double arrows on the left-hand margin indicate that permanent income and domestic outputs are

Figure 1—Flow chart of the simplified system

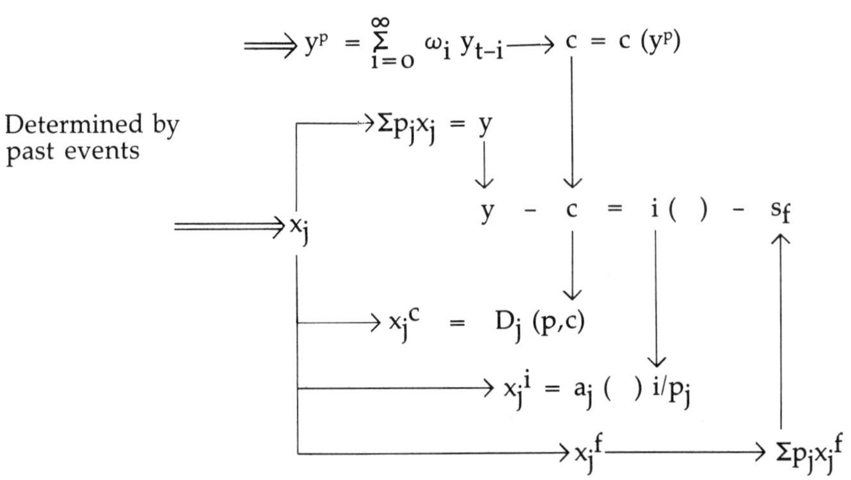

predetermined. The chart is drawn in such a way that it would be very easy to generalize to more than two sectors. Note that in this version investment is predetermined. Consequently, the traded quantities are residuals and the foreign savings, s_f, are determined by the system.[9]

Dynamics

In the short run, the economy simply distributes available supplies. Over a longer time, the quantity of the supply changes. Clearly, some changes in output take place in any interval. However, these changes take place largely within the framework of existing resource allocation among firms within sectors rather than between sectors. As this study focuses on intersectoral allocation and distribution, the short-run variations are ignored in order to concentrate on the long-run variations that can be measured from year to year.

The effect of resource allocation and technology on output is summarized by the production functions. These are assumed to be homogeneous of degree one, and are written in terms of total output, Nx_j, where N is population:

$$Nx_1(t) = F_1 [K_{11}(t), K_{12}(t), L_1(t), A(t), t], \tag{3.20}$$

and

$$Nx_2(t) = F_2 [K_2(t), L_2(t), t]. \tag{3.21}$$

These functions assume that both sectors use capital (K) and labor (L) and that agriculture also uses land (A). Agriculture uses two types of capital: K_{11}, which are units of capital that originate in agriculture (for example, livestock), and K_{12}, which are units of capital that originate in nonagriculture (for example, machines).

The fundamental assumptions that resource allocations and technology at any one time are given determine the marginal productivities at time t. That is, the left-hand sides of the following equations are predetermined:

$$\begin{aligned} MP_{1L}(t) &= w_1/p_1, & MP_{2L}(t) &= w_2/p_2, \text{ and} \\ MP_{1k}(t) &= r_1/p_1, & MP_{2k}(t) &= r_2/p_2. \\ MP_{1A}(t) &= R/p_1, & & \end{aligned} \tag{3.22}$$

The right-hand sides of the equations (3.22) indicate the ratios of factor prices to product prices. Because these ratios are equal to the marginal productivities, they are determined by the same variables that determine outputs. These factor prices can be referred to as shadow prices to emphasize the fixity of resources in the short run. However, assuming that each sector is competitive, the shadow prices will actually be the factor prices. With product prices given, factor prices are uniquely determined at time t. As a consequence, factor prices are endogenous in the system but are determined recursively.

An important feature of this framework is that factor prices need not be equal in all sectors, because factor mobility is imperfect. It is the discrepancy in returns between

[9]The notation x^f here replaces x^e and x^m used in the rest of the discussion.

sectors that generates the intersectoral mobility of resources. The process of resource allocation is formulated explicitly. Starting with labor, let m denote the rate at which labor in agriculture migrates to nonagriculture during a year.[10] This rate is considered to be endogenous in the economic system as it depends on the wage differential and on other variables that are determined by the state of the economy. The actual formulation of the equation is discussed in Chapter 9.

It is assumed that population grows at an exogenous rate, n, which need not remain constant over time, and that this is also the rate of growth of the labor force. Consequently, the rates of change in sectoral employment are

$$\hat{L}_1 = n - m, \tag{3.23}$$

and

$$\hat{L}_2 = n + m\, L_1/L_2, \tag{3.24}$$

where $\hat{x} = d\ln x/dt$ is the rate of growth of x.[11]

The new labor allocation is thus

$$L_j(t + 1) = L_j(t)\,[1 + \hat{L}_j(t)]. \tag{3.25}$$

The investment that takes place in time t changes the allocation of capital between sectors. It is assumed here that this is the only mode for allocation of capital. The distribution of new investment between the sectors is determined by the function θ, as indicated by equations (3.10) and (3.11). Let I_j be total investment in sector j; then the rates of sector accumulation of capital, by origin, are

$$\hat{K}_{11} = [(\lambda I_1 p)/K_{11}] - \Delta_{11},$$

$$\hat{K}_{12} = [(1 - \lambda) I_1/K_{12}] - \Delta_{12},$$

and

$$\hat{K}_2 = (I_2/K_2) - \Delta_2, \tag{3.26}$$

where Δ_j is the rate of depreciation of K_j and

$$K_j(t + 1) = K_j(t)\,[1 + \hat{K}_j(t)]. \tag{3.27}$$

The size of the cultivated land is determined by the economic environment. The land equation is discussed in Chapter 9.

The change in resources, combined with technical change, which at the present is assumed to be completely exogenous, determines output in year t + 1. Having new outputs and new income, a new equilibrium position for the economy is achieved at t + 1 through the selection of an appropriate amount of exports and imports. This is the process that generates the growth path of the economy.

[10]Let M be the size of net sectoral migration per year, then $m = M/L_1$.

[11]In this it is assumed that employment is equal to the labor force.

The Economy at Time t, Second Representation

The Treatment of Nontradable Products

In the foregoing discussion it was assumed that product prices, measured in a foreign currency, are determined by the international market. Using the first-order conditions given by equation (3.22), factor prices are determined in terms of foreign currency. This simple determination of factor prices holds when all goods are traded. Here a good part of the nonagricultural product is not traded and the analysis has to be modified accordingly. The direct and the common approach to dealing with nontradables is to identify them as a separate sector. If competition prevails so that factor prices are equal in all sectors and if the number of traded sectors is larger than the number of factors, then the price of the nontraded product, in a small open economy, is determined by the prices of the traded product.[12] Once intersectoral factor mobility is restricted this result does not apply. To see this, consider the case where sector 2 produces only nontradables. With resources and technology predetermined, the first order conditions for this sector are:

$$MP_{2L} = w_2/p_2, \tag{3.28}$$

and

$$MP_{2K} = r_2/p_2, \tag{3.29}$$

where the product price p_2 fulfills the Euler condition:

$$p_2 = (w_2L_2 + r_2K_2)/X_2. \tag{3.30}$$

However, this equation is not independent of the other two and p_2 cannot be determined. This is as much as can be said for this case.

Note that this result holds true no matter what the number of additional traded sectors as long as factor mobility is restricted. Thus, to overcome this difficulty in empirical analysis it is necessary to identify tradable sectors that maintain perfect factor mobility with the nontraded sector. Alternatively, knowledge of the demand function for nontradables will facilitate the determination of their price, relative to that of tradables, for any predetermined amount of output.

In the present study nontradables are a part of nonagriculture and are not identified with a separate sector. The foregoing discussion facilitates an appropriate interpretation of this analysis. To begin, it is assumed that within sector 2 there is perfect mobility of resources between tradables and nontradables. In that case the short-run equilibrium position of the sector can be obtained by the same technique used for a two-sector closed economy with a general demand function.[13] This is described in terms of Figure 2. The demand curve for the nontraded product can be derived from the income-consumption curve of consumers' theory. Point A is uniquely determined under the classical conditions of the supply side for any given

---

[12] See for instance R. Komiya, "Non-Traded Goods and the Pure Theory of International Trade," *International Economic Review* 8 (June 1967): 132–152.

[13] See Yair Mundlak and R. Mosenson, "Two-Sector Model with Generalized Demand," *Metroeconomica* 22 (September–December 1970): 227–258.

Figure 2—Short-run equilibrium position of nonagriculture

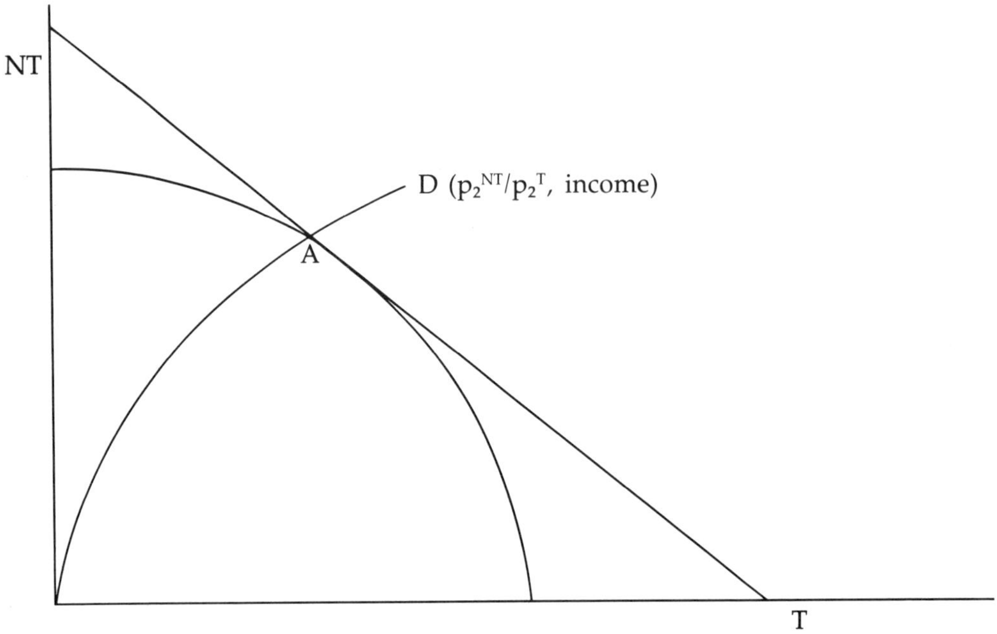

Notes: NT is a nontradable product. T is a tradable product. D is demand.

amount of resources and technology.[14] The price ratio p_2^T/p_2^{NT} is determined at the equilibrium point A. Since p_2^T is given from abroad, it is also possible to compute p_2^{NT}. It is then possible to aggregate the two products, and to compute the price for that aggregate domestic product in sector 2:

$$p_2^d = (p_2^{NT} X_2^{NT} + p_2^T X_2^T)/X_2, \tag{3.31}$$

where

$$X_2 = X_2^{NT} + X_2^{NT}.$$

p_2^d is observed in domestic currency. National accounting data generally report neither the two output components, X_2^T and X_2^{NT}, nor their prices. Instead the data report domestic outputs, imports, and exports. Thus, instead of p_2^T, the domestic price of the imported good, p_2^{nd}, is observed. Assuming that p_2^{nd} moves as p_2^T, the short-run equilibrium position of the economy will be characterized by the price ratio p_2^{nd}/p_2^d.

[14]When factor mobility between the two subsectors is partially restricted, the feasible production set of the economy will be a subset of that obtained with perfect mobility. In that case factor prices will not be the same in the two subsectors. However, short-run equilibrium exists, but need not be unique. This model, in the framework of a closed economy, is discussed in Yair Mundlak and Z. Tropp, "Distortion in the Factor Market and the Short-Run Equilibrium," in *On the Stability of Contemporary Economic Systems*, ed. O. Kyn and W. Schretti (Göttingen: Vanderhoeck and Ruprecht, 1980), pp. 130–156.

A use is also made in the analysis of price of the aggregate supply of sector 2, which consists of output and imports:

$$p_2 = \omega p_2^d + (1 - \omega)p_2^{nd}, \quad (3.32)$$

$$\omega = X_2/(X_2 + X_2^m).$$

Intervention in Foreign Trade

The actual influence of world prices on domestic prices is affected by the exchange rate, tariffs, and taxes. The analysis is now modified to take explicit account of those determinants.

Let the international prices of the products of the two sectors be p_j^f, in dollars per unit of j, then, to convert them to pesos,

$$p_j^e = (RE)\, p_j^f, \quad (3.33)$$

with (RE) being the exchange rate.[15] Let t_m and t_x be the rates of taxation on imports of the nonagricultural products and exports of the agricultural products. Then,

$$p_1 = p_1^e\,(1 - t_x), \quad (3.34)$$

and

$$p_2^{nd} = p_2^e\,(1 + t_m), \quad (3.35)$$

where p_1 is the local price of agricultural products and p_2^{nd} is the local price of imported agricultural products. The aggregate price of nonagricultural products is given by equation (3.32). At this point the tax rates, the exchange rate, and the international prices are taken to be exogenous. Thus the price ratio $p = p_1/p_2$ is uniquely determined by ω of (3.32). The price ratio p is affected by the tariffs and in turn affects the short-run behavior of the economy and, therefore, its growth path.

Whereas the change in price affects equilibrium values, it does not change the set of equations that solve simultaneously for the short-run equilibrium. This set of equations is affected, however, by the income effect of the tax on consumption. Let the per capita tax collection on foreign trade be given by

$$y^{tf} = t_x p_1^e x_1^e + t_m\, p_2^e\, x_2^m.$$

The total per capita income is then

$$y = p_1 x_1 + p_2^d\, x_2 + y^{tf}.$$

It is clear that the tax depends on x_1^e and x_2^m. Its effect on consumption, and thus on the simultaneous system, is traced in the following section.

[15]At this point no differentiation is made between the nominal and real rates of exchange. Thus, RE can be interpreted here as the nominal rate. Later on this notation is used for the real rate.

Intervention in Domestic Trade

In addition to the indirect taxes on foreign trade, indirect taxes on domestic trade are considered. Such taxes create the difference between market prices and factor prices. Let t_j be the rate applied to sector j:

$$p_1^* = p_1 (1 + t_1), \tag{3.36}$$

$$p_2^{d*} = p_2^d (1 + t_2), \tag{3.37}$$

and

$$p_2^* = \omega p_2^{d*} + (1 - \omega) p_2^{nd}, \tag{3.38}$$

where the asterisk now indicates market prices. Given t_1 and t_2 and having determined factor prices, the market prices are determined immediately from equations (3.36) to (3.38). Consequently,

$$p^* = p_1^*/p_2^*. \tag{3.39}$$

The per capita indirect tax collected from domestic sales is

$$y^{td} = t_1 p_1 (x_1 - x_1^e) + t_2 p_2^d x_2.$$

Combining y^{tf} and y^{td}, the total per capita indirect tax is

$$y^t = y^{td} + y^{tf}, \tag{3.40}$$

and per capita income is the sum of per capita product in factor prices and indirect taxes:

$$y = p_1 x_1 + p_2^d x_2 + y^t. \tag{3.41}$$

Referring to the consumption function in equation (3.5), this equation now expresses the per capita consumption of the private sector, c^p. As government is not treated explicitly here, it is simply assumed that all of y^t is consumed. Thus per capita consumption is

$$c = c^p + y^t. \tag{3.42}$$

It is assumed that all government consumption is of nonagricultural products. Consequently, the demand function in equation (3.4) is for the private sector alone. For that reason private demand for the products is denoted as $x_2^{c,p}$, whereas x_2^c is the total demand. Consequently,

$$x_2^c = x_2^{c,p} + y^t. \tag{3.43}$$

The Simultaneous System

The present system cannot be solved recursively along the lines of Figure 1. To begin with, p^* depends on x_2^m, which in turn depends on x_2^c and x_2^i, both of which depend on p_2^*. Also, x_2^m depends on the expenditure by government, y^t, which itself depends on x_2^m, as well as on x_1^e. These relationships are summarized by seven equations and identities:

$$x_2^{c,p} = D_2\,(p_2^*,\, x_2^m, \text{ exogenous variables}), \tag{3.44}$$

$$x_1^c = (c^p - p_2^*\, x_2^{c,p})/p_1^*, \tag{3.45}$$

$$x_2^i = [i_2 + (1 - \lambda)i_1]/p_2^*, \tag{3.46}$$

$$x_1^e = x_1 - x_1^c - x_1^i, \tag{3.47}$$

$$x_2^m = -\,x_2 + x_2^{c,p} + x_2^i + (y^t/p_2^*), \tag{3.48}$$

$$y^t = t_1 p_1\,(x_1 - x_1^e) + t_x\, p_1^e\, x_1^e + t_2\, x_2 + t_m\, p_2^e\, x_2^m, \tag{3.49}$$

and

$$p_2^* = x_2^m/(x_2 + x_2^m)\,(p_2^{nd} - 1 - t_2) + (1 + t_2). \tag{3.50}$$

The system solves for the endogenous variables $x_2^{c,p}$, x_1^c, x_2^i, x_2^m, x_1^e, y^t, and p_2^*.

Equation (3.44) expresses the demand for x_2 in terms of the two endogenous variables p_2^* and x_2^m. It also depends on several exogenous variables to be discussed in Chapters 4 and 8. Equation (3.45) is simply the consumption budget identity of the private sector. Equation (3.46) transforms the investment demand for nonagricultural output into quantities. Equation (3.47) is the resource identity given in equation (3.16). Similarly, equation (3.48) is the resource identity for nonagriculture, where x_2^c is decomposed into the two components according to equation (3.43). Equation (3.49) is indirect tax collection, whereas equation (3.50) gives the aggregate price in terms of imports, x_2^m.

Endogenous Technology and Other Extensions

The model implicitly assumes that technology is exogenously given, as it usually is in economic analysis. This study takes an additional step by making technology endogenous. This is discussed in Chapter 7, which deals with production functions, but this extension of the model does not affect its structure as discussed here. It does affect the dynamics of the model. Most importantly, it introduces an additional channel for affecting the differential growth of the two sectors.

Subsequently, the real rate of exchange is also made endogenous. This proves to be an important variable in the development of the economy. In addition, the rate of unemployment and changes in the rate of participation in the labor force are incorporated. These are explained later.

Summary and Perspective

The essence of the present model is that at any one time the allocation of resources in the economy is largely predetermined, and the response to prices within one year is limited. Given the technology, and abstracting from short-term fluctuations, supply is predetermined. The short-run problem is to clear the product market. In a closed economy this is accomplished through prices. In an open economy prices are influenced by outside forces, and the domestic markets are cleared through foreign trade. The allocation of products to outlets is determined by the demand for them.

Resource allocation and technology determine the marginal productivity of the factors. Given the foreign prices, exchange rate, and indirect taxes, factor prices are determined. Such prices need not be the same for all sectors. Intersectoral differences in the factor prices cause the factor mobility. This mobility, along with the overall expansion of the labor force and capital stock, changes the resource allocation in time $t+1$. This new allocation and technical change increase output and the system reaches a new equilibrium in time $t+1$.

The model has been described in detail to facilitate interpretation of the results. In so doing no explicit reference was made to the literature. The model is similar to a two-sector general equilibrium model. However, the discussion in this chapter indicated that it differs from an equilibrium model of the comparative static type in that the returns to factors in the two sectors are not equal. It also differs from models dealing with distortions in the factor markets that assume that the differences in the sectoral returns to factors are fixed.[16] Such models may be useful for short-run analysis.[17] In a long-run analysis it is necessary to explain the rate of distortion. This is what the present model is doing. It also deals with all factor markets without imposing the assumption that labor but not capital can be allocated instantaneously. Such an assumption is unnecessary in a general framework of the type used here. This is independent of the possibility that the assumption may be wrong empirically for Argentina. This is not to say that the rate of adjustment to differential returns is the same for all factors but rather that such adjustment rates have to be determined from the data. In that it follows suggestions made to deal with micro data.[18] The present formulation is designed to allow economic data to be analyzed and interpreted correctly. As such the framework is used in the actual computation used to fit the model with the data as explained in Chapter 4.

---

[16]Such models are surveyed in S. P. Magee, "Factor Market Distortion and Trade: A Survey," *Oxford Economic Papers* 25 (No. 1, 1973).

[17]The short-run equilibrium under distortion is discussed in Mundlak and Tropp, "Distortion in the Factor Market."

[18]Yair Mundlak, "Long-Run Coefficients and Distributed Lag Analysis: A Reformulation," *Econometrica* 35 (April 1967): 278–293.

4

THE EMPIRICAL IMPLEMENTATION OF THE MODEL

Before confronting the model with actual data, the procedures used must be described, the variables defined, and the assumptions specified. That will make it possible to illustrate the working of the model and thereby link the description of it in Chapter 3 to the empirical analysis. In so doing, the empirical equations that were used to fit the model are needed. Because the empirical equations are discussed in more detail in later chapters, only a short description of the equations actually used to fit the model is given here. Once the equations and the working of the model are presented, the fit of the model will be presented. This is done graphically in a set of figures comparing the simulated and actual values. The performance of the model in explaining the Argentine experience is evaluated. A complete listing of all the variables used, their definitions, and their symbols, is presented in Appendix 1. Some summary data are presented as Appendix 2.

The reader who prefers continuity of the discussion may prefer to leave the discussion of the equations for later and begin with the working of the model.

Empirical Equations

Some of the variables are determined within the system by using empirical equations whose coefficients are estimated from past data. The estimation is discussed in the last three chapters. Only the results used in the simulator are presented here.

Because the main focus of the study is on the process of growth, some of the random variations can be ignored by working with three-year moving averages. Such a procedure somewhat complicates the empirical analysis because it introduces serial correlation in the equations that did not exist in the annual data.

The equations were originally estimated for the period 1940–72. Because the simulation begins with 1946, the equations were reestimated using only the data for 1946–72. The equations shown here are obtained for that period.[19] All the variables, unless indicated otherwise, are for year t.

Production Functions

The basic idea is that the production function itself is determined by economic forces. More technically, such forces are referred to as state variables. A system of equations is formulated that explains the variations of the coefficients of the production functions. Starting with nonagriculture,

$$\ln (X_2/L_2) = \Gamma_2 + S_{K2} \ln(K_2/L_2), \tag{4.1}$$

where the average labor productivity (X_2/L_2) is determined by the capital/labor ratio (K_2/L_2). The coefficients are the level of the function or simply the intercept (Γ_2) and the factor share of capital (S_{K2}). The state variables that determine the level and the factor share are the total per capita stock of capital in the economy (K/N), the average investment per worker (I_2/L_2),

[19]Except for the equations for labor migration and production functions.

the price of imported goods (p_2^{nd}), the rate of return on capital (r_2), and the wage rate (w_2). The function is formulated to allow for a discrepancy between the factor share and the elasticity of production in an imperfect factor market. The equations for sector 2 are:

$$\Gamma_2 = -0.799 + 0.512 \ln (K/N) + 0.158 \ln (I_2/L_2)(t-1) - 1.135 \ln p_2^{nd} - 0.591 \ln r_2 (t-1) + 1.358 \ln w_2 (t-1) - 0.077 [\ln (K_2/L_2)]^2 - 0.655 \ln (X_2/L_2)(t-1), \quad (4.2)$$

and

$$S_{K2} = 0.006 + 0.004 \ln (K/N) - 0.035 \ln (I_2/L_2)(t-1) + 0.135 \ln r_2 (t-1) + 0.141 \ln p_2^{nd} - 0.066 \ln w_2 (t-1) + 0.153 \ln (K_2/L_2). \quad (4.3)$$

The system for sector 1 is similar except that there are more inputs: land (A) and two components for capital stock, that which came from agriculture (K_{11}) and that which came from nonagriculture (K_{12}). The function is thus

$$\ln (X_1/L_1) = \Gamma_1 + S_A \ln (A/L_1) + S_{K11} \ln (K_{11}/L_1) + S_{K12} \ln (K_{12}/L_1). \quad (4.4)$$

Only three state variables, similar to those mentioned above, are used for the agricultural production function. With obvious modification of sectoral indexes, the equations are:

$$\Gamma_1 = 4.491 - 0.046 \ln p_A - 0.078 \ln (I_1/L_1) - 0.833 \ln r_1 (t-1) - 0.154 [\ln (A/L_1)]^2 - 0.0118 [\ln (K_{11}/L_1)]^2 - 0.0015 [\ln (K_{12}/L_1)]^2; \quad (4.5)$$

$$S_A = 0.509 + 0.128 \ln p_A + 0.043 \ln (I_1/L_1) + 0.113 \ln r_1 (t-1) + 0.215 \ln (A/L_1) - 0.074 \ln (K_{11}/L_1) - 0.040 \ln (K_{12}/L_1); \quad (4.6)$$

$$S_{K11} = -0.0017 - 0.0409 \ln p_A + 0.0085 \ln (I_1/L_1) + 0.0799 \ln r_1 (t-1) + 0.109 \ln (A/L_1) + 0.012 \ln (K_{11}/L_1) - 0.007 \ln (K_{12}/L_1); \quad (4.7)$$

and

$$S_{K12} = -0.369 - 0.007 \ln p_A - 0.014 \ln (I_1/L_1) + 0.009 \ln r_1 (t-1) - 0.056 \ln (A/L_1) + 0.064 \ln (K_{11}/L_1) + 0.034 \ln (K_{12}/L_1). \quad (4.8)$$

Consumption

Consumption consists of two components, private and government. Government consumption is assumed to equal the indirect tax collection. The consumption of the private sector is estimated to allow the consumption coefficients to vary by their sources of income. Specifically, wage and nonwage income are differentiated in the two sectors; therefore, there are four sources of income. The empirical analysis indicates that all sources except nonwage income in agriculture have the same coefficient, which amounts to 70 percent of factor income. The nonwage income in agriculture is represented by the value of agricultural land, which is used as a measure of agricultural wealth. The consumption coefficient of this variable is 4.5 percent of wealth.

The consumption function is

$$c^p = 8.49 + 0.045\, p_A A/N + 0.70\, (x_2 + w_1 L_1/N); \quad (4.9)$$

$\rho = 0.846;$

where ρ is the estimate of first-order autocorrelation coefficient.

Demand

The demand system consists of two demand equations, one for each sector, and the budget constraint given by consumption, as derived from the consumption function. Consequently, only the demand for nonagricultural products is estimated. Then the demand for agricultural products is obtained as a residual from the budget constraint.

The main arguments of the demand system are per capita private consumption, c^p, and the price ratio, p^*. Two more variables are added. The first is the share of imports in the total supply of sector 2, $\omega = x_2^m/(x_2 + x_2^m)$. This variable serves two purposes. First, it represents the availability of imported goods. There were years when imports were restricted, and therefore the consumption of imported durables was postponed. Second, it plays a technical role in the aggregation of the two components of p_2^*, as explained in Chapter 8.

The second variable is the share of income generated in agriculture in total income, $p_1 x_1/(p_1 x_1 + x_2)$. This variable also serves two purposes. It may reflect different demand coefficients according to the source of income. It may also reflect the availability of food that was not fully reflected in relative prices due to government intervention. The foregoing refers to the private component of demand. The equation for this component is

$$x_2^{c,p} = 4.84 + 0.603\, c^p + 29.25\, p^* + 295.07\, x_2^m/(x_2^m + x_2) - 237.88\, p_1 x_1/(p_1 x_1 + x_2) + 0.221\, x_{2\,t-1}^{c,p}; \quad (4.10)$$

$\rho = 0.407$

Consumption by the government is assumed to equal per capita indirect taxes, y^t.

As indicated, the per capita demand for agricultural goods, x_1^c, is obtained by using the demand for x_2^c and the budget constraint:

$$x_1^c = (c^p - p_2^* x_2^{c,p})/p_1^* \quad (4.11)$$

Investment

Per capita investment is postulated to depend on the rate of capital utilization (K/X) and on the growth of per capita output $(x - x_{t-1})$. The investment function is

$$i = 60.78 - 27.74\, K/X + 0.49\, (x_t - x_{t-1}) + 0.87\, i_{t-1}; \quad (4.12)$$

$\rho = 0.202$

where $K = K_1^N + K_2$, and K_1^N is the agricultural capital stock evaluated in terms of sector 2 prices; that is, $K_1^N = p^* K_1$. X is total output at factor cost, that is, $X = N(x_1 p_1 + x_2)$. In 1952 and 1953 the intercept was set at 52.0 instead of 60.78. It takes into account the reduction in public investment and restrictions on imports of investment goods that were imposed by the government immediately after the severe balance-of-payments crisis of 1951.

It is postulated that investment is allocated to the two sectors according to their expected profitability. Empirically, the expected profitability variable is measured by the ratio of the average productivities of capital in the two sectors, δ_r, as well as by the price of land, p_A. The effects of changes in profitability on investment allocation cause the ratio of agriculture in total investment (θ) to deviate from its ratio in the total capital stock (K_1^N/K). The allocation of investment was also affected by the availability of credit for agriculture (CRED) because the amount of credit that banks could extend was rationed during the period. The function is

$$\ln \theta = -1.29 + 0.54 \ln (K_1^N/K) - 0.60 \ln \delta_r + 0.3 \ln CRED + 0.29 \ln p_A + 0.72 \ln \theta_{t-1} - 0.45 \ln \theta_{t-2}, \quad (4.13)$$

where

$$\delta_r = (X_2/K_2)/(p_1 X_1/K_1^N).$$

The share of agricultural investment originating in agriculture (λ) is determined by the lagged price of agricultural goods, p_1 (t − 1). Again, it is assumed that in the long run this price causes deviations from the ratio of capital originating in agriculture to total agricultural capital (K_{11}/K_1). The equation is

$$\ln \lambda^* = -0.212 - 3.13 \ln (K_{11}/K_1) + 1.97 \ln p_1 (t-1) - 2.60 \ln \lambda(t-1) + 1.81 \ln \lambda(t-2), \quad (4.14)$$

where

$$\lambda^* = [1/(\lambda - 0.27)] - 1.$$

Labor Migration

The migration of agricultural labor from agriculture to nonagriculture expressed as a proportion of the labor force (m) is determined by the intersectoral wage differential lagged one year $(w_2/w_1)(t-1)$. The effect of this wage differential is adjusted by the rate of unemployment and variations in the participation rate in nonagriculture. Thus

$$\ln [m(t-1) + 0.6] = -0.26 + 0.08 \ln [(w_2/w_1)(t-1) - 1.25] - 0.13 \ln [UN(t-1) + 1] + 0.87 \ln [m(t-2) + 0.6]. \quad (4.15)$$

For t = 1947 the intercept is set at 0.195 instead of 0.26 to account for the strong migration caused by Peronist policies.

Land

Cultivated land (A) includes land sown with crops and artificial pasture. It does not include natural pasture. Cultivated land is responsive to the price of land lagged two years, p_A (t − 2), and to current and lagged values of p_{LS}/p_C. The net effect of the lags is negative so that the smaller the price ratio, the more land is cultivated. When the price ratio favors crops, more land is brought under cultivation. The equation is

$$\begin{aligned}\ln A = {} & 0.529 + 1.329 \ln A(t-1) - 0.490 \ln A(t-2) + 0.17 \ln p_A(t-2) \\ & - 0.142 \ln (p_{LS}/p_C) + 0.264 \ln (p_{LS}/p_C)(t-1) \\ & - 0.281 \ln (p_{LS}/p_C)(t-2) \\ & + 0.247 \ln (p_{LS}/p_C)(t-3) - 0.138 \ln (p_{LS}/p_C)(t-4). \qquad (4.16)\end{aligned}$$

Rate of Exchange

The real rate of exchange (RE) is obtained by deflating the nominal rate by the domestic price of nonagriculture (p_2^d). To allow for inflation abroad, the dependent variable in the empirical analysis is the product of RE and a weighted average of foreign prices relevant to the Argentine economy (p^f). Variations in the rate of exchange thus defined are accounted for in terms of the foreign terms of trade (p_1^f/p_2^f) and commercial policy as represented by t_x and t_m. In addition, the rate of exchange is affected by macro variables, such as the expansion of domestic credit over and above the expansion of nominal income (EC) and the surplus in the current account as a proportion of the total quantity of money in the previous period (EM/M_3). The equation is

$$\begin{aligned}\ln [(RE)(p^f)] = {} & 0.024 - 0.635 \ln(1 - t_x) - 0.338 \ln(1 + t_m) \\ & + 0.511 \ln (p_1^f/p_2^f) - 1.054 \ln (p_1^f/p_2^f)(t-1) \\ & + 0.491 \ln (p_1^f/p_2^f)(t-3) - 0.388 \ln (p_1^f/p_2^f)(t-4) \\ & - 0.236\, EC - 0.469 (EM/M_3)(t-1), \qquad (4.17)\end{aligned}$$

where

$$p^f = \delta_f p_1^f + (1 - \delta_f) p_2^f \text{ and } \delta_f = x_1^e/(x_1^e + x_2^m).$$

The Determination of the System

The components can now be combined to show schematically how the system is determined for a given year t. The description basically follows the order in which computations were actually made in the simulation. The recursive nature of the system is fully used.

The inputs to the program consist of the coefficients of the empirical equations and the exogenous variables. The coefficients of the empirical equations were given in the previous section. The exogenous variables are entered into the simulator every year. These variables are: foreign prices, p_1^f and p_2^f; the price of livestock relative to the price of crops, p_{LS}/p_C; taxes on foreign trade, t_x and t_m; indirect domestic taxes, t_1 and t_2; population, N; unemployment, UN; depreciation rates, Δ_{11}, Δ_{12}; the proportion of rationed bank credit given to agriculture, CRED; and the expansion of domestic credit over and above the rate of growth of nominal income, EC.

Given the exogenous variables, the model determines the values of the endogenous variables for each year. The simulated values are shown in the figures below as broken lines; the moving averages of the actual observations as solid lines.

The real rate of exchange (RE) is determined by equation (4.17). Having determined RE, the following prices can then be determined:

$$p_1^e = p_1^f RE,$$

$$p_2^e = p_2^f RE,$$

$$p_1 = p_1^e(1 - t_x),$$

$$p_2^{nd} = p_2^e(1 + t_m),$$

$$p_1^* = p_1(1 + t_1),$$

$$p_2^{d*} = (1 + t_2).$$

RE, p_1, and p_2^{nd} are plotted in Figures 3-5.

Factor prices depend on the amount of inputs, which are determined by the process of resource allocation. The pattern of resource allocation is determined by equations (3.23) to (3.27). In implementing these equations, other effects on each of the inputs are also accounted for, as is explained below.

The capital stocks at the beginning of the year are given by the following equations:

$$K_{11} = K_{11}(t-1)(1-\Delta_{11}) + I_{11}(t-1)/p_1^*(t-1),$$

$$K_{12} = K_{12}(t-1)(1-\Delta_{12}) + I_{12}(t-1)/p_2^*(t-1),$$

and

$$K_2 = K_2(t-1)(1-\Delta_2) + I_2(t-1)/p_2^*(t-1).$$

Thus the capital stocks are fully determined by variables that are known at the beginning of year t.

In fitting the model, the values used for the depreciation rates were the actual values used in the construction of the capital series in the national accounts. To get some idea of those values, their extreme values are reported for the period under consideration:

	Minimum	Maximum
Δ_{11}	0.030	0.056
Δ_{12}	0.040	0.120
Δ_2	0.028	0.067

The sectoral capital stocks are plotted in Figures 6 and 7.

When the labor force in the two sectors is fully employed, its size is determined by its natural rate of growth and the migration equation (4.15). Variations in the rate of participation in the labor force or in unemployment affect sectoral employment and therefore should be taken into account. At this stage unemployment and variations in the rate of participation are treated as if they were exogenous.[20] Furthermore, it is assumed that variations in these two variables are fully absorbed by nonagriculture. That leads to the

[20]The empirical analysis of the determinants of unemployment appears in Chapter 9.

Figure 3—Real rate of exchange (RE), 1941–71

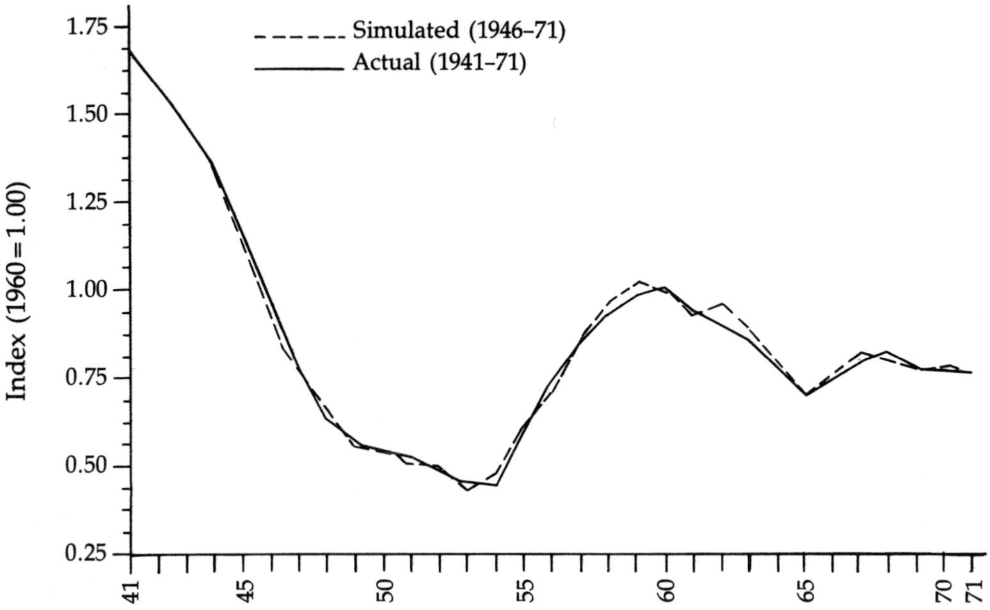

Figure 4—Factor price of agricultural products (p_1), 1941–71

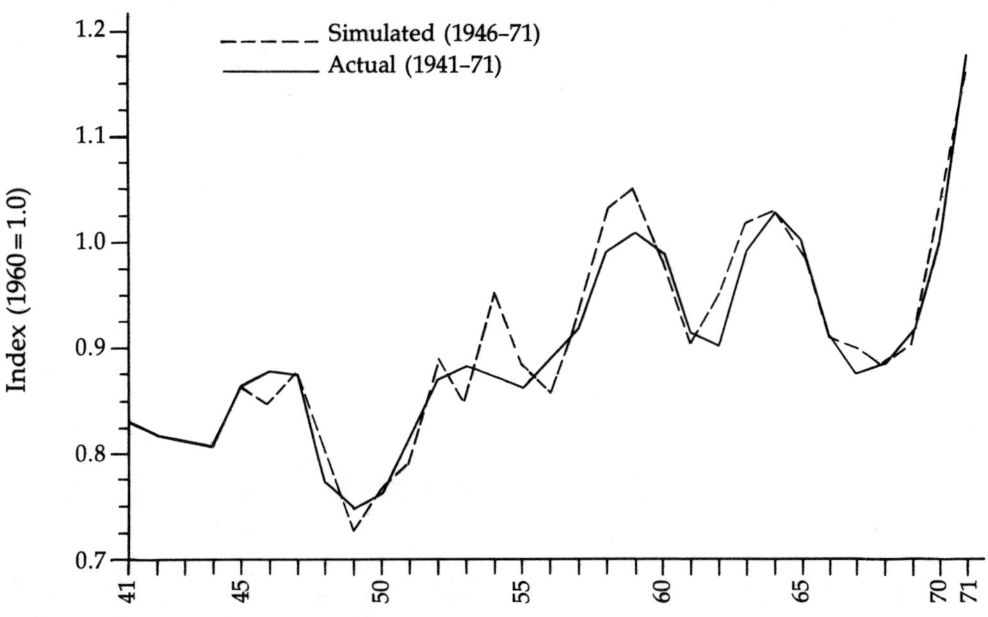

Figure 5—Market price of imported nonagricultural products (p_2^{nd}), 1941–71

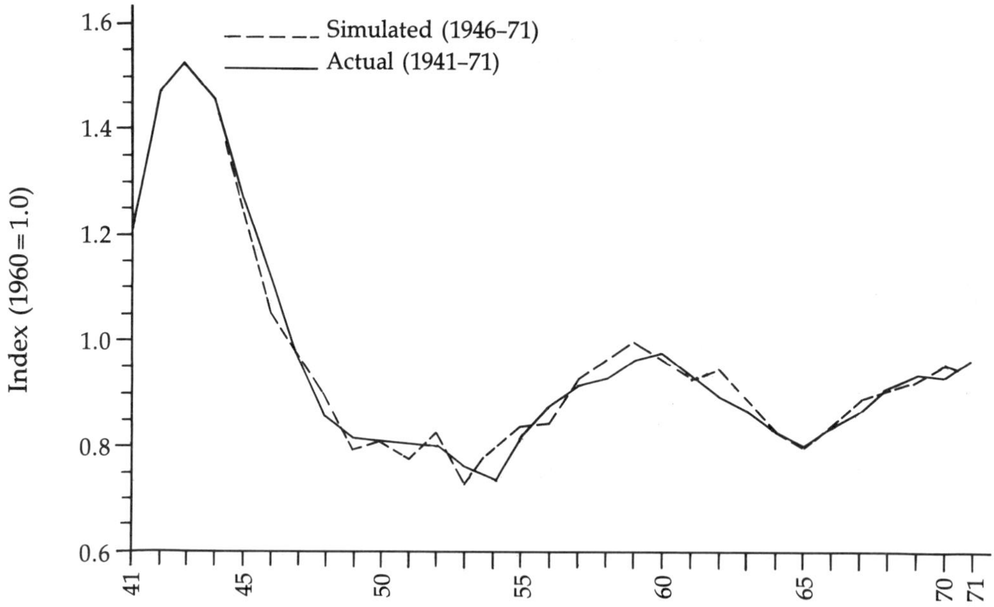

Figure 6—Composition of capital stock (K), 1941–71

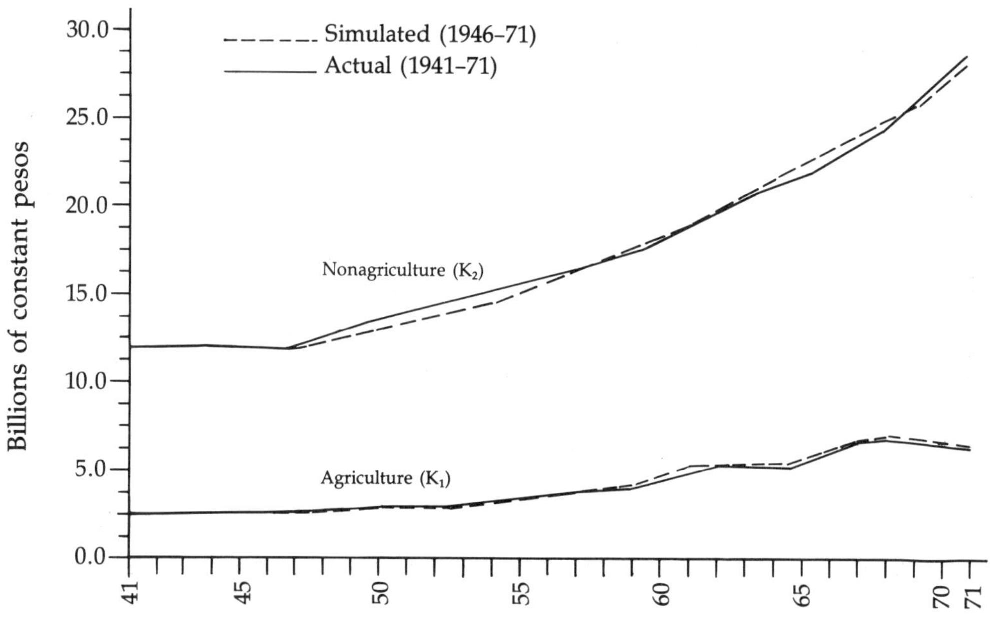

Figure 7—Composition of agricultural capital (K_1) by sector of origin, 1941–71

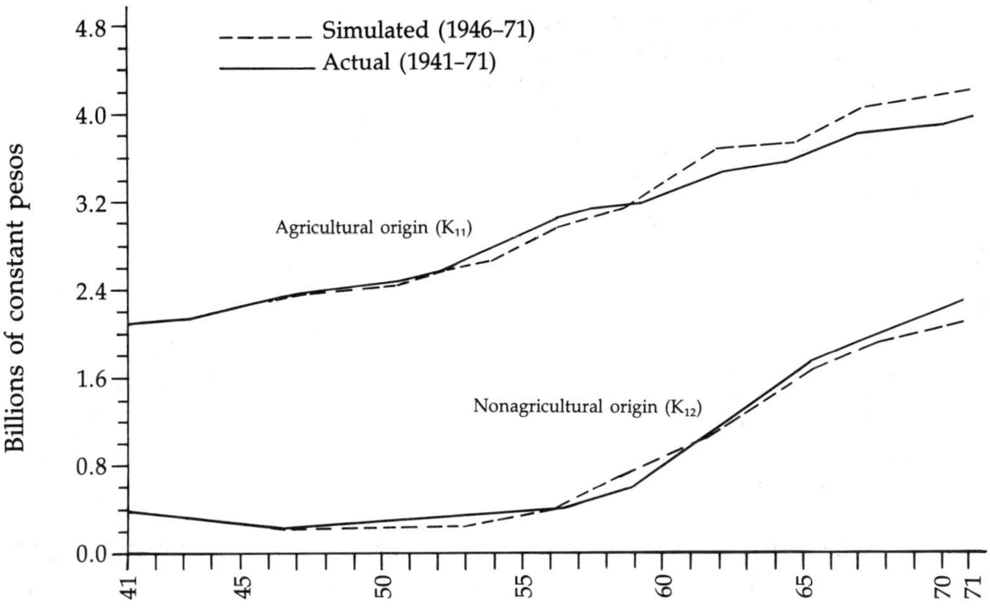

following equation for the labor force in sector 2, in which the migration equation (4.15) is used to determine the portion of the agricultural labor force that migrates to nonagriculture:

$$L_2 = (L_2 + UN)(t-1)(1+\hat{N}) + mL_1(t-1) - UN,$$

whereas for sector 1 it is simply

$$L_1 = L_1(t-1)(1+\hat{N}-m).$$

This derivation is based on the assumption that the natural rate of population growth is given exogenously. The migration equation is plotted in Figure 8 and the composition of the labor force in Figure 9.

The size of the cultivated land is determined by equation (4.16). Simulated values are plotted in Figure 10. Because the inputs are known, the production functions given in equations (4.1) to (4.8) can be used to determine the output of each sector. Note that all the state variables except I_1 are known at the time they enter the production functions in year t. To keep the system recursive, I_1 is lagged one year. The simulated output per capita is plotted in Figures 11 and 12 for agriculture and nonagriculture.

The estimation of the production functions also involves estimation of the factor shares as given by equations (4.3), (4.6), (4.7), and (4.8) and plotted in Figures 13-16 for agriculture and nonagriculture. The factor shares are used to determine the factor prices. For sector 2,

$$r_2 = S_{K2}X_2/K_2,$$

and

$$w_2 = (1 - S_{K2})X_2/L_2.$$

Figure 8—Labor migration (m), 1941–71

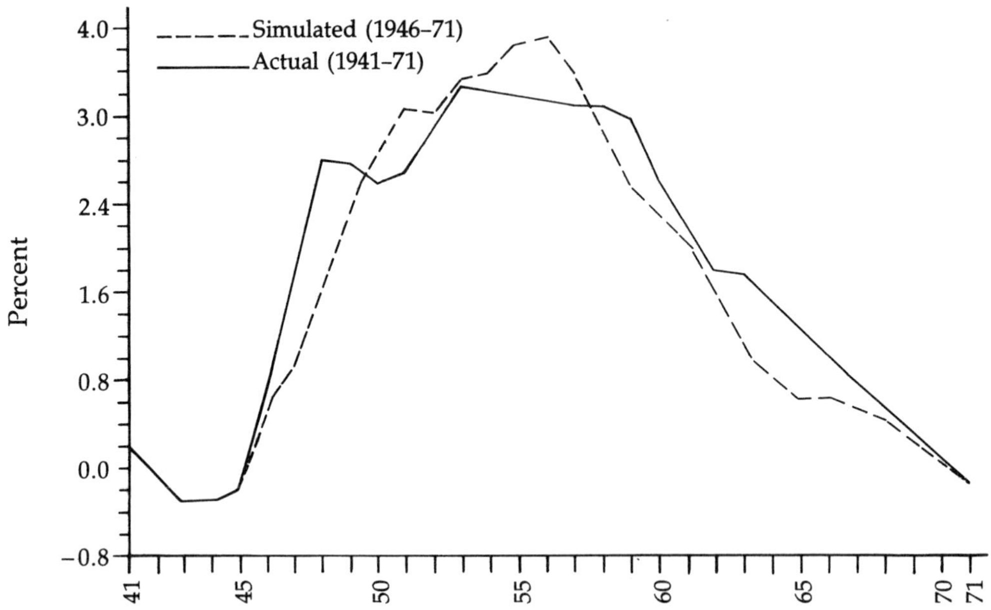

Thus, the factor prices in year t are determined by the sectoral inputs in that year and the state variables that determine productivity.

Factor prices in agriculture are determined under the hypothesis that the rates of return are the same for each alternative. Thus,

$$r_1 = (S_{K11} + S_{K12})p_1X_1/K_1,$$

$$w_1 = (1 - S_{K11} - S_{K12} - S_A)\, p_1X_1/L_1,$$

and

$$R = S_A p_1 X_1/A.$$

Knowing the rent on land and the rate of return on capital, land price is determined from

$$p_A = R p_1^*/r_1.$$

The factor prices are plotted in Figures 17-20.

The production functions determine the outputs. Once prices are determined, factor income can also be determined. It is now possible to determine the product utilization. The major components are private consumption, government consumption, investment, and foreign trade.

For computation, this part of the system can be subdivided into two subsystems, recursive and simultaneous. The recursive subsystem determines each endogenous variable individually in terms of known variables. This subsystem includes private per capita consumption, c^P, which is determined by equation (4.9) and plotted in Figure 21. Per capita investment is determined by equation (4.12). Having determined overall investment, equation (4.13) is used to compute the allocation of investment to the two sectors (θ)

Figure 9—Composition of the labor force (L), 1941–71

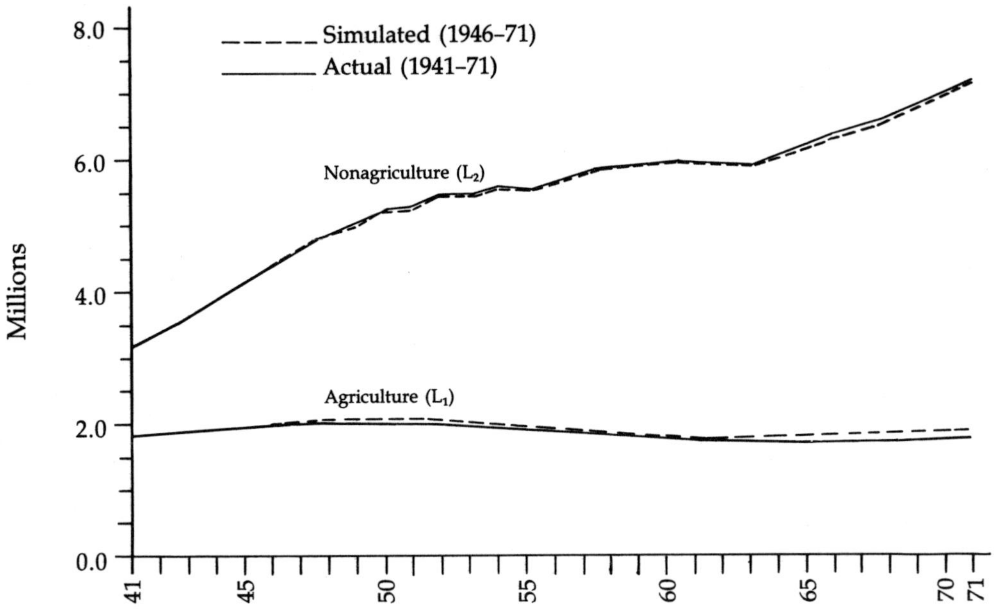

Figure 10—Cultivated land (A), 1941–71

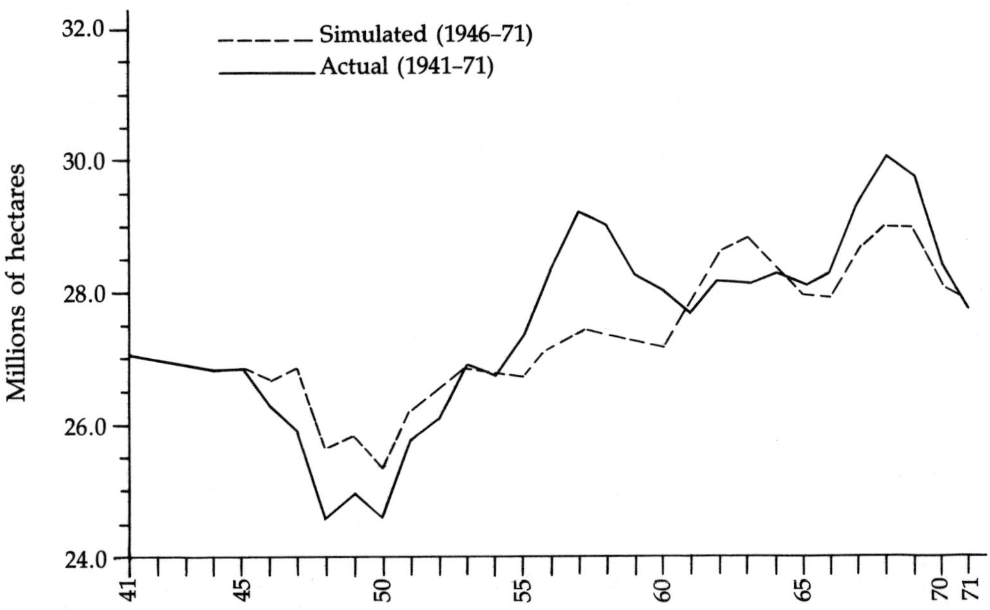

Figure 11—Per capita output and domestic utilization, agriculture, 1941–71

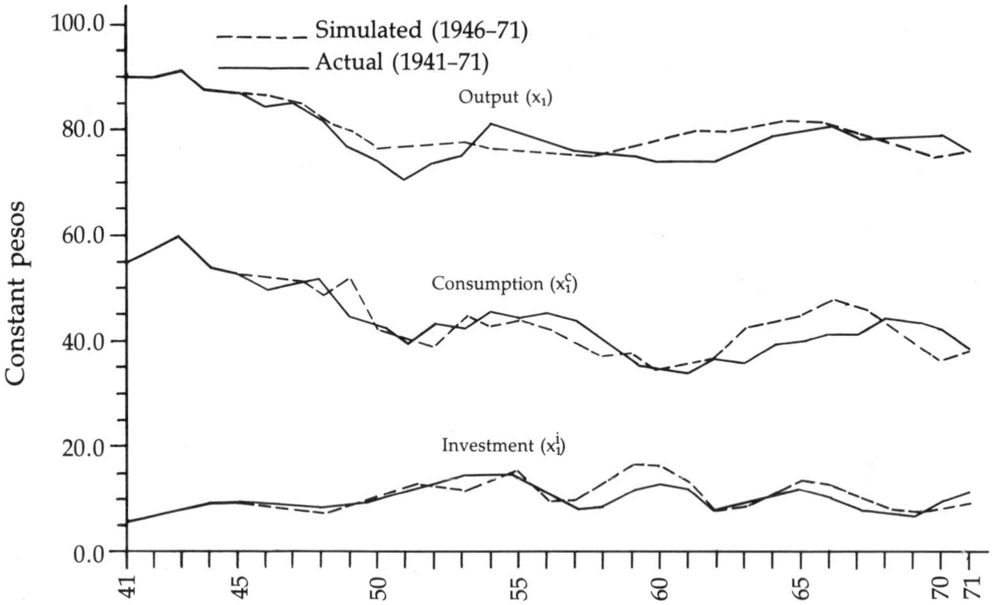

Figure 12—Per capita output and domestic utilization, nonagriculture, 1941–71

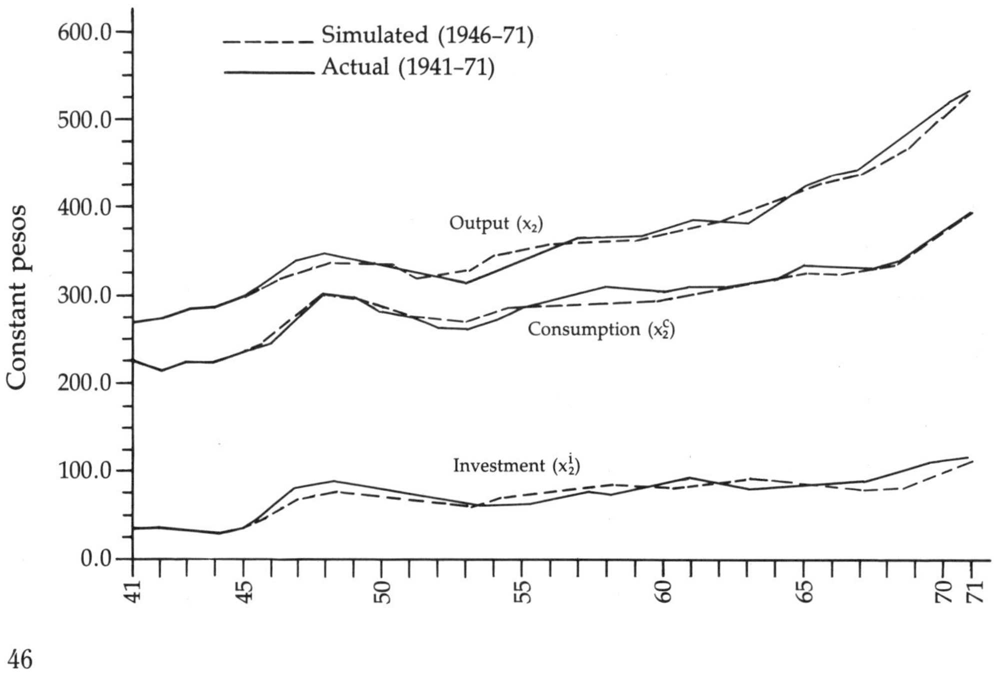

Figure 13—Share of land in agricultural output (S_A), 1941–71

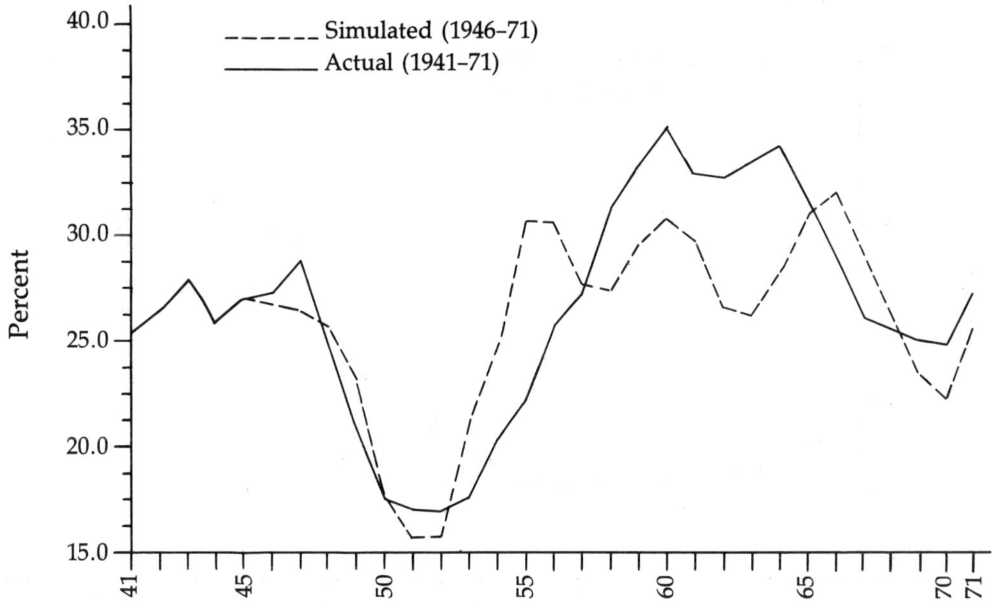

Figure 14—Share of capital originating in agriculture in agricultural output (S_{K11}), 1941–71

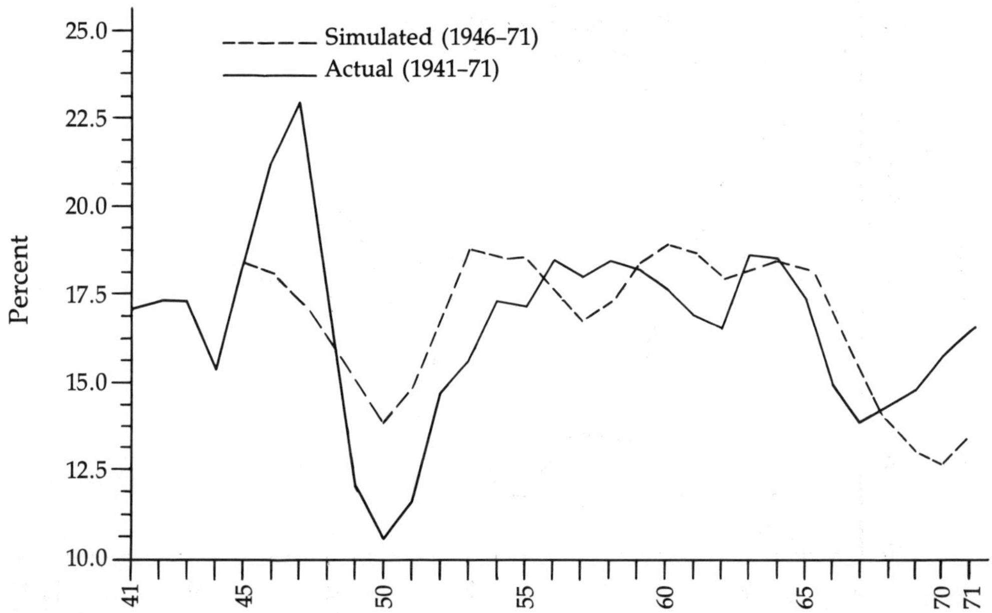

Figure 15—Share of capital originating in nonagriculture in agricultural output (S_{K12}), 1941–71

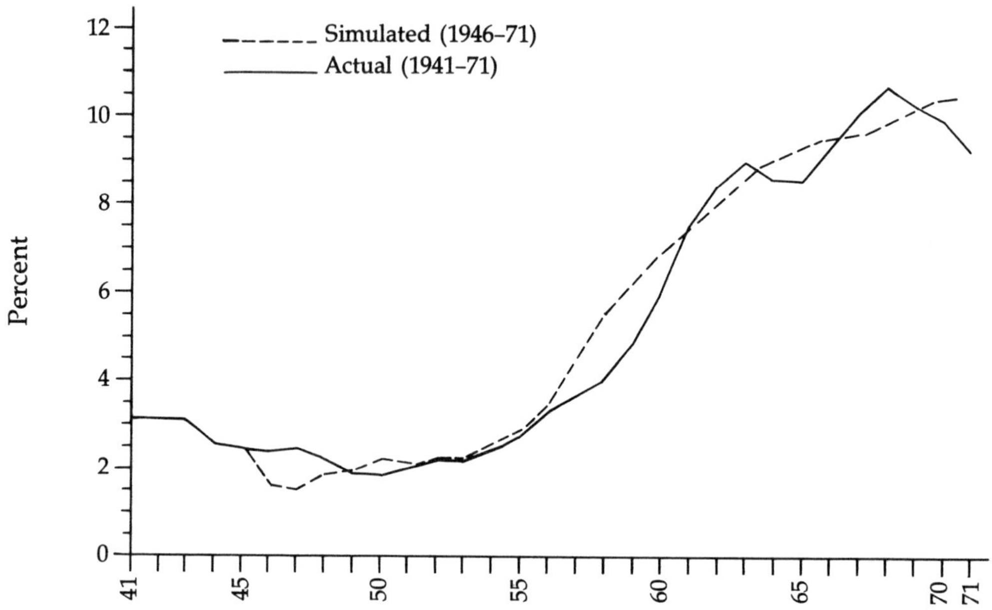

Figure 16—Share of capital in nonagricultural output (S_{K2}), 1941–71

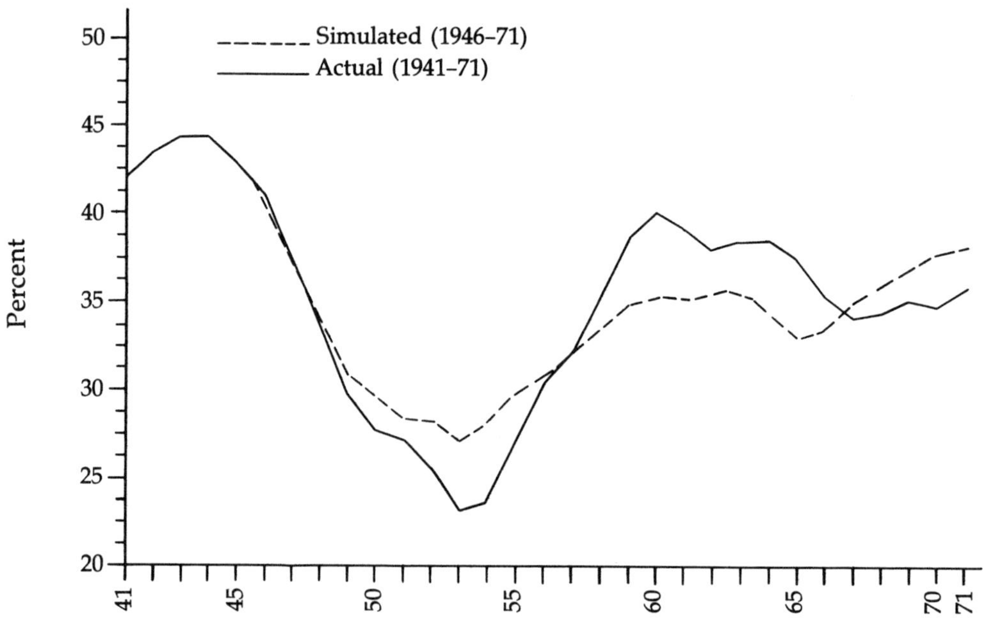

Figure 17—Returns to capital (r), 1941–71

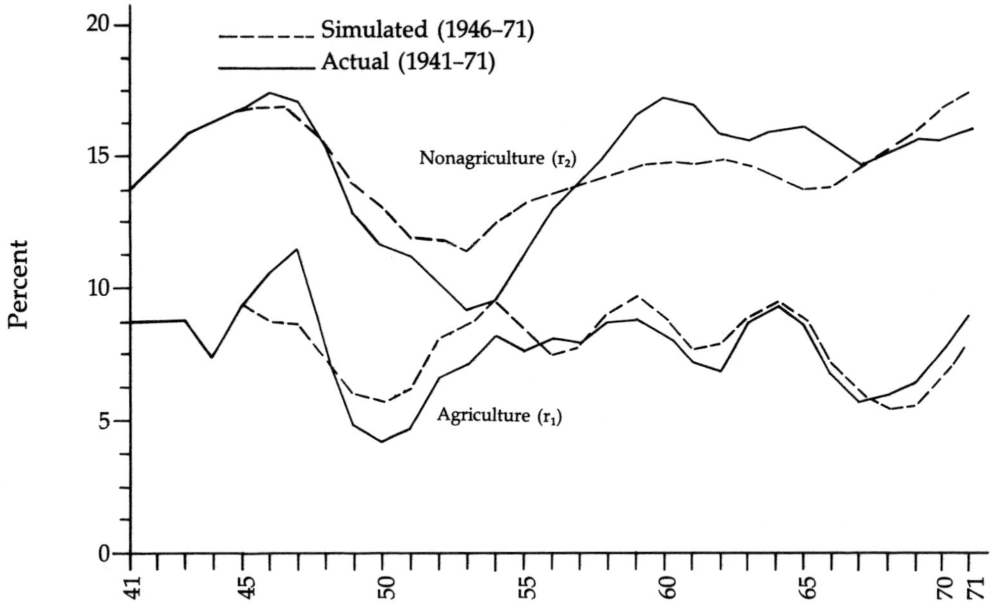

Figure 18—Wage rates (w), 1941–71

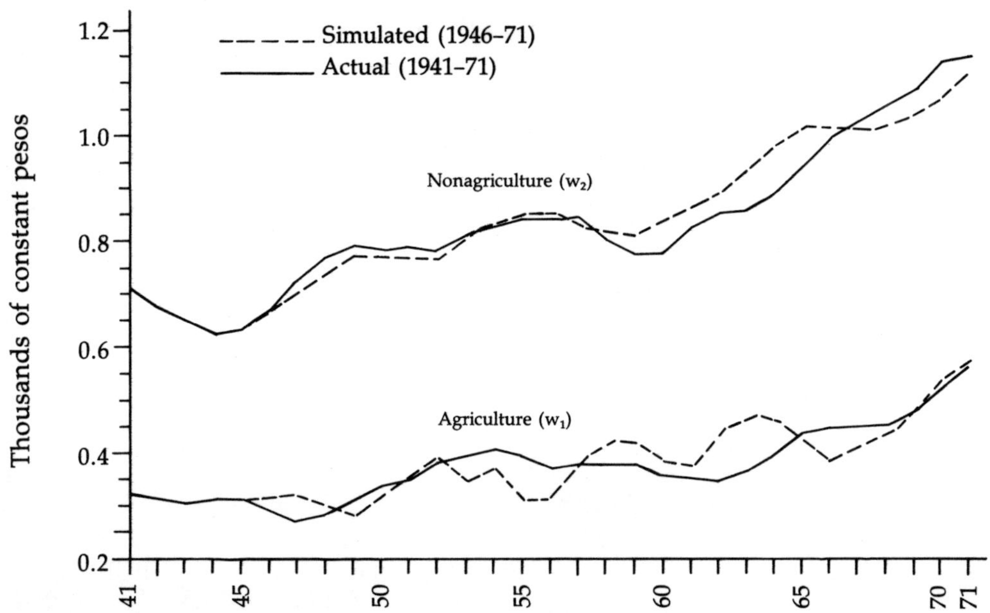

Figure 19—Rent on land (R), 1941–71

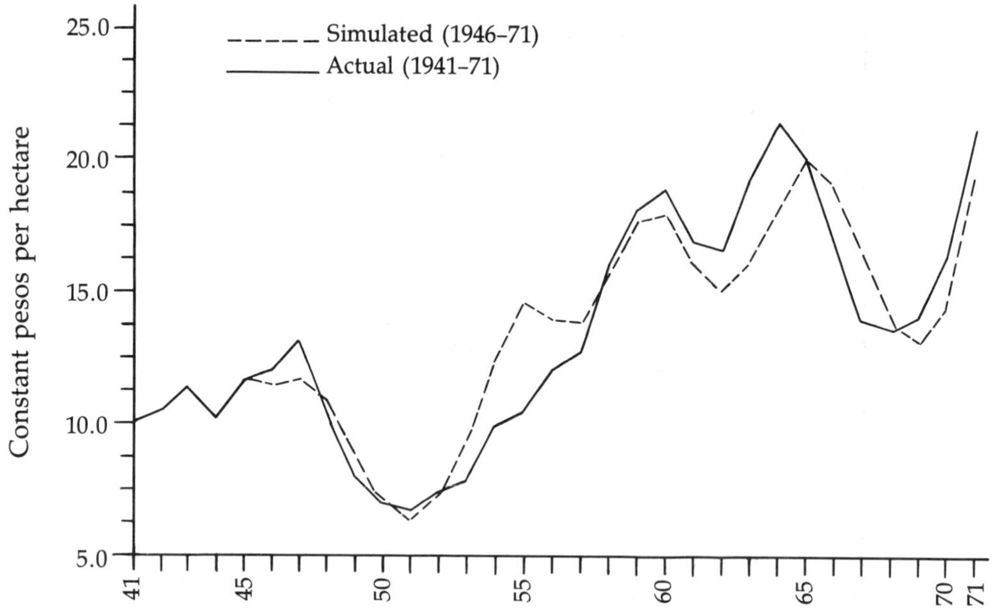

Figure 20—Price of land (p_A), 1941–71

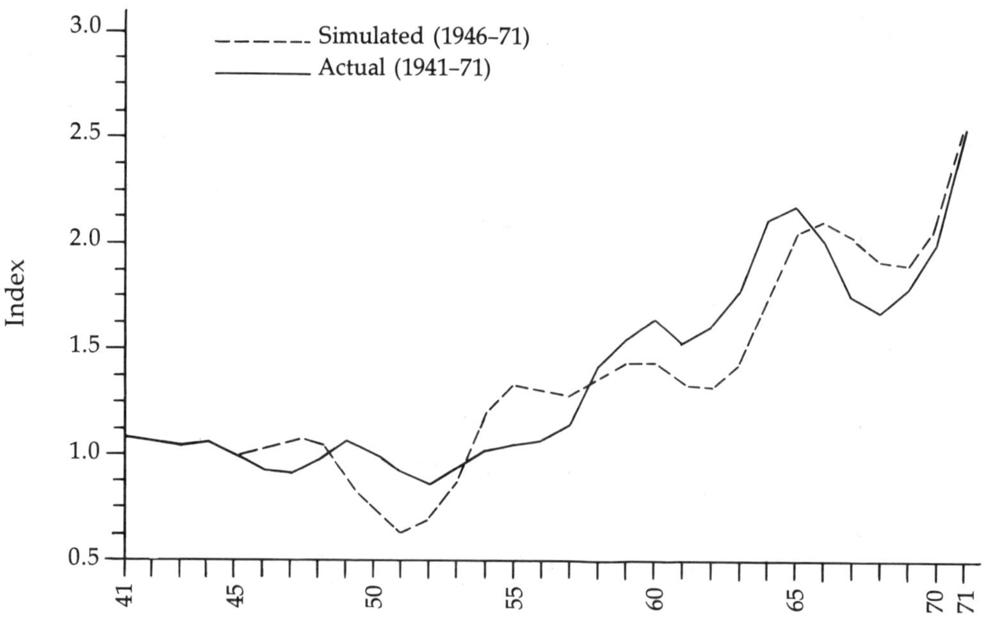

according to the opportunities they offer. θ is plotted in Figure 22. The resulting per capita investments in each sector are

$$i_1 = \theta i,$$

and

$$i_2 = (1 - \theta) i.$$

They are plotted in Figure 23.

Equation (4.14) is used to determine λ, which allocates agricultural investment according to its sources:

$$i_{11} = \lambda i_1,$$

and

$$i_{12} = (1 - \lambda)\, i_1.$$

In passing, it should be noted that these are the same components of investment used to determine the capital stocks. The plots for λ are given in Figure 24. Having determined i_{11}, it is now possible to compute x_1^i using equation (3.14), $x_1^i = \lambda \theta i / p^*$. This variable is plotted in Figure 11. The rest of the product utilization is determined simultaneously, using the following subsystem of equations and identities to solve for $x_2^{c,p}$, x_1^c, x_2^i, x_2^m, x_1^e, and p_2^*:

$$x_2^{c,p} - A_0 + A_1 c^p + A_2 p_1^*/p_2^* + A_3\, x_2^m/(x_2 + x_2^m) + A_4 p_1\, x_1/x + A_5\, x_2^{c,p}(t-1),$$

$$x_1^c = (c^p - p_2^* x_2^{c,p})/p_1^*,$$

$$x_2^1 = [i_2 + (1 - \lambda)\, i_1]/p_2^*,$$

$$x_2^m = x_2^{c,p} + x_2^i + y^t/p_2^* - x_2,$$

$$x_1^e = x_1 - x_1^c - x_1^i,$$

$$y^t = t_1\, p_1\, (x_1 - x_1^e) + t_x\, p_1^e x_1^e + t_2\, x_2 + t_m\, p_2^e x_2^m,$$

and

$$p_2^* = x_2^m/(x_2 + x_2^m)\,(p_2^{nd} - 1 - t_2) + (1 + t_2).$$

The coefficients of the $x_2^{c,p}$ function are given in equation (4.10). As explained in Chapter 8, this system is estimated together with the consumption function. In this simulation a few modifications were made to make the system recursive. The weight variable $x_2^m/(x_2 + x_2^m)$ is set exogenously. That modification makes p_2^* at time t predetermined. As a consequence, the market price ratio $p^* = p_1^*/p_2^*$ is determined and plotted in Figure 25. Per capita private consumption of nonagriculture ($x_2^{c,p}$) can then be determined. This is also true for x_1^c, x_2^i, and x_1^e. The system reduces to the two equations with the left-hand variables, x_2^m and y^t. These two variables are determined by solving the two

Figure 21—Per capita income and expenditures, 1941–71

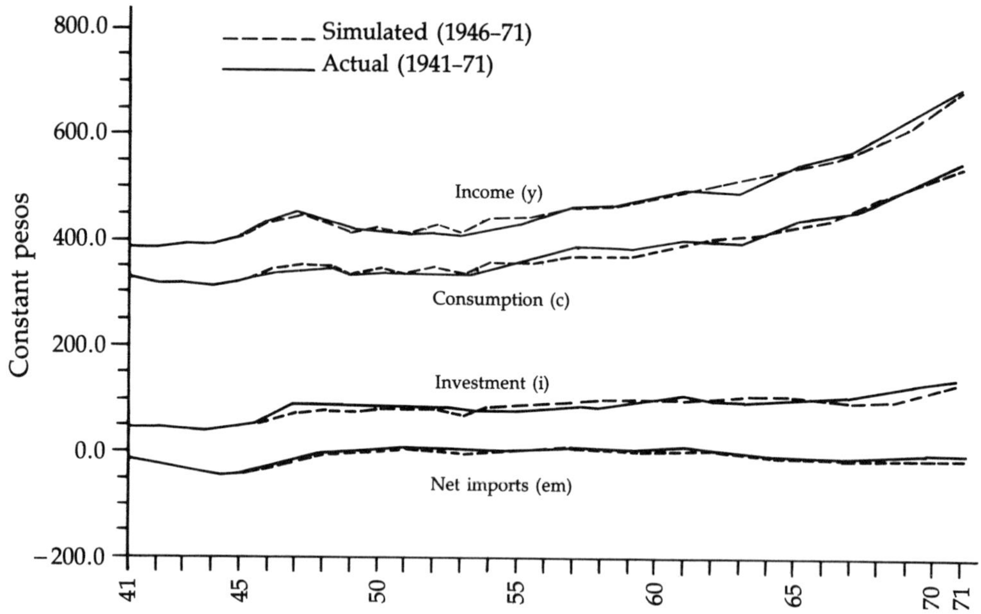

Figure 22—Share of agriculture in total investments (θ), 1941–71

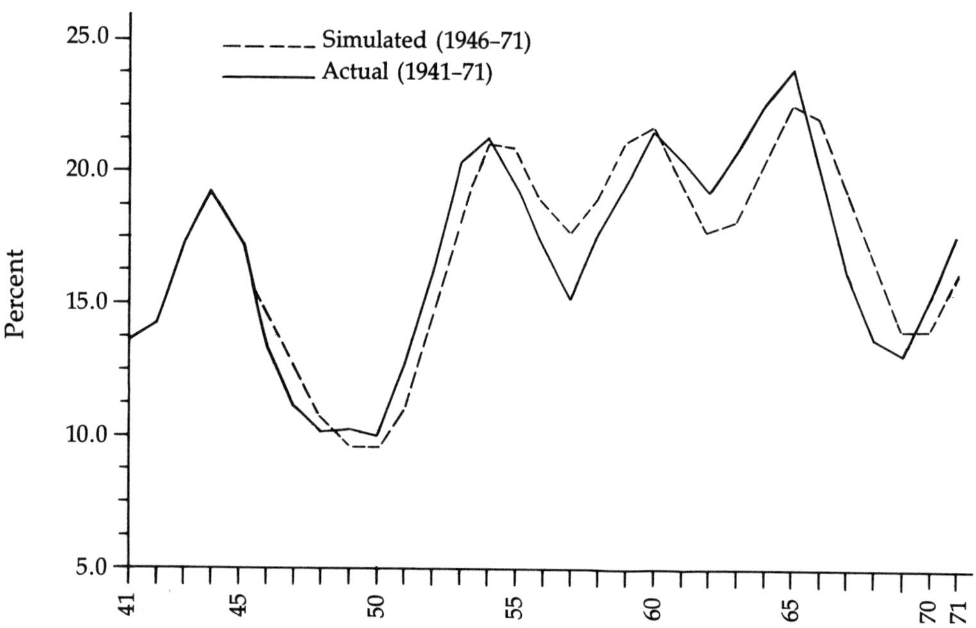

Figure 23—Per capita investment (i) by sector, 1941–71

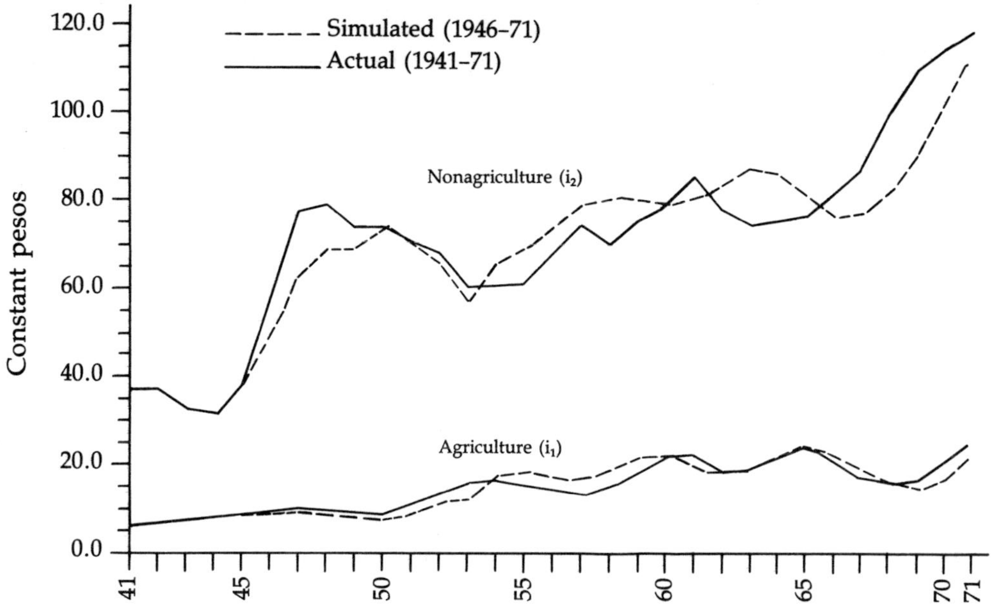

Figure 24—Share of agricultural products in agricultural investment (λ), 1941–71

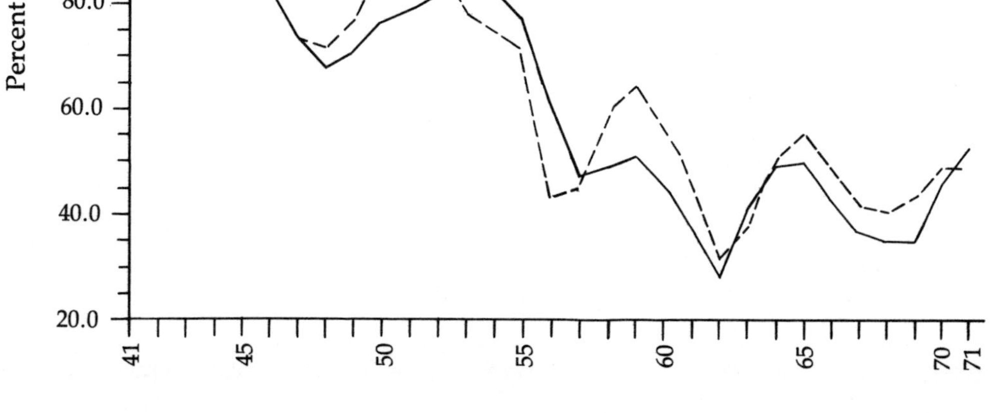

equations simultaneously. Note that they determine the amount of imports, x^m_2, as a function of the amount of indirect tax, y^t, which is used for government consumption. These two variables are positively correlated; the larger the government expenditures, the larger the imports. It should be noted that they are determined independently of the size of $x_2^{c,p}$ and x_2^i, which have already been determined. The plots of x_2^c and x_2^i appear in Figure 12. The plots of x^m_2 and x_1^e appear in Figure 26, of x_i^c in Figure 11, and of y^t in Figure 27.

Having solved the system for time t, it is now possible to compute the following aggregates:

$$y = x + y^t = \text{total income in market prices},$$

$$c = c^p + y^t = \text{total per capita consumption},$$

and

$$em = c + i - y = \text{foreign savings}.$$

All are plotted in Figure 21; em is also plotted in Figure 28.[21]

The Confrontation of the Model with the Data

The model was fitted to the data for the years 1946–72.[22] The study begins with the postwar years to avoid some of the abnormalities that existed during 1940–45. The figures are obtained by a dynamic simulation in which all the endogenous variables of the model are actually generated by the model.

The first important period, referred to in Chapter 2 as the upward swing of the Peronist cycle, is characterized by a rapid increase of GDP, which arises exclusively from nonagriculture, and by a decline in agricultural output. The model captures these movements, as can be seen in Figures 11, 12, and 21. These changes are also reflected in the sectoral investments and the labor migration in Figures 8, 22, 23, and 24. The fit of the model verifies that all these changes can be accounted for by the economic forces of the period. These were not the only forces, however. There was also strong government investment in nonagriculture. As government behavior is not explicitly included, the model somewhat underestimates the investment and output of sector 2 in that period. Figure 26 indicates that the dramatic changes in postwar imports and exports are captured closely. It should be recalled that these two variables are computed as the residuals of the system.

By 1950 the Peronist boom was over and the country faced difficult problems. The stagnation of agriculture affected the traditional exportation of agricultural products. This phenomenon is described in Figure 26. It should be noted that this decline in exports is a natural outcome of Peronist policies. The situation was worsened by the droughts of 1951 and 1952. The yield decline due to the drought is not explained by the model; consequently, discrepancies between the simulated and actual outputs for the period 1950–54 can be observed. Similarly, the model does not explain the high agricultural production of 1954, which was due to extremely favorable weather conditions (see Figure 11).

During the early 1950s the Peronist policies were changed to favor agriculture. This caused the direct investments of government to shift from nonagriculture to agriculture. The

[21]The scale in Figure 21 is too large for tracing the detailed variations in em.

[22]This section relies on the description of Chapter 2 and on the annual reports on the performance of agriculture issued by the central bank (Banco Central de la República Argentina, *Memorias del Banco Central* [Buenos Aires: BCRA, 1951–72]).

Figure 25—Market price ratio (p*), 1941–71

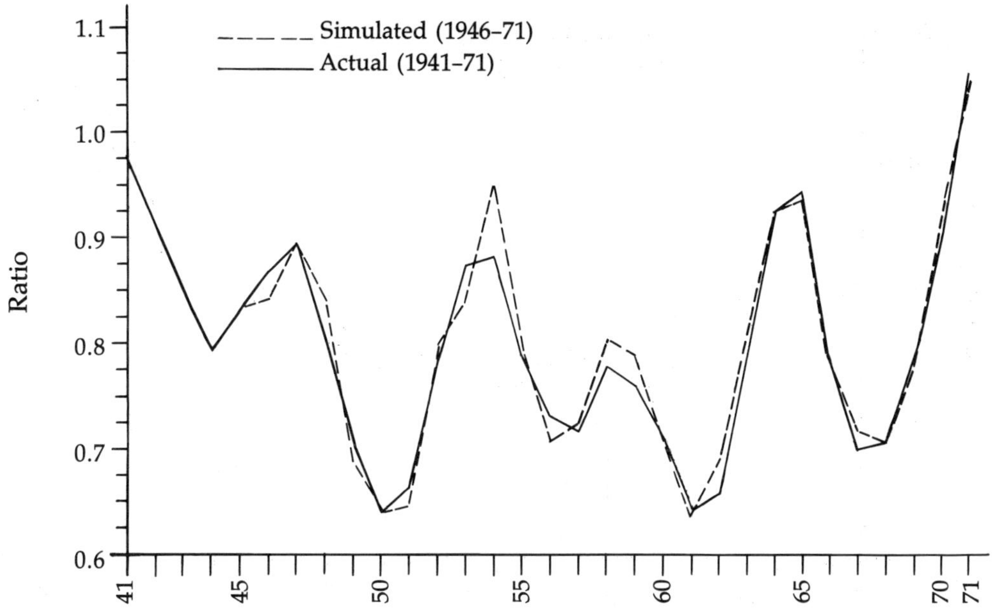

Figure 26—Per capita exports (x_1^e) and imports (x_2^m), 1941–71

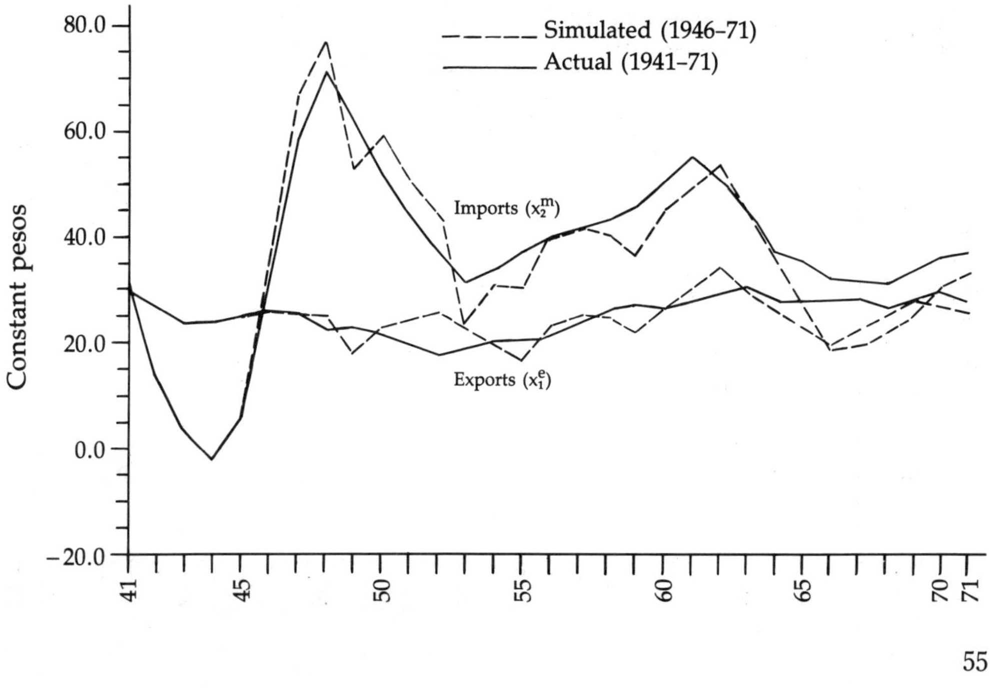

Figure 27—Per capita indirect taxes (y^t), 1941–71

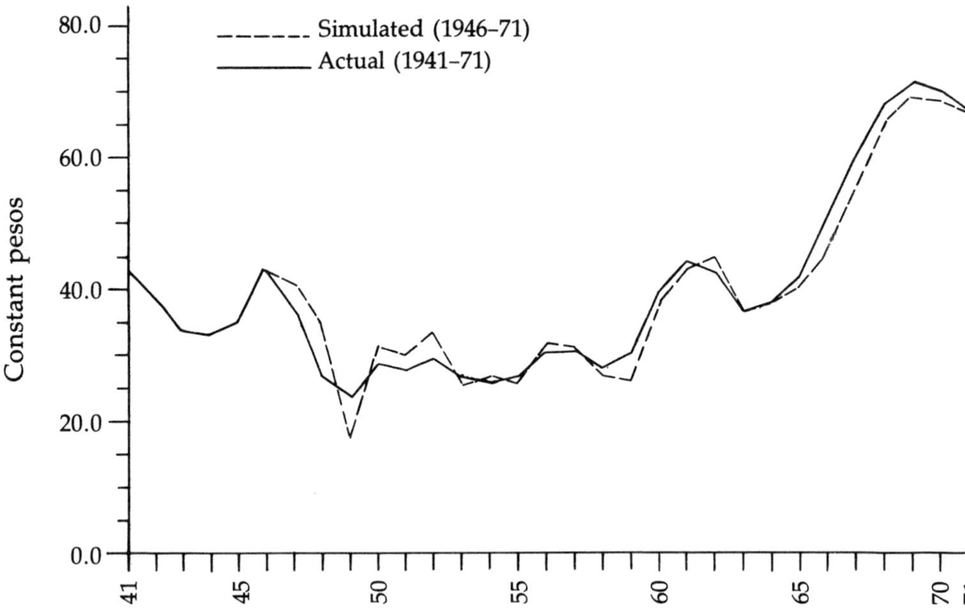

Figure 28—Per capita net imports (em), 1941–71

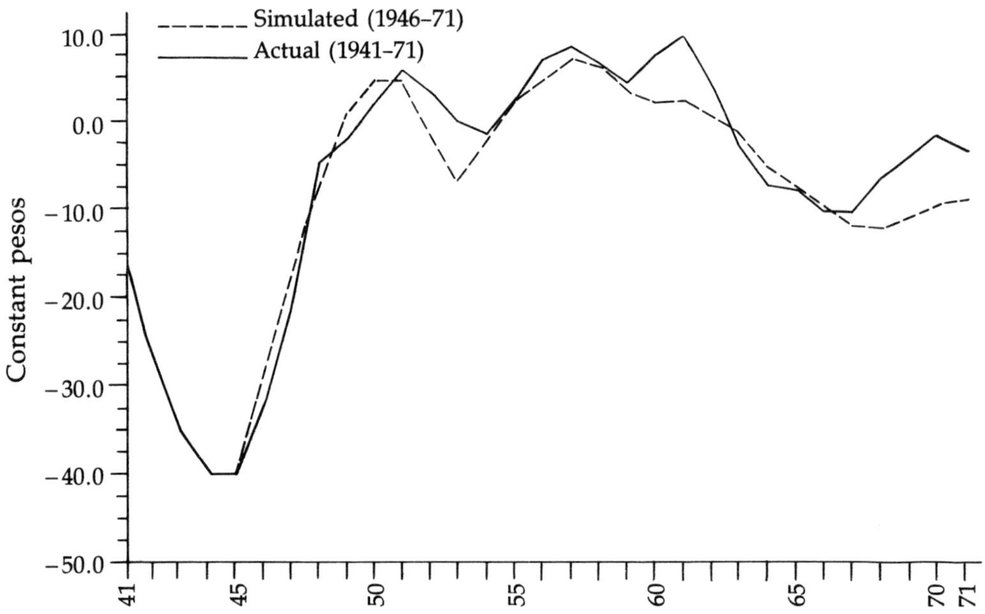

effects of direct government intervention that are not reflected in prices are not captured by the model. As a consequence, the performance of nonagriculture is overestimated, as can be seen in Figure 12.

In the late 1950s government policies became even more favorable toward agriculture when the real exchange rate was increased. The model describes this well, as can be seen in Figures 3-5. The response of resource allocation to these favorable policies can also be seen in the reversal of migration in Figure 8 and the sharp increase in agricultural investment in Figures 22, 23, and 24. During this period there were important changes in the price ratio of crops to livestock, leading to a pronounced change in output composition—a shift toward crops at the beginning of the period and back to livestock at the end. The production function shows aggregate output and does not capture fully the changes in output resulting from these changes in composition. Consequently, the model overestimates the performance of agriculture during that period, as can be seen in Figure 11.

The policies of the early 1960s had little effect on agriculture. The model describes the trend in agricultural output well. The model also captures the reversal of export and import trends that took place between 1955 and the early 1960s, indicating that it was a response to the underlying economic forces. So was the reversal that took place after 1962, although the model somewhat exaggerates the response. This may reflect the discrepancy in agricultural output resulting from the changes in the composition of trade in the late 1950s (Figure 26).

Figures 3-5 also reflect the policies unfavorable to agriculture of the late 1960s. They document the reduction in the real exchange rate. Again, the model captures the changes in resource allocation well. (See Figure 8 for labor migration and Figures 22, 23, and 24 for sectoral investment.) The model anticipates the decline in agricultural production, which in reality started in 1966. The rapid growth of nonagriculture, which began in 1955, is also described well (see Figure 12). It does, however, miss the recession of 1962–63 resulting from the policies implemented to cope with severe balance-of-payments problems, which are not explicitly dealt with in the model.

In sum, a model consisting of a small number of behavioral equations suggested by basic economic theory is able to explain the main patterns of Argentine growth in the postwar period. It reproduces the postwar decline in agricultural production and the slow recovery in the 1960s. It describes quite well the postwar boom in nonagricultural output, the downward turn of the Peronist cycle in the early 1950s, and nonagriculture's rapid growth in subsequent decades. Moreover, the model satisfactorily reproduces the trend of factor prices, in spite of extensive government intervention in setting wages and other prices. These policies apparently only dampened the cyclical variations of real wages (Figure 18) and exacerbated the variability of the returns to capital (Figure 17).

How can the patterns of economic growth be explained so simply when they usually require elaborate arguments taking into account a large number of social, institutional, and other considerations? The keys to the explanation are in the formulation of the process of resource allocation and the changes in productivity. It is essential in explaining the response of the economy to economic forces to take the current state of the economy explicitly into account. It is difficult to explain the economic process by starting with concepts of long-term equilibrium and inferring from them current movements of the economy. On the contrary, present movements are determined largely by the state of the economy. Whether or not the economy will move to the long-term equilibrium point presently perceived depends largely on the economic signals that develop along the path of convergence.

5

THE EFFECT OF TRADE LIBERALIZATION, EXCHANGE RATE POLICIES, AND DOMESTIC TAXATION

Savings and Flow of Funds

A transfer of funds from agriculture is considered by some to be an important instrument for economic development.[23] The idea is that the transferred funds provide financing for the development of nonagriculture. In a market economy a transfer will take place if the rates of return in nonagriculture are sufficiently favorable. This voluntary flow takes into account not only the potential returns in nonagriculture but also the opportunity cost in agriculture. Many times, however, countries do not wait for the market to allocate the funds and use taxes to perform the task. That has been true in Argentina. In what follows, the sizes of the kinds of transfers that have been made in Argentina are reviewed. The consequences of these transfers will be evaluated in subsequent discussions.

Domestic Savings

The transfer or flow of funds is defined here as the difference between the savings generated by a sector and the investment in the sector. It is therefore natural to start the discussion by evaluating saving behavior in the private sector. This is done by using the estimates of the consumption function in Chapter 8. Taking equation (4.9) as a description of the consumption function, the following conclusions about savings generated by the sources of income can be derived. The coefficient of consumption for nonagricultural income and agricultural wages is 0.70. That amounts to a saving rate of 30 percent. The consumption rate of disposable income is somewhat higher, as indicated in Chapter 8. It is obtained by adjusting the output figure for direct personal and corporate taxes. Thus, if such taxes amount to 10 percent, the marginal propensity to consume out of disposable income will be 0.78 and the corresponding saving rate will be 0.22.

This illustration should help to interpret the results, making them comparable to savings studies where savings are related to disposable income. For other purposes, it would be more meaningful to consider the rate corresponding to output or to compare private savings to tax extraction.

Savings generated by agricultural income have two components, wage and nonwage. Thus the per capita saving function can be written in the following form:

$$S_1 = p_1x_1 - 0.70\ w_1L_1/N - 0.045\ p_AA/N,$$

Dividing S_1 by the per capita agricultural output in factor cost (p_1x_1) gives the saving rate (s_1). This information is summarized in Table 2 and plotted in Figure 29. The average saving rate is 51 percent. It ranged from 39 to 61 percent. This is considerably higher than for

[23]The term transfer of funds is used as it is in the literature. Clearly, this term applies to a monetary economy. The framework here is of a real economy and therefore it would have been more appropriate to refer to a transfer of resources. The discussion should be interpreted in this sense.

Table 2—Rates of agricultural saving, tax extraction, and transfer, 1940-72

Variable	Mean	Standard Deviation	Coefficient of Variation
Saving	50.9	5.1	0.10
Export tax extraction			
Direct	15.4	11.2	0.73
Indirect	34.5	28.4	0.82
Flow of funds			
Saving	30.6	7.3	0.24
Saving and tax extraction	80.5	44.7	0.56

Notes: The means and standard deviations are expressed as percentages. For definitions of the variables see the text.

nonagriculture. Because the rate of saving from agricultural wages is equal to that of nonagricultural income, the difference originates in the higher saving rate of nonwage income. The overall saving rate can be written as a weighted average of savings out of wage (s_w) and nonwage income (s_π):

$$s = s_w S_L + s_\pi (1 - S_L).$$

Applying it to agriculture, the average value of the labor share in total agricultural income (S_L) is 0.52. Using the average value of agricultural savings of 0.51 for s, $s_w = 0.3$, the marginal propensity to save out of nonwage income (s_π), is solved for, giving a value of 0.74.

Export Tax

Agriculture has been taxed heavily over the years, especially agricultural exports. The effective rates of this taxation are plotted in Figure 30. The tax rate varied widely, reaching a peak of 60 percent in 1947 and a trough of 2 percent protection (rather than tax) in 1954. The average rate for the whole 1940–72 period was 29 percent.

With such high rates of taxation, what share of the agricultural product did not generate private consumption? Ignoring supply and demand responses to the export tax, the question is answered in terms of the direct and indirect effects of the export tax. The direct extraction from agriculture is equal to the tax rate as applied to actual agricultural exports, that is, ($t_x p_1^e x_1^e$). This amount is given as a share of $p_1 x_1$, the value of per capita agricultural output, so that it is expressed in the same terms as the saving rate. The values of the direct tax extraction are plotted in Figure 31. They fluctuated widely, reaching a peak value of 44 percent in 1947. The average value for the period was 15 percent.

The indirect effect of the export tax is the reduction of domestic prices. The indirect extraction from agriculture from this reduction, expressed as a proportion of the same base as the other rates, is $t_x \cdot p_1^e (x_1 - x_1^e)/p_1 \cdot x_1$. The indirect extraction was far more important than the direct extraction. Its average for the period was 34 percent. Its fluctuations follow the same pattern as the rate of direct extraction. The rate of total tax extraction, plotted in Figure 31, is the sum of the direct and indirect extractions. The peak value in 1947 was 148 percent. That is, the effect of the tax was to transfer resources out of agriculture valued at 148 percent of agricultural income at factor cost.

These rates declined after 1947, sinking to 2 percent protection in 1954. They again reached about 40 percent in the period 1956–62 and declined for the rest of the 1960s. The average value for the whole 1940–72 period was 50 percent, about the same as the private agricultural saving rate.

Figure 29—Private savings out of agricultural income (s_1), 1940–73

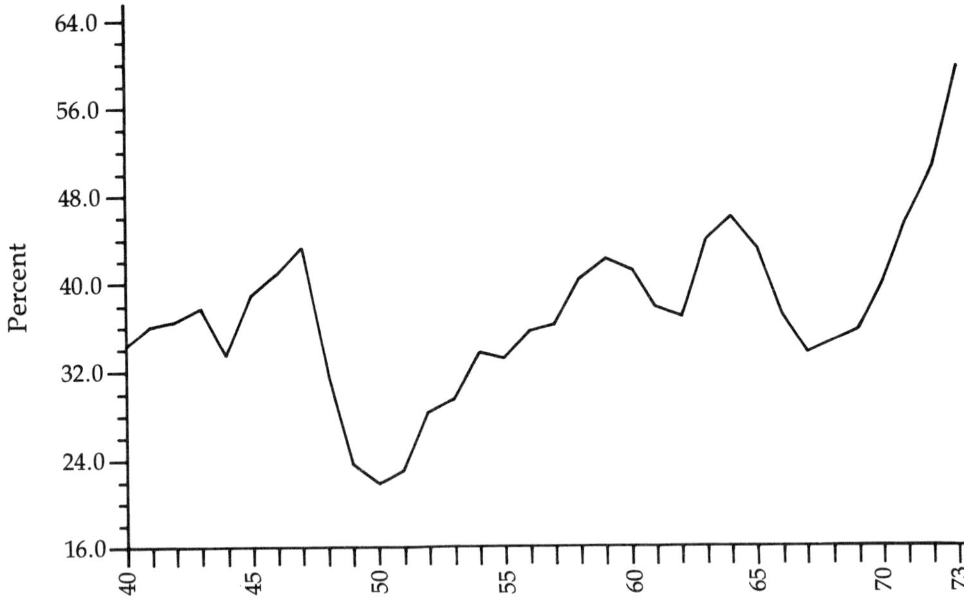

Figure 30—Export tax rate (t_x), 1940–73

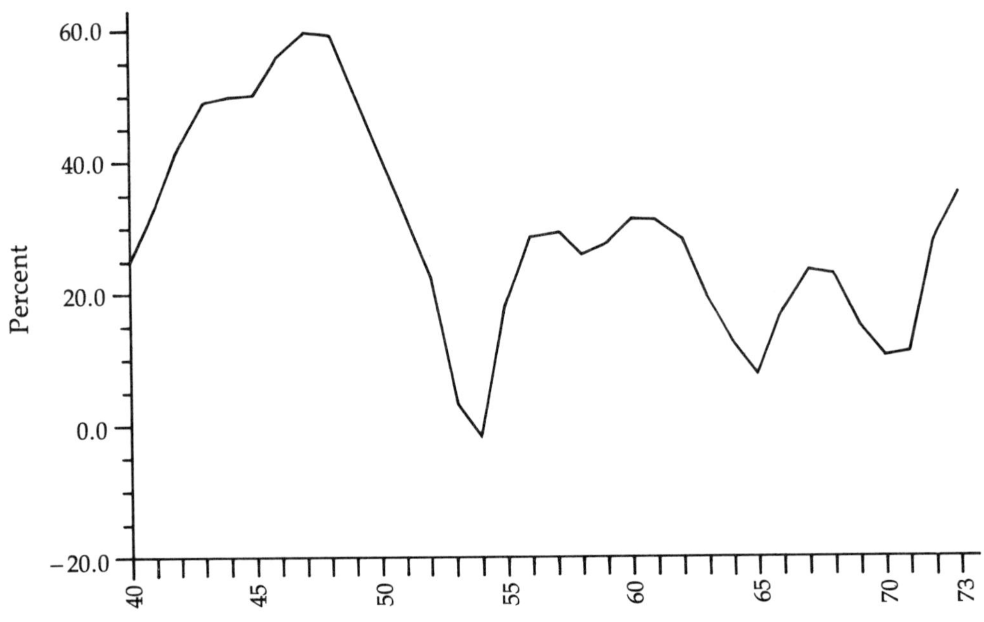

Flow of Funds

In considering the contribution of agriculture to the rest of the economy, the rates of several flows are computed. The flow of savings out of agriculture is defined as savings generated by agricultural income less investment in agriculture. As before, it is more informative to express this variable as a proportion of agricultural output valued at factor cost. The rate of flow thus expressed is plotted in Figure 32. This flow is quite large. The average value for the period was 30.6 percent with a standard deviation of 73 percent. Thus the coefficient of variation is 0.238 as compared with 0.1 for private savings. Thus, the flow fluctuates relatively more than savings. This can be explained by noting that market conditions affect the two components of the flow in a complementary way, taking the sign into account. More favorable conditions in agriculture increase its share in total investment and probably the ratio of investment to output. At the same time, these conditions are also reflected in land prices and the amount of cultivated land, leading to more wealth and more consumption. This results in a decline in the rates of savings and flow. Thus, the flow is accounted for in terms of market conditions without estimating a flow equation directly.

The actual flow of funds out of agriculture is, of course, far larger because it also includes the transfer due to extraction. This can be seen in Figure 32 where the flow is plotted cumulatively, taking extraction into account.

Foreign and Domestic Terms of Trade

From the previous discussion it is clear that agriculture was heavily taxed, both directly and indirectly, through the protection of nonagriculture. The situation can be summarized clearly by looking at the difference between the domestic and foreign terms of trade of agriculture, measured as the ratio of the prices of the two sectors. The data are plotted in Figure 33. It is evident that the domestic terms of trade are considerably less than the international. The discrepancy between the domestic and foreign price ratios is lowest in 1958, when the foreign price ratio was 31 percent greater than the domestic. Throughout the period the discrepancy was much larger and was around 60 percent during the 1960s.

As expected, and as supported by the empirical analysis, the system responds to prices. But what effect did this diversion from the foreign terms of trade have on the Argentine economy in general and on agriculture specifically? This question is evaluated below under alternative assumptions and specifications of some key relations. The method used is to introduce some modifications in the basic model presented in Chapter 4 and to simulate the economy under such changes. Selected results will be presented in plots comparing the results of the experiments, joined by plots of the results of the base run described in Chapter 4.

Before the results are presented, a caveat about the interpretation of the simulation should be considered. It is possible that changes in policy generate changes in parameters that are not captured by a model estimated from past data. It is claimed that this is particularly true when the model contains agents' expectations of the future values of the variables affecting their decisions.[24] It is felt that using rational expectations to replace the unobserved values of agents' expectations will alleviate the problem. Without going into detail, it is enough to point out here that using rational expectations implies a joint solution for the expected values of the

[24]Compare R. E. Lucas, Jr., "Econometric Policy Evaluation: A Critique," in *The Phillips Curve and Labour Markets,* a supplement to the *Journal of Monetary Economics,* ed. K. Brunner and A. H. Meltzer (1976): 19–46.

Figure 31—Extraction of agricultural output as a proportion of agricultural output at factor cost, 1940–73

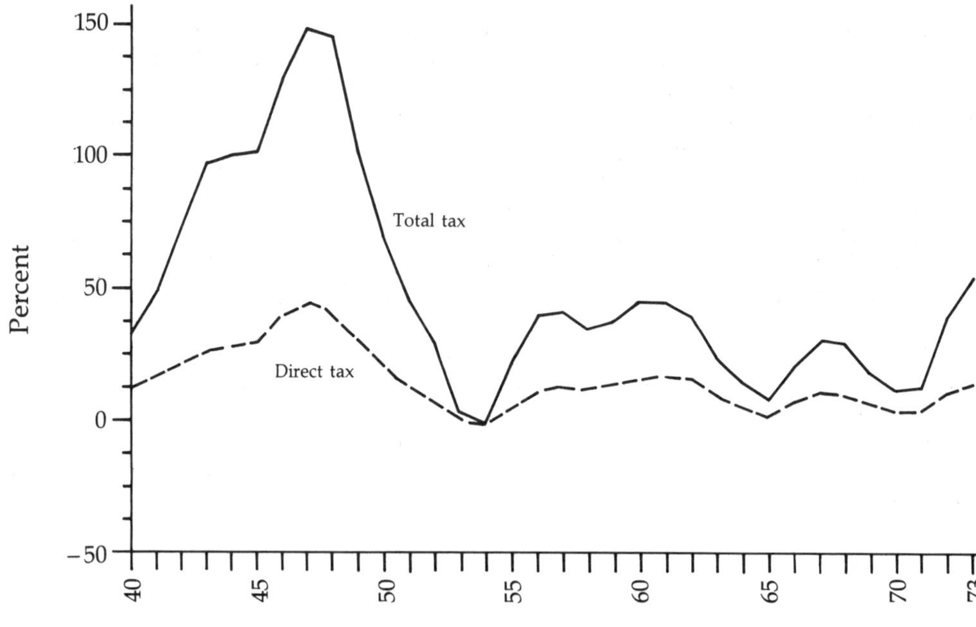

Figure 32—Rates of flow of funds out of agriculture, 1940–73

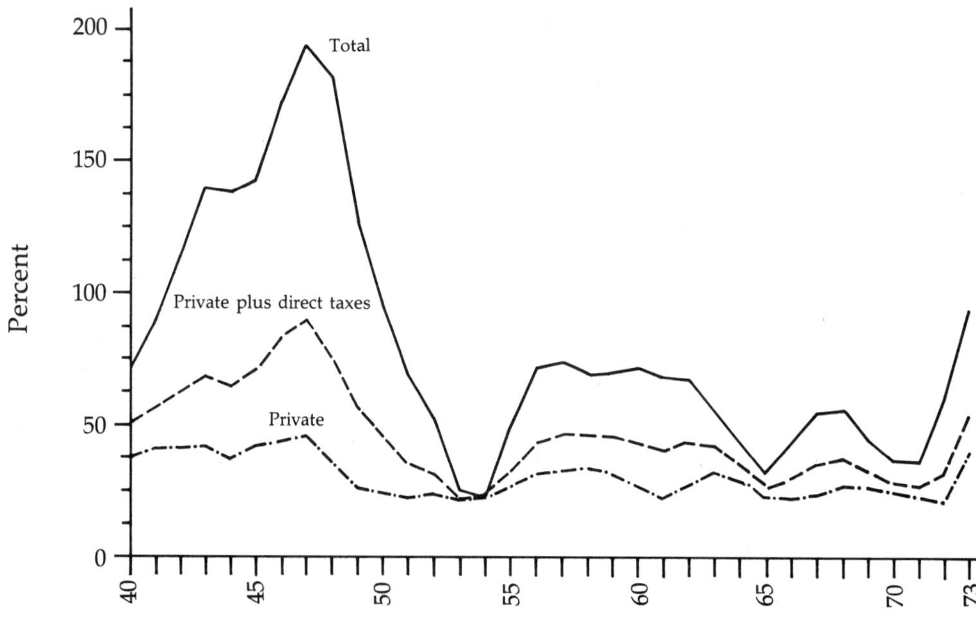

variables in question and for the coefficients based on the sample.[25] It therefore follows that if the coefficients depend on policies, a solution obtained for a given sample is still not applicable when different policies are adopted. Thus, the problem is not resolved.

The question of whether coefficients might be dependent on policies is somewhat broader. Policies affect the economic environment, but so do other variables. If such effects are to be allowed for explicitly, the model should be formulated accordingly. This is basically the approach taken here in the formulation and estimation of the production sector. It is explained in more detail in Chapter 7.

Any empirical analysis requires a limit to the number of coefficients to be estimated. That limit requires that some coefficients be constant. What implications does this have for the interpretation of the simulated results? It is suggested that the simulations show how an economy such as the one described by the empirical model for Argentina responds to changes in its exogenous variables. As such, they help us to draw conclusions from the postulated model. Reluctance to draw such conclusions implies reluctance to attribute to the model empirical significance. This applies to any economic analysis. Yet the purpose for making such an analysis is to draw empirical propositions from it.

Elimination of Export Taxes and Import Tariffs

The first exercise examines the effects of eliminating export taxes and import tariffs. This is done using the model described in Chapter 4 with the following modifications:

Instead of beginning in 1946, the exercise begins in 1950, after the main abnormalities of the war and the postwar period disappeared and world trade was developing rapidly. The main change of this experiment is to set t_x and t_m equal to zero. In terms of Figure 33, this implies that beginning in 1950 the domestic terms of trade jumped to equal the foreign terms of trade and remained identical to them thereafter.

The elimination of t_x and t_m reduces the indirect tax revenue (y^t). In order to isolate the effect of changes in the terms of trade from changes in tax collection, it is necessary to restore the tax revenue. This is done by increasing the domestic indirect tax rates, t_1 and t_2, by applying an additional tax with a uniform rate t on all domestic utilization. The rate t is determined so that it maintains the ratio of tax collections to output, y^t/x, equal to that of the base run. Thus t is determined from the following equation:

$$(y^t/x)^{exo} = \frac{t_1 p_1 (x_1 - x_1^e) + t_2 x_2 + t\,[p_1(x_1 - x_1^e) + x_2 + x_2^m]}{x} \tag{5.1}$$

where $(y^t/x)^{exo}$ is the value of the base run imposed exogenously. At any time none of the variables on the right-hand side of equation (5.1) are determined independently of t, so to avoid interdependence, t can be solved approximately for lagged values of all the variables in equation (5.1). This means that the ratio y^t/x will be approximately $(y^t/x)^{exo}$.

The elimination of t_x and t_m affects the terms of trade between agriculture and the traded subsector of nonagriculture. However, the effect of this step on the economy as a whole depends also on the terms of trade between the traded and nontraded sectors. These terms of trade are measured by the real rate of exchange. Recall that $p_2^{nd} = p_2^f RE(1 + t_m)$. If t_m is set to be zero, then for any given foreign price, p_2^{nd} is determined by the exchange rate, RE. From here on, this expression for p_2^{nd} is evaluated for real values of RE and p_2^{nd}. Recall that RE is

[25] Yair Mundlak, "Elements of a Pure Theory of Forecasting and After-Keynesian Macroeconomics," in *Development in an Inflationary World,* ed. M. June Flanders and Assaf Razin (New York: Academic Press, 1981), pp. 359-373.

actually computed by deflating the nominal exchange rate, NRE, by p_2^d and p_2^{nd} is also deflated by p_2^d. Therefore RE determines the terms of trade between the traded and nontraded sectors of nonagriculture. A similar calculation can be done for the terms of trade of the nontraded sector and agriculture.

The elimination of t_x and t_m affects the real rate of exchange. That in turn has a strong effect on the economy. Thus any simulation of trade liberalization is affected by the assumptions for RE. That of course emphasizes the fact that RE is a policy instrument.

To introduce the subject it is noted that RE is related to the size of t_x and t_m. From the empirical analysis in Chapter 9 it appears that the effect of t_x on RE dominates that of t_m. Consequently, trade liberalization causes RE to fall. Figure 34 illustrates the simulated values of RE obtained with liberalized trade and with the other variables in the RE equation kept at their historical values.[26] The decline can be attributed to the increase in liquidity generated by the increase in exports. As a result, the response of the economy to a policy of trade liberalization fails to produce the gains anticipated in the literature on trade distortion. This can be shown by examining closely the simulation where the determinants of RE are kept at their historical values, except for the changes introduced by the trade liberalization explained above. Summary results for year 21 (1971) of this exercise appear in Table 3.

The decline in RE due to trade liberalization reached 20 percent of the base-run value, as can be seen in Figure 34. This decline was enough to encourage a shift of resources toward nontraded goods. This can be inferred from the resulting changes in domestic prices received by producers of the two traded commodities. The new values of p_1 and p_2^{nd} are plotted in Figures 35 and 36. Those values reflect the decline in RE. As such p_1 did not increase by the full amount of t_x, and p_2^{nd} declines by more than the amount called for by the elimination of t_m.

The economy responded to those changes in prices. Agricultural production increased gradually and reached the largest deviation from the base run in 1963 with a growth of 4.7 percent, as can be seen in Figure 37. At the same time there was a reduction in the consumption of food. This decline reflects the increase in food prices caused by the elimination of t_x and, to some extent, by the compensatory increase in the domestic tax.

The response of nonagricultural output was also in line with the price change. As Figure 38 shows, per capita output in sector 2 went down drastically following the change. This decline is produced by the sharp decline in p_2^{nd}, which appears as a state variable in nonagriculture's production function. Basically p_2^{nd} allocates resources between the traded and nontraded activities in nonagriculture. Thus a decline in p_2^{nd} signifies a shift of resources toward services and away from manufacturing. It should be noted that the decline in per capita output, x_2, continued for four years, whereas the decline in overall income, which is plotted in Figure 39, lasted only three years. The economy recovered from then on. The recovery was produced by an increase in agricultural output that took place gradually while the response in x_2 was more immediate. It thus took several years for income to stabilize and for investment, which responded to growth in output, to begin an upward trend. This process led the gap in x_2 to close gradually, but after 20 years x_2 was still less than the base-run value. The behavior of the economy followed the pattern of changes in RE. After its initial downward adjustment, it started to move up, following the main trends observed for the base run, but remaining below it for most of the period.

Looking at the overall performance of the economy in Figure 39, it can be seen that at the end of the period, income measured in terms of nonagriculture was still less than the historical value as given by the base run. It should, however, be pointed out that as a result of the changes, net imports (em) were reduced and the country improved its foreign asset

[26]In Figures 34–71, the base run is the simulated run in Figures 3-28 for 1946–71 plus the actual values for 1941–45. The actual estimation begins in 1950, but it is connected by a line to the 1949 value of the base run.

Figure 33—Foreign and domestic terms of trade, 1941–71

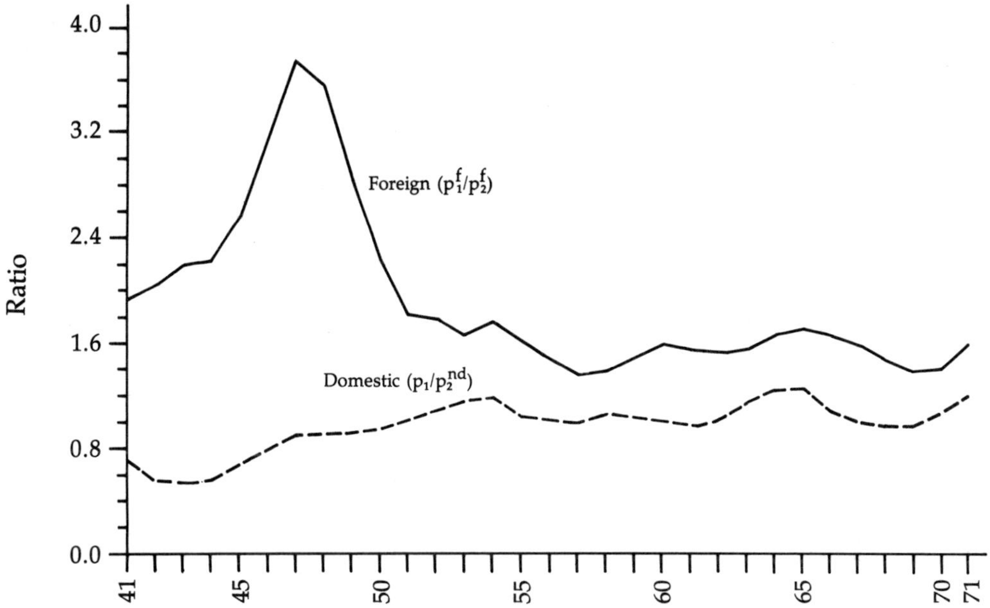

Figure 34—Effects of trade liberalization on the real exchange rate (RE), 1941–71

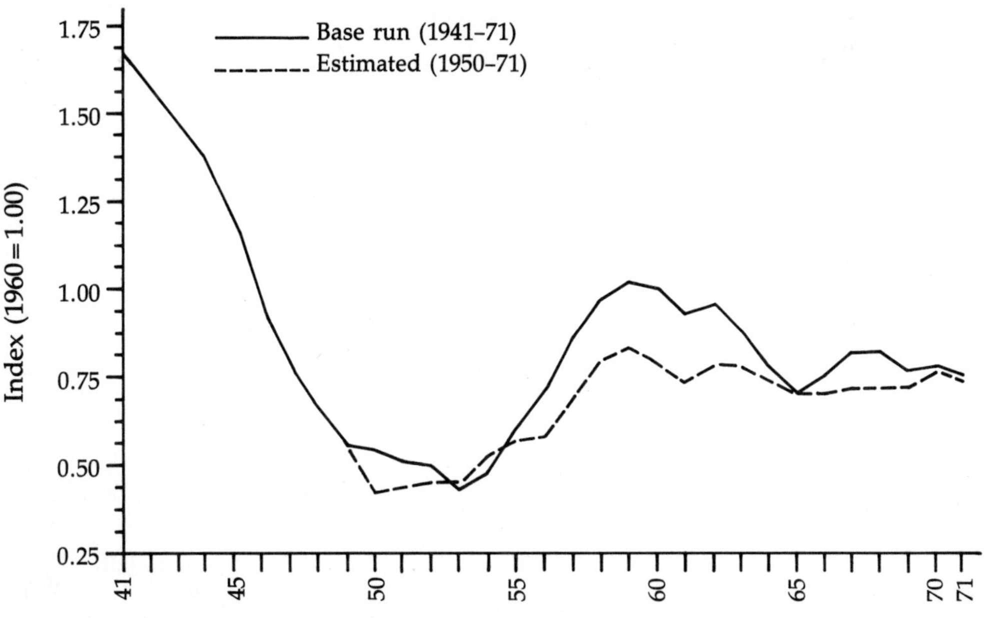

Figure 35—Effects of trade liberalization on agricultural prices (p_1), 1941–71

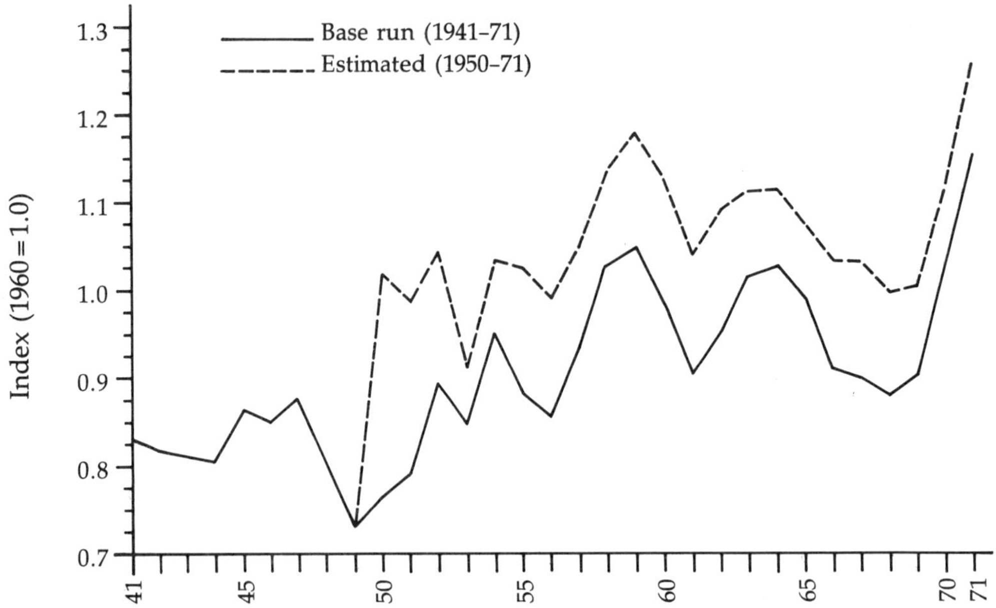

Figure 36—Effects of trade liberalization on the market price of imported nonagricultural products (p_2^{nd}), 1941–71

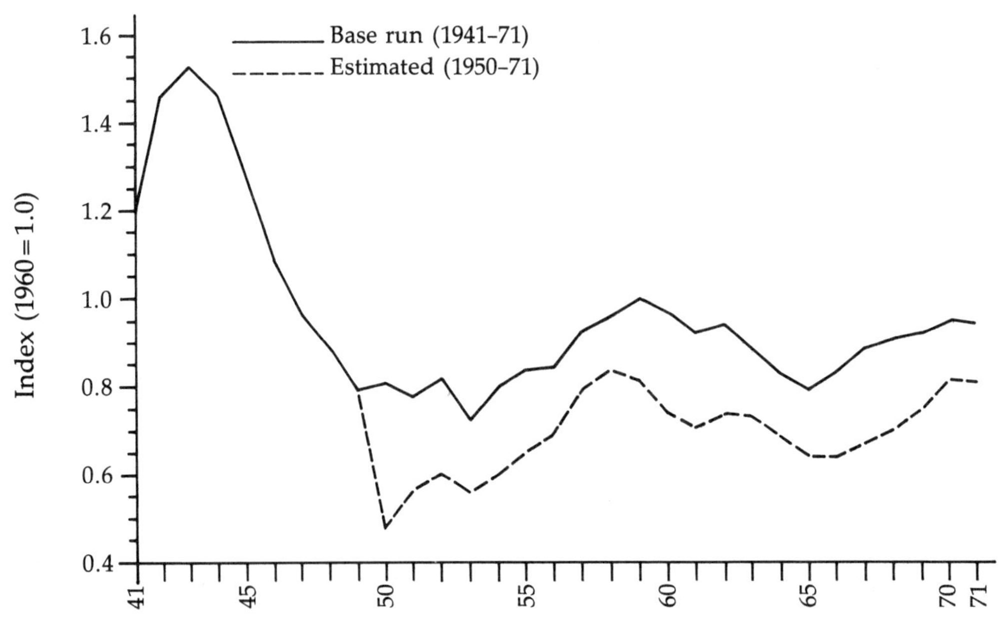

Figure 37—Effects of trade liberalization on per capita output and domestic utilization, agriculture, 1941–71

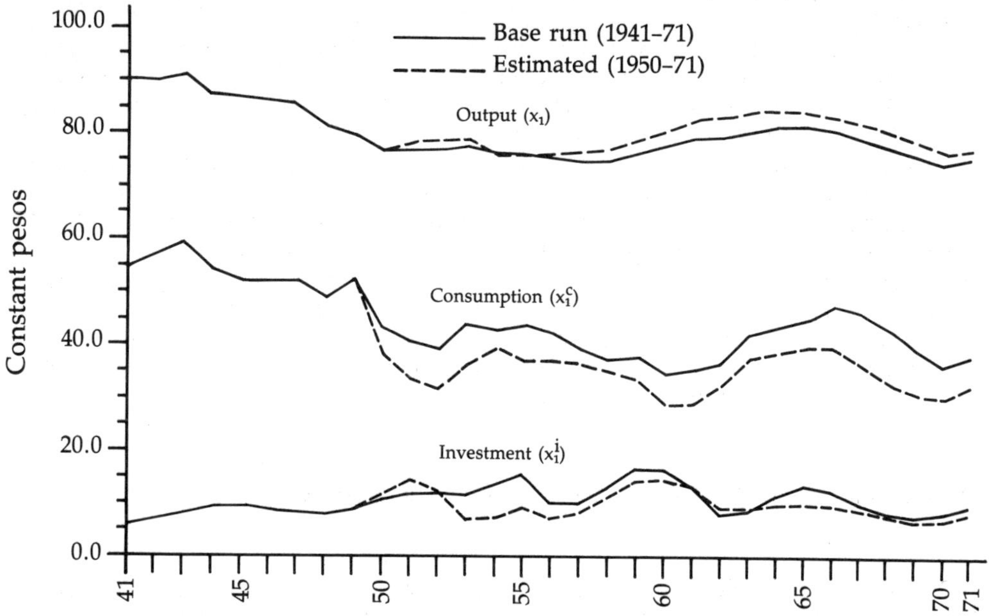

Figure 38—Effects of trade liberalization on per capita output and domestic utilization, nonagriculture, 1941–71

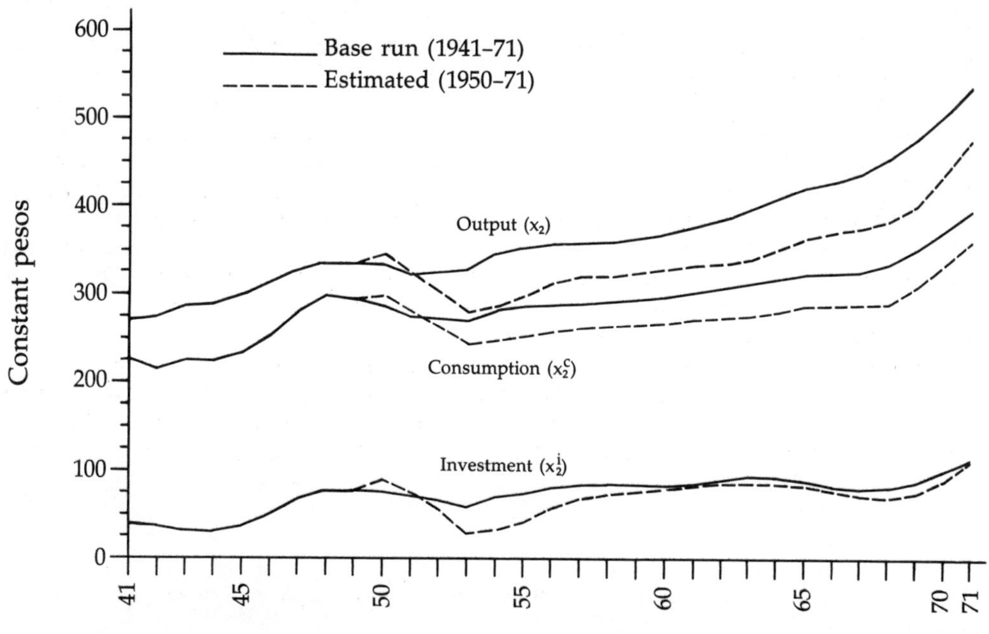

position. This improvement over the 20-year period amounts to approximately 24 percent of the income at the end of this period. If a 10-percent real return on capital is applied to this change, per capita income increases by about 2.4 percent, which reduces the gap with the base-run value.

The policy under review had a result that was particularly unfavorable for the wages of nonagricultural labor in actual values and even more so for the relationships of these wages to the market price of food as measured by the ratio w_2/p_1^*. The plots of food wages, the wage rates relative to food prices, appear in Figure 40.

To summarize this exercise it is noted that the elimination of taxes and tariffs on foreign trade did produce the sectoral effects expected. However, the overall effect on the economy was negative in the sense that per capita consumption of both products was dominated for the whole period by the base run. If one also takes into account the foreign assets of the country, the situation is somewhat improved but not enough to justify the loss of production and consumption over such a long period. This outcome has been attributed to the deteriorating effect that the policy had on the real exchange rate. The decline in the exchange rate is claimed to have diverted resources away from the traded sectors. It is therefore desirable to examine the response of the economy when RE is prevented from declining.

Trade Liberalization with Exchange Rate Management

The exchange rate can be kept from deteriorating in the simulation by fixing RE exogenously at any predetermined level. But it is more desirable to introduce such changes through the RE equation and thereby show the nature of the economic policies needed to accompany trade liberalization. Basically, the policy should be designed to reduce the expansion of net domestic credit creation to offset the growth in the money supply associated with the accumulation of foreign reserves. In terms of the exchange rate equation (4.17) this can be accomplished by controlling the variable EC. The exercise to be described here sets EC at -1 for the period 1950–53 and -0.5 thereafter.[27] The choice of the level of RE will be discussed in the last section of this chapter. Other than that, the condition in (5.1) that prevents a change in the share of tax revenue in total income is maintained.

The effect of this change on the rate of exchange is shown in Figure 41, where the value of RE is initially greater than that of the base run. The effect on prices is shown in Figures 42 and 43. The agricultural price increases considerably, whereas the price of the imported goods is less than its base-run value, as it should be, though the difference is relatively small. This change in prices results in a strong effect on agricultural output, as can be seen in Figure 44. Referring to the column on trade liberalization and exchange rate management in Table 3, it is seen that at the end of the period agricultural output is about a fourth greater than its base-run value. At the same time, the per capita output of nonagriculture also increased continuously and never declined below the value of the base run (Figure 45). The overall picture of the economy is shown in Figure 46. At the end of the 20-year period of this experiment, per capita income increased around 33 percent and consumption and investment changed similarly. The economy accumulated foreign assets, which by the end of the period represented 18 percent of the new augmented income. This accumulation of foreign assets reflects the developments in exports and imports, as can be seen from Figure 47. At the end of the period exports were 44 percent greater than in the base run. Imports also rose

[27] In this and all other experiments, the variable EM/M_3 was kept exogenously at its historical values.

Table 3—Growth under trade liberalization, summary results for 1971

Variable	Base	TL	TL,ERM	TL,FS	ERM	Ratio to Base Run: TL	TL,ERM	TL,FS	ERM
y	691.7	636.9	920.2	811.2	790.2	0.92	1.33	1.17	1.14
c	479.0	443.6	620.3	546.9	548.5	0.93	1.29	1.14	1.15
i	136.6	132.0	192.6	162.7	150.8	0.97	1.41	1.19	1.10
em	−8.8	−3.8	−14.6	−19.3	−13.7	0.43	1.64	2.18	1.54
y^t	66.7	63.6	92.2	81.4	76.6	0.95	1.38	1.22	1.15
x_1	75.8	77.3	93.3	89.5	80.6	1.02	1.23	1.18	1.06
x_1^c	38.1	32.6	42.2	38.9	39.6	0.85	1.11	1.02	1.04
x_1^i	9.5	7.9	10.7	9.5	8.5	0.83	1.12	1.00	0.90
x_1^e	28.2	36.8	40.4	41.2	32.4	1.31	1.44	1.46	1.15
x_2	537.6	475.1	701.1	608.2	613.2	0.88	1.30	1.13	1.14
x_2^c	396.5	362.1	505.6	443.8	452.9	0.91	1.27	1.12	1.14
x_2^i	114.5	109.8	160.0	134.5	127.2	0.96	1.40	1.17	1.11
x_2^m	34.1	54.0	47.5	43.0	36.2	1.58	1.39	1.26	1.06
A	27.9	29.0	30.6	29.5	29.3	1.04	1.10	1.06	1.05
L_1	1.9	1.8	1.706	1.924	1.981	0.99	0.91	1.03	1.06
L_2	7.1	7.2	7.305	7.087	7.030	1.00	1.02	0.99	0.98
K_1	6,253.7	6,428.8	9,263.0	8,099.3	7,616.4	1.03	1.48	1.29	1.22
K_2	28,165	23,750	32,229	29,337	30,993	0.84	1.14	1.04	1.10
K_{11}	4,200	3,706	4,613	4,514	4,254	0.88	1.10	1.07	1.01
K_{12}	2,130	3,137	5,720	4,408	3,746	1.47	2.68	2.07	1.76
S_A	0.255	0.336	0.417	0.360	0.315	1.32	1.63	1.41	1.23
S_{K11}	0.136	0.121	0.119	0.126	0.094	0.90	0.87	0.93	(0.69)
S_{K12}	0.106	0.102	0.125	0.120	0.110	0.96	1.18	1.13	1.04
S_{L1}	0.503	0.447	0.339	0.394	0.481	0.89	0.67	0.78	0.95
S_{K2}	0.381	0.312	0.380	0.370	0.422	0.82	1.00	0.97	1.11
S_{L2}	0.619	0.688	0.620	0.630	0.578	1.11	1.00	1.02	0.93
RE	0.756	0.737	0.789	0.789	0.815	0.97	1.04	1.04	1.08
p_2^{nd}	0.944	0.811	0.867	0.869	1.019	0.86	0.92	0.92	1.02
p_1	1.154	1.268	1.358	1.357	1.245	1.10	1.18	1.17	1.08
p^*	1.037	1.152	1.230	1.182	1.114	1.11	1.19	1.14	1.07
$1+t_1$	0.987	1.008	1.007	0.972	0.987	1.01	0.001	0.98	1.00
$1+t_2$	1.109	1.130	1.129	1.134	1.109	1.02	1.07	1.02	1.00
w_1	565.5	561.3	604.1	597.5	585.3	0.99	1.07	1.06	1.03
w_2	1,120.9	1,096.5	1,431.9	1,299.2	1,213.0	0.98	1.28	1.16	1.08
r_1	0.082	0.083	0.081	0.089	0.065	1.01	0.99	1.08	0.79
r_2	0.175	0.150	0.199	0.185	0.201	0.86	1.14	1.06	1.15
r	19.325	27.377	41.6	35.7	26.0	1.42	2.15	1.85	1.34
p_A	2.523	3.966	6.584	4.951	4.600	1.57	2.61	1.96	1.82
w_2/p_1^*	983.7	857.2	1,046.4	983.7	986.5	0.87	1.06	1.00	1.00

Notes: The variables are defined and the sources are described in Appendix 1. TL stands for trade liberalization; ERM, for exchange rate management; and FS, for food subsidy.

Figure 39—Effects of trade liberalization on per capita income and expenditures, 1941–71

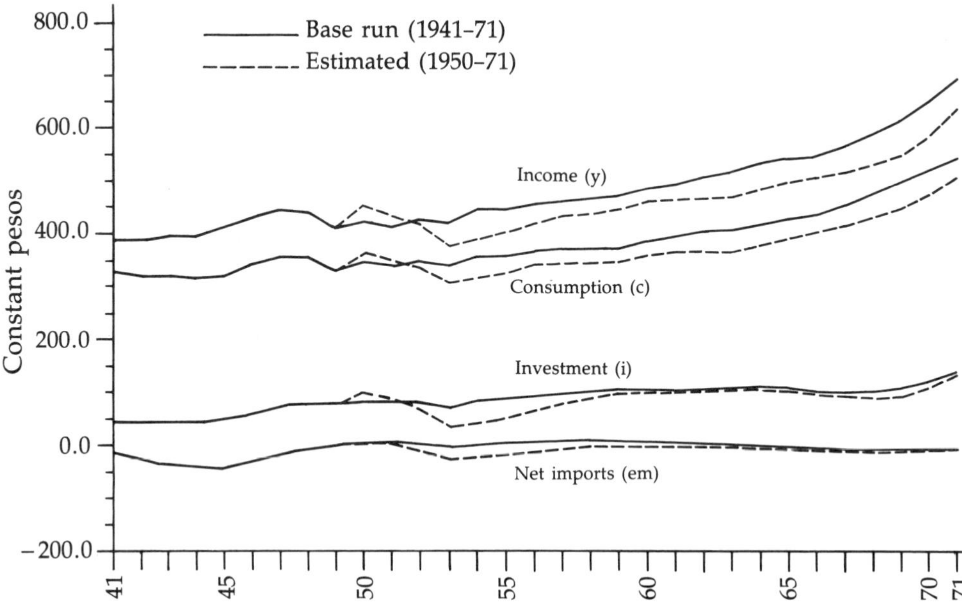

Figure 40—Effects of trade liberalization on food wages (w/p_1^*), 1941–71

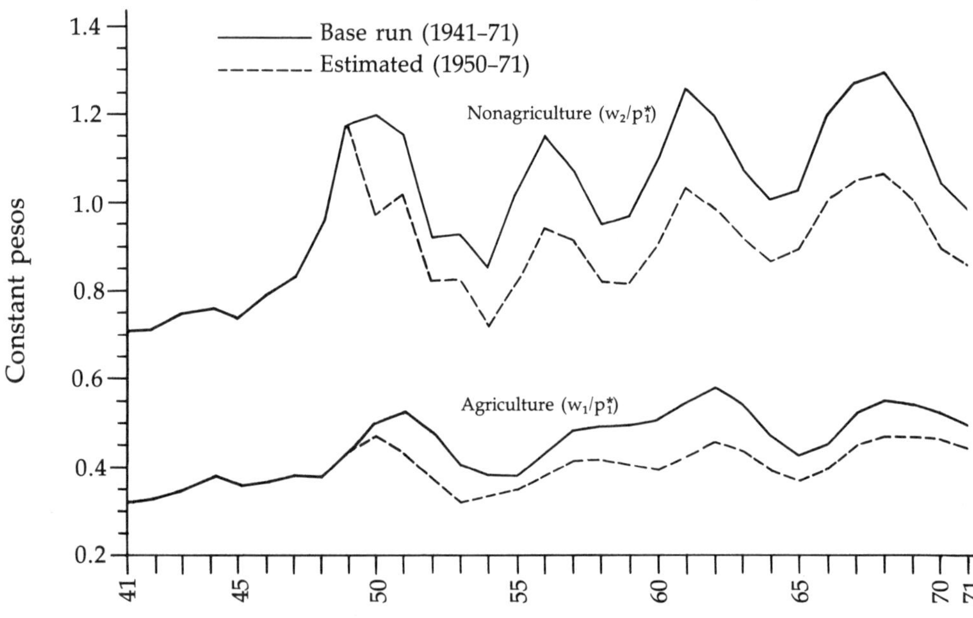

Figure 41—Effects of trade liberalization with exchange rate management on the real exchange rate (RE), 1941–71

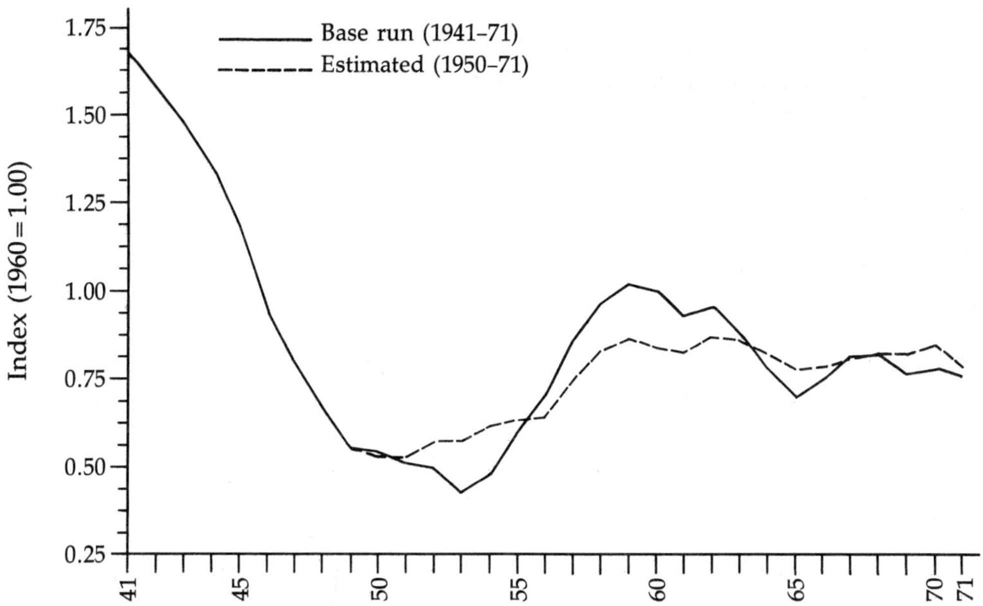

Figure 42—Effects of trade liberalization with exchange rate management on agricultural prices (p_1), 1941–71

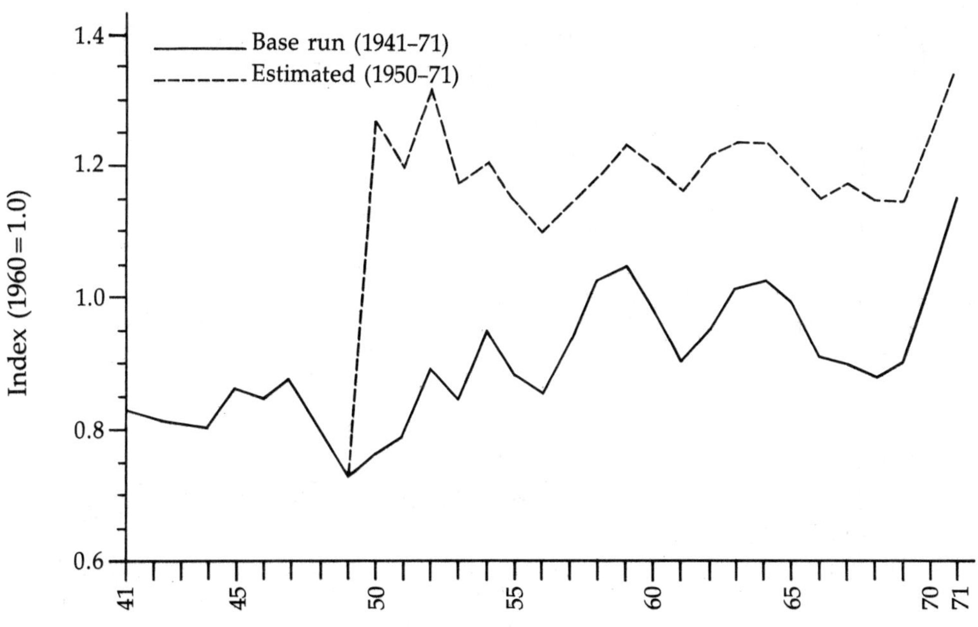

Figure 43—Effects of trade liberalization with exchange rate management on the market price of imported nonagricultural products (p_2^{nd}), 1941–71

Figure 44—Effects of trade liberalization with exchange rate management on per capita output and domestic utilization, agriculture, 1941–71

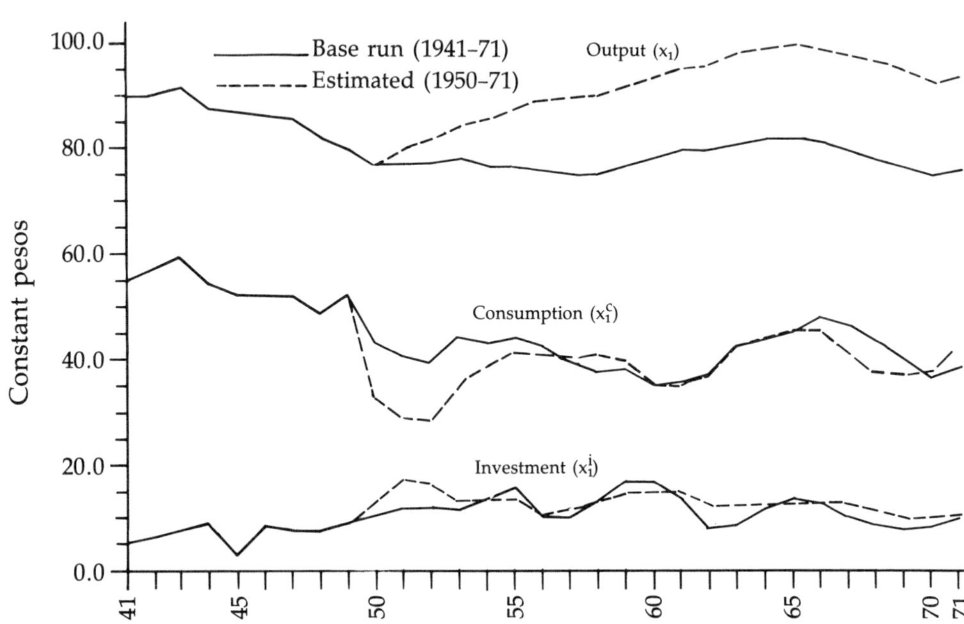

Figure 45—Effects of trade liberalization with exchange rate management on per capita output and domestic utilization, nonagriculture, 1941–71

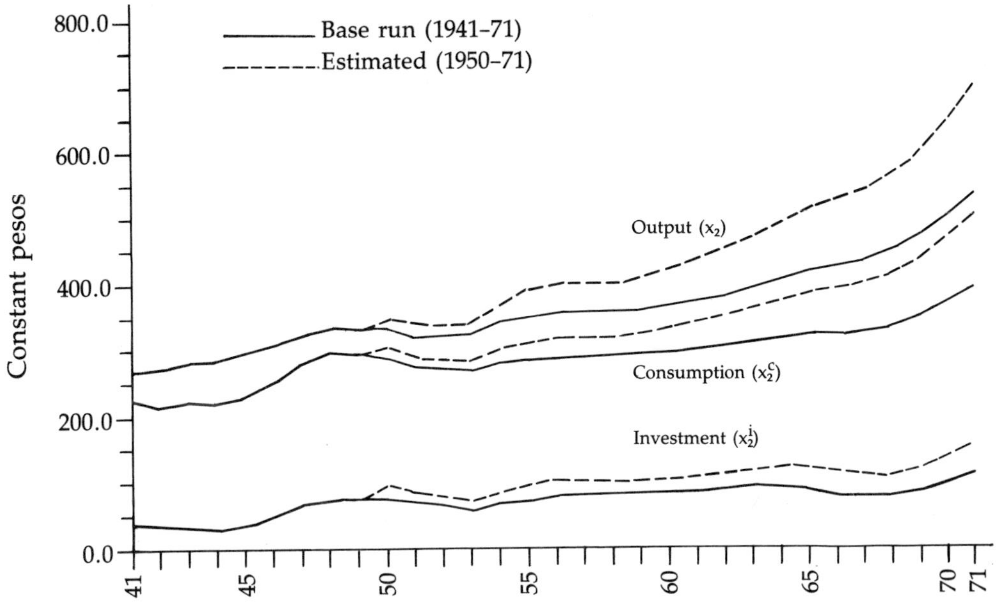

Figure 46—Effects of trade liberalization with exchange rate management on per capita income and expenditures, 1941–71

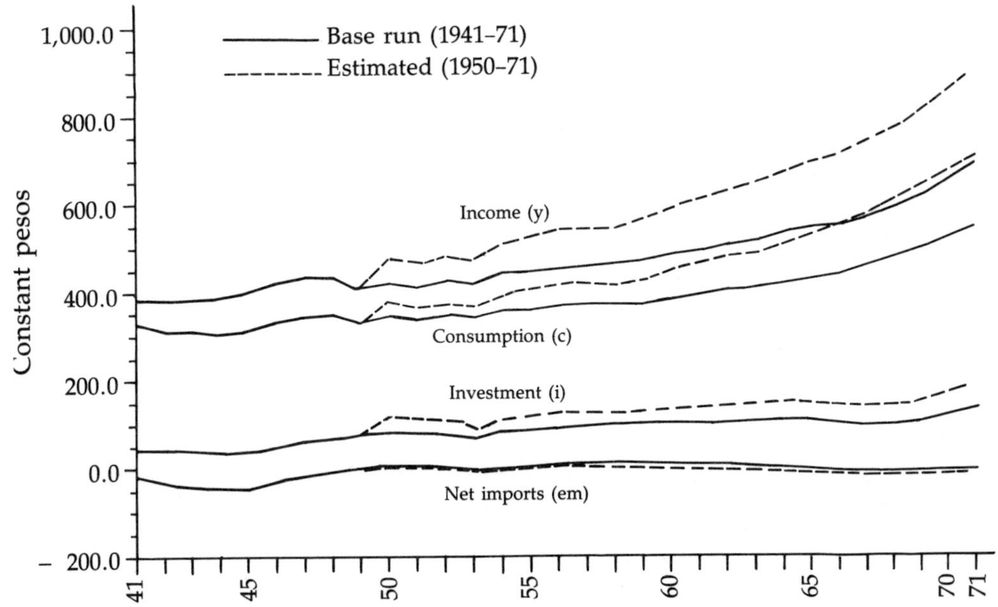

considerably, becoming 60 percent greater than in the base run and declining to 40 percent greater at the end of the period.

The sources of the sectoral growth can be seen in Figures 48, 49, 50, and 51, which show that cultivated land increased about 10 percent and agricultural capital, 50 percent. The latter increase was mostly of capital originating in nonagriculture, which indicates that most of the growth in agricultural output comes from crops and not livestock. While land and agricultural capital increased considerably, there was a decline in the agricultural labor force toward the end of the period. This reflects a response to wages, as is shown below. This shift of labor to nonagriculture did not cause a significant change in the labor force of that sector. On the other hand, its capital stock at the end of the period was 15 percent larger than in the base run.

It should be noted that there was a significant change in productivity in both sectors. The residual technical change, obtained by using the historical factor shares, is about 0.7 percent a year for agriculture and 1.2 percent for nonagriculture. Thus, although the terms of trade of agriculture improved more than those of nonagriculture, the latter showed a better performance in technical change. This result is attributed to the reflection of historical data by the state variables. At no time in the past under investigation was agriculture exposed to conditions as favorable as those in this exercise. This opens up an important question that will be discussed in the next chapter.

This differential increase in productivity has some other repercussions. In spite of the new, favorable terms of trade of agriculture, there is a decline in the share of agriculture in the labor force. The reason is that industrial wages grew faster than agricultural wages, as can be seen in Figure 52. At the end of the period, nonagricultural wages were about 28 percent higher than in the base run whereas agricultural wages only increased by 7 percent. The reason for nonagricultural wages to increase faster is again the stronger increase in productivity. However, in this case the differential effect of productivity is also related to factor bias. In nonagriculture, the share of capital declines at the beginning of the period, as can be seen in Figure 53. It exceeds the base-run value only at the end of the period. The result is a decline in the share of capital, which implies an increase in the total share of labor. For agriculture, on the other hand, the changes in technology increase the shares of land and capital originating in nonagriculture, as can be learned from Figures 54, 55, and 56. The net effect is a decline in the share of labor. Thus the technical change was labor saving in agriculture and capital saving in nonagriculture. Furthermore, that change was land using in agriculture, as the share of land increased considerably above its value in the base run. This is in contrast to the experience of countries that enjoyed a rapid increase of productivity in their agriculture during the period under consideration. This point, too, will be discussed below. It is, however, indicated that this change is well reflected in the price of land, which more than doubled, as can be seen in Figure 57. The implications of these changes are the returns to capital presented in Figure 58.

The policy examined here produces favorable results. But it may be difficult to implement such a policy, as it has some effects on distribution to be considered. While wage rates increased favorably, they increased less than the market price of agricultural products (p_1^*). Consequently, when measured in terms of food, wages declined, particularly at the beginning of the period, as can be learned from Figure 59. Thus the cost of this policy was a decline in the ability of workers to purchase food. As was explained in Chapter 2, the real wage measured in terms of food was an important variable observed by policymakers. In general, past policies were directed to keep it high and thereby increase the welfare of the urban workers. What the present exercise shows is that such policies had a high cost in terms of economic growth. The question is whether or not it was possible to use part of the potential growth forgone to keep the real wages in terms of food at their historical values using different policies from those pursued in the past. This question is taken up in the next section.

Figure 47—Effects of trade liberalization with exchange rate management on per capita exports (x_1^e) and imports (x_2^m), 1941–71

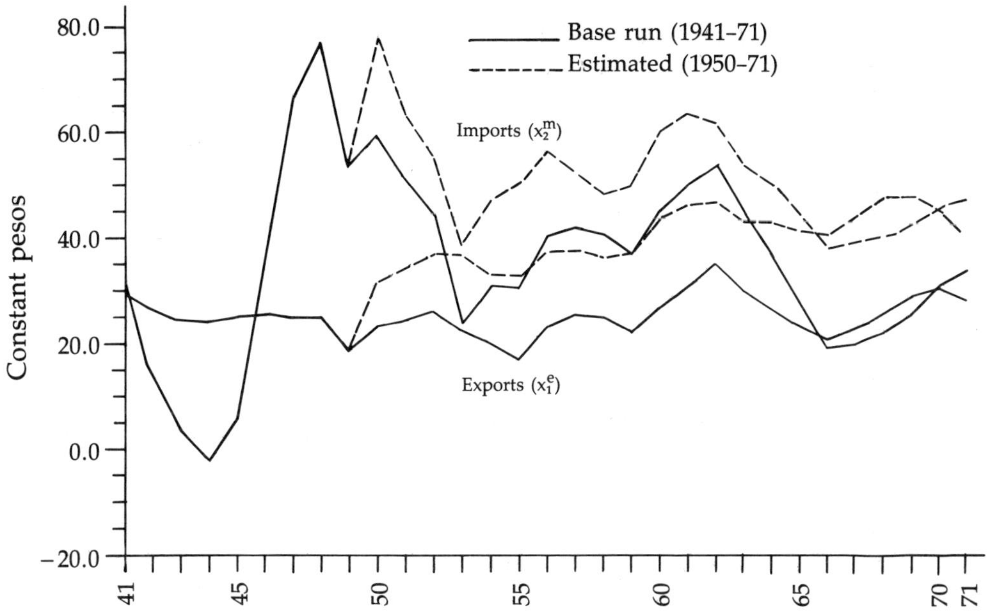

Figure 48—Effects of trade liberalization with exchange rate management on cultivated land (A), 1941–71

Figure 49—Effects of trade liberalization with exchange rate management on the composition of the labor force (L), 1941–71

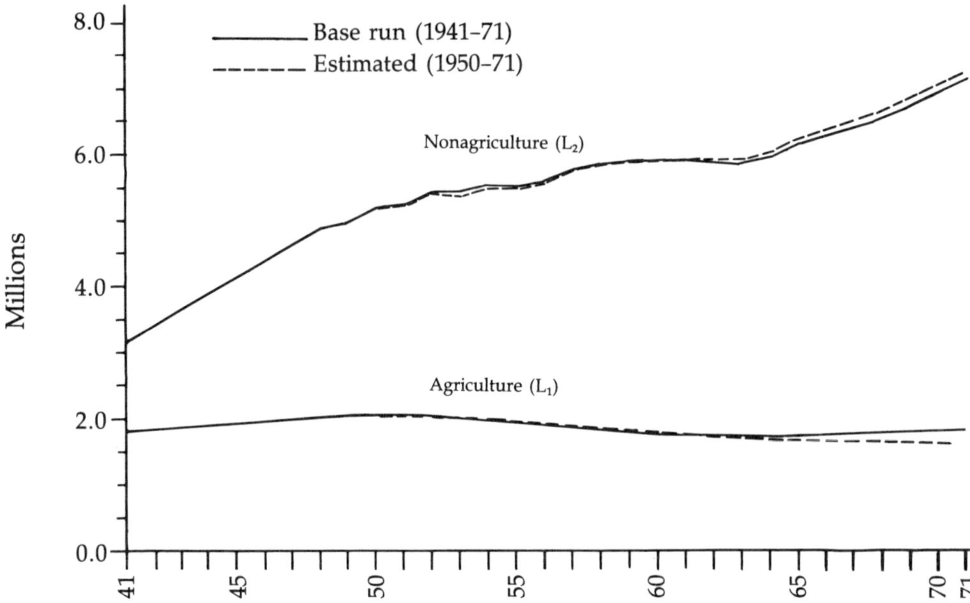

Figure 50—Effects of trade liberalization with exchange rate management on the composition of capital stock (K), 1941–71

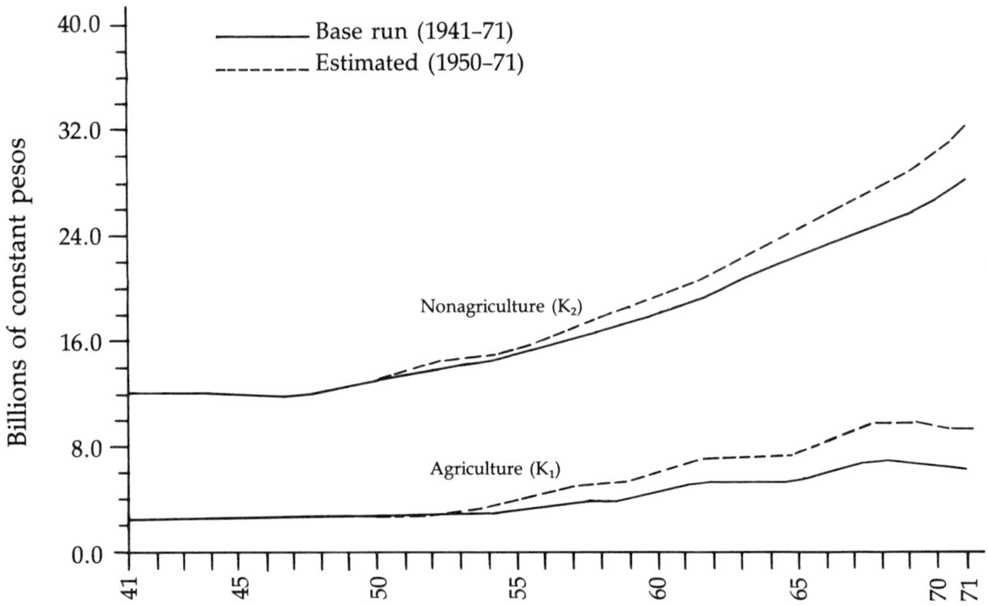

Figure 51—Effects of trade liberalization with exchange rate management on the composition of agricultural capital (K_1), 1941–71

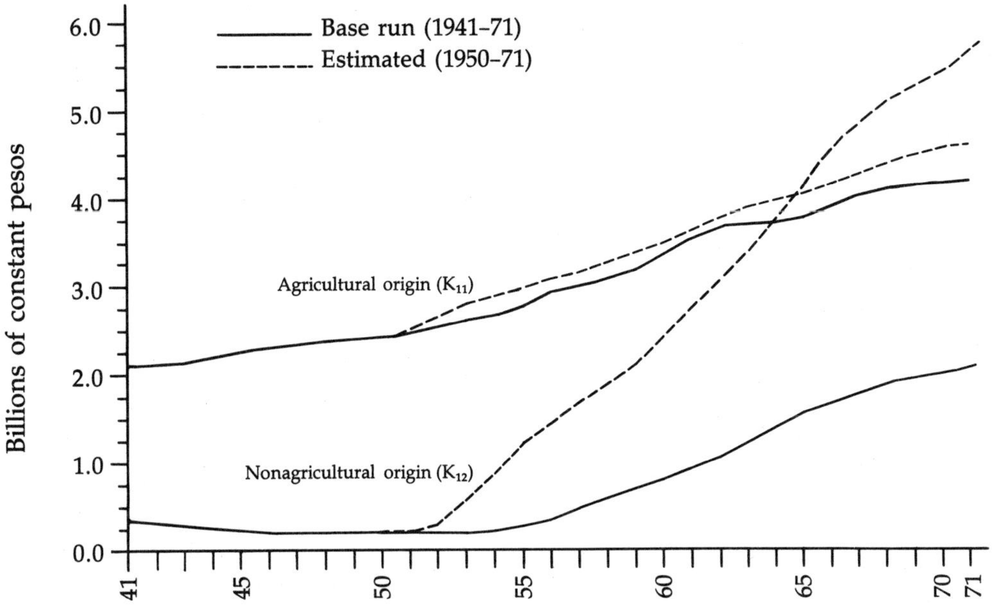

Figure 52—Effects of trade liberalization with exchange rate management on real wages (w), 1941–71

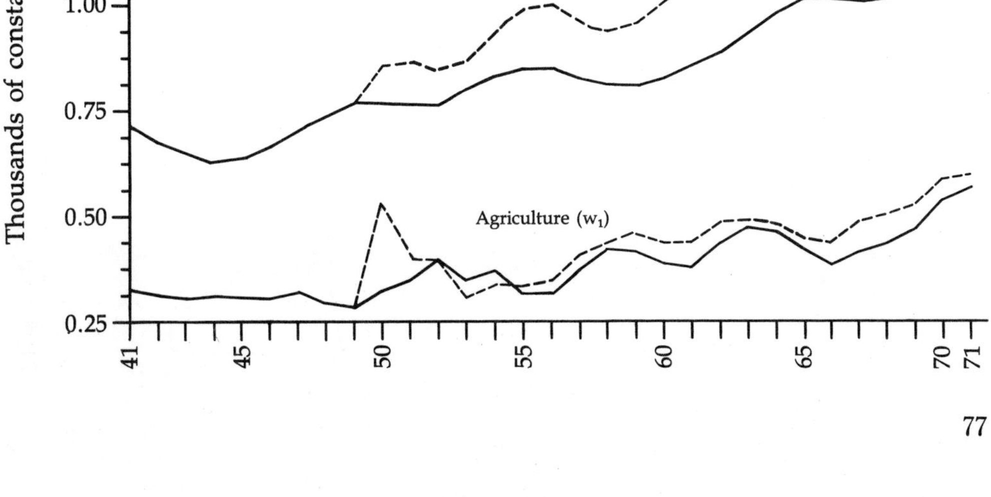

Figure 53—Effects of trade liberalization with exchange rate management on the share of capital in nonagricultural output (S_{K2}), 1941–71

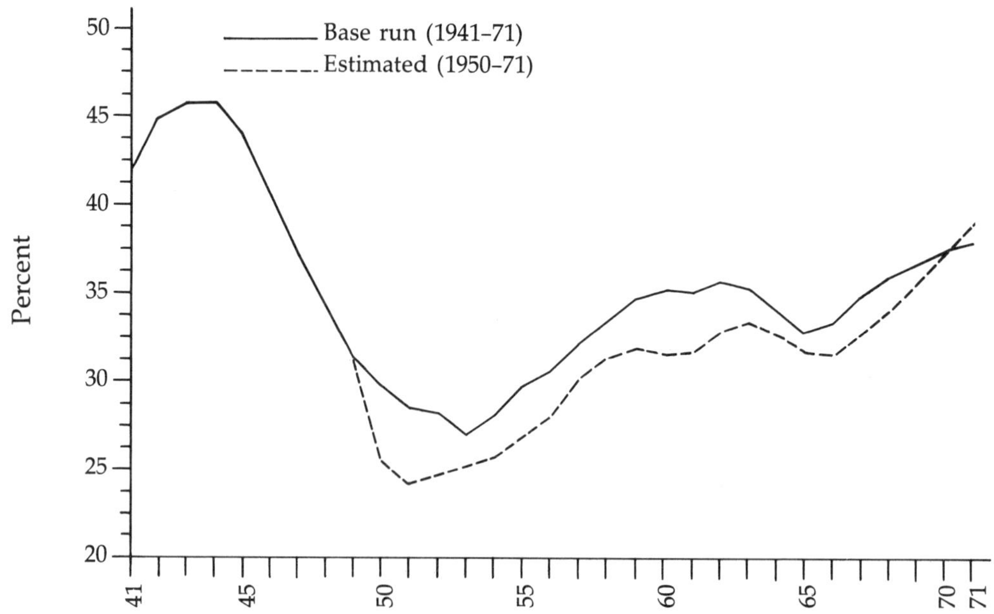

Figure 54—Effects of trade liberalization with exchange rate management on the share of agricultural capital originating in agriculture (S_{K11}), 1941–71

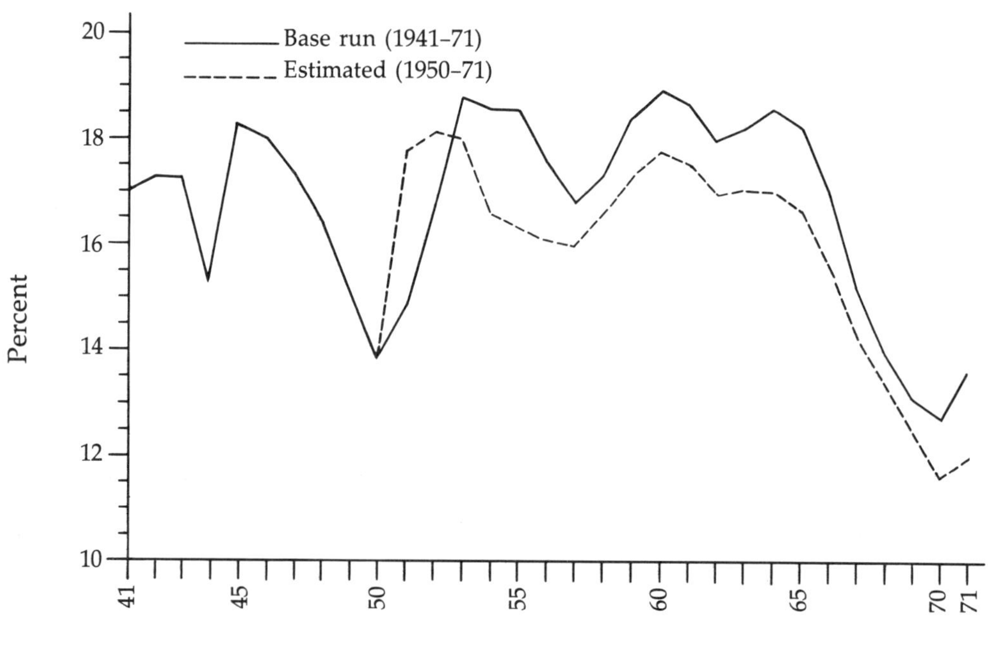

Figure 55—Effects of trade liberalization with exchange rate management on the share of agricultural capital originating in nonagriculture (S_{K12}), 1941–71

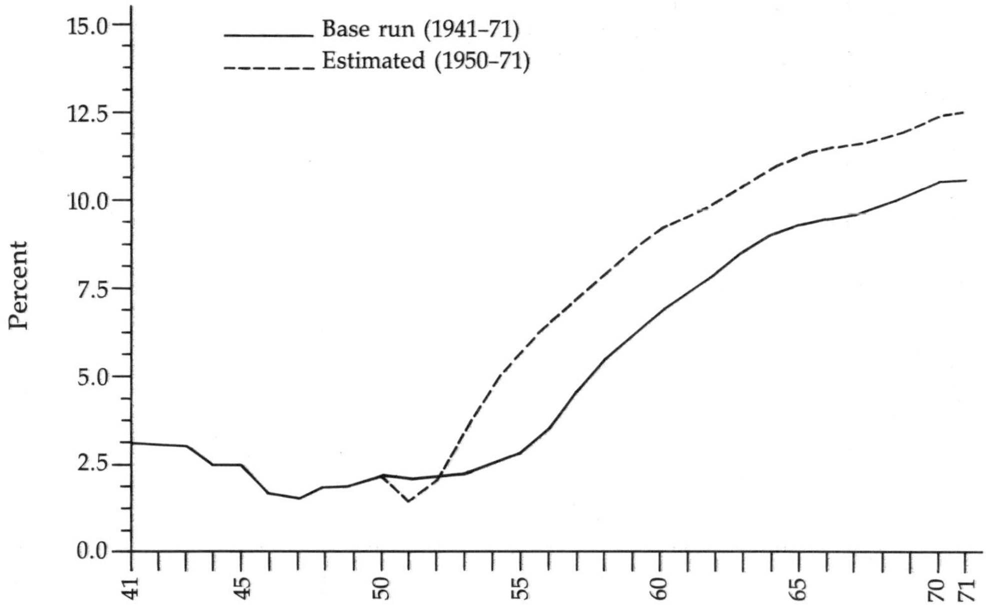

Figure 56—Effects of trade liberalization with exchange rate management on the share of land in agricultural output (S_A), 1941–71

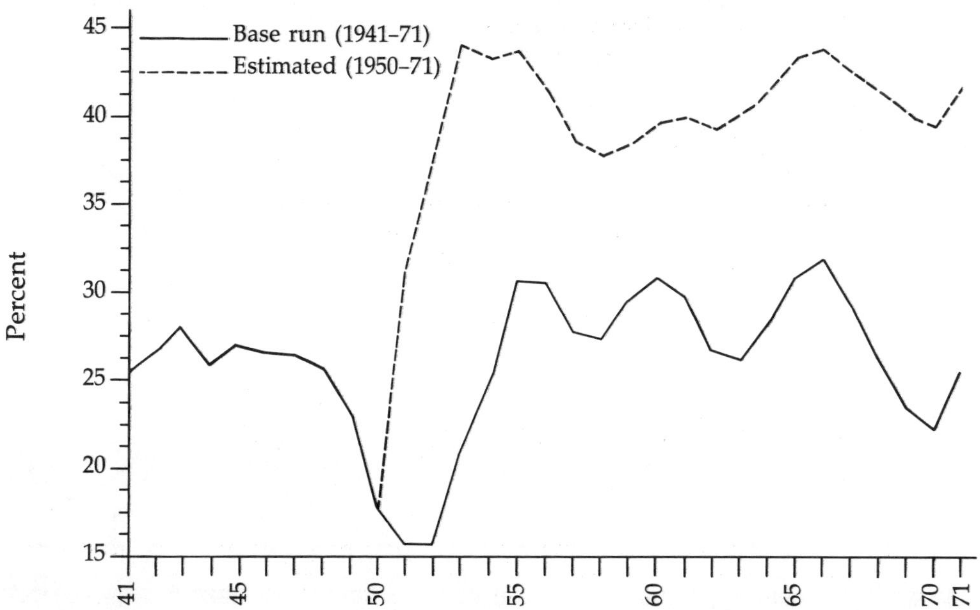

Figure 57—Effects of trade liberalization with exchange rate management on the price of land (p_A), 1941–71

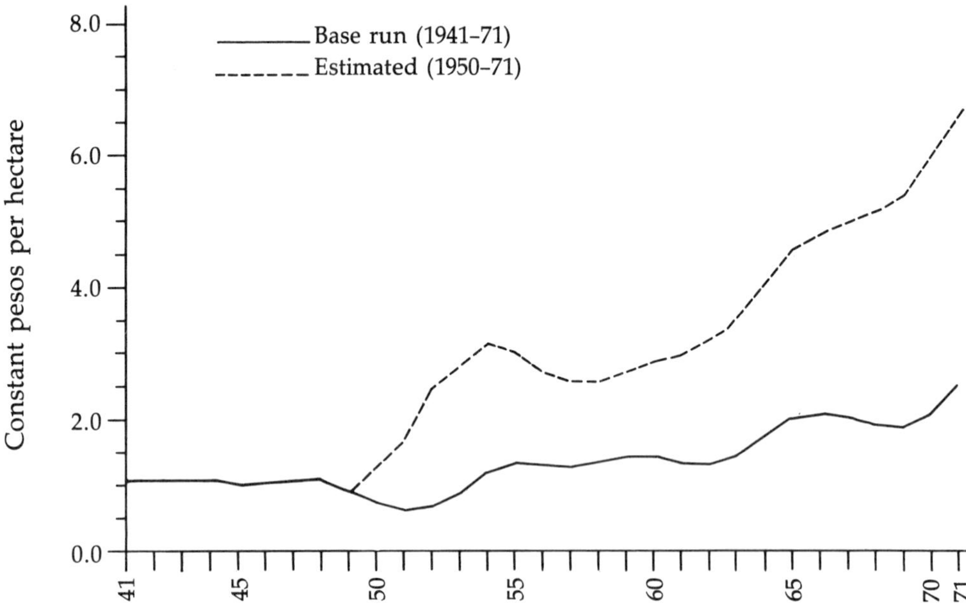

Figure 58—Effects of trade liberalization with exchange rate management on the returns to capital (r), 1941–71

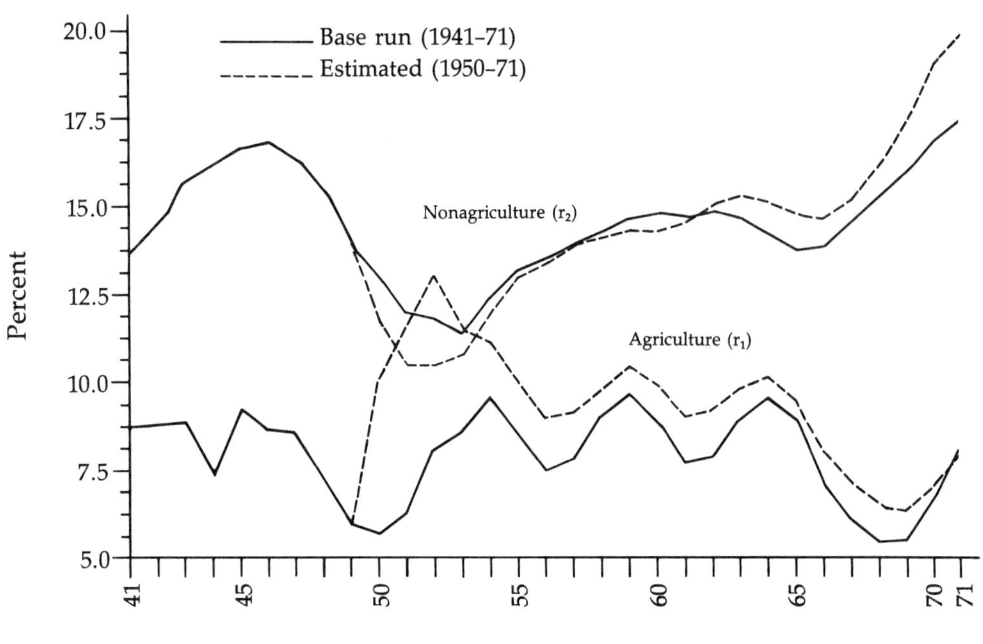

Trade Liberalization with Food Subsidy

In this section the previous experiment is repeated — liberalizing trade while managing the exchange rate, but the condition that wages in terms of food (food wage) will not decline is imposed. The historical food wages are taken from the base run. Thus w_2/p_1^* is introduced exogenously into the model. w_2 is determined by the production system; knowing w_2/p_1^* and w_2, p_1^* is determined. But $p_1^* = p_1$ (RE)$(1+t_1)$, p_1^f is exogenous, and RE is determined by equation (4.7); consequently t_1 can be determined. To restore tax revenue, t_2 must be determined so that the ratio y^t/x is the same as in the base run. That means that y^t/x is introduced exogenously as before to determine the tax rate (t_2) on nonagricultural utilization. Consequently,

$$t_2 = [(y^t/x)^{exo}\, x - t_1 p_1 (x_1 - x_1^e)]/(x_2 + x_2^m). \tag{5.2}$$

The effect of this policy on the tax (subsidy) imposed on the consumption of the agricultural product is shown in Figure 60, where t_1 expressed in percentages is plotted. It is seen that at the beginning, there is a great decline in t_1. In the first year (1950), t_1 declines from -0.16 to -0.44. In the second year t_1 increases to -0.37 and two years later to -0.30. Thereafter the value of t_1 fluctuates with changes in the other economic variables, but toward the end of the period it converges to its base-run value. It should be noted that the historical values for t_1 were realized in a regime that taxed agricultural exports, which in turn kept agricultural prices down so that when t_1 was actually used as a subsidy, rather than a tax, its value was not large in absolute terms. Thus, what this calculation shows is that it is possible to liberalize with a food subsidy that gradually declines. This subsidy kept the food wage unchanged in nonagriculture, as can be seen in Figure 61. The changes in food wages in agriculture were not affected in an important way.

The cost of this program in terms of the tax on the expenditures on nonagricultural products is shown in Figure 62. Immediately after the initiation of the program, t_2 increased from 3.5 percent to 14 percent. In the second year the increase was from 6.3 percent to 16 percent. However, in subsequent years the gap showed a downward trend, so that in the last year the difference between the base-run value and that obtained under the experiment was only 2 percent.

The increase in t_2 does not mean a decline in welfare. It only implies a restoration of a price structure that does not deviate sharply from historical values in variables with important political implications. The effect of this change on income and expenditures is seen in Figure 63. It is quite clear that this policy resulted in a pronounced increase, compared to the base run, in all the aggregates, income, consumption, investment, and foreign asset possessions. This is, of course, a result of changes in the economy that are similar in nature to those reviewed in the previous section.

It is thus possible to liberalize trade while protecting the food wage. This policy is, however, not costless. The performance of the economy under this policy is inferior to that without the food subsidy. This can be seen from Table 3, which summarizes for the last year of the simulation (1971) the results of the base run, trade liberalization with real exchange rate management, and the latter combined with food subsidy. After 21 years, per capita income reached, under the latter policy, 811.2 pesos as compared to 920.2 without food subsidy. This loss of 13 percent in income resulted in a decline in the per capita consumption of the agricultural product from 42.2 pesos to 38.9, a decline of 8 percent. So, even though such a policy may be appealing and acceptable for other reasons, less food and fewer nonagricultural goods are consumed under it.

Figure 59—Effects of trade liberalization with exchange rate management on food wages (w/p_1^*), 1941–71

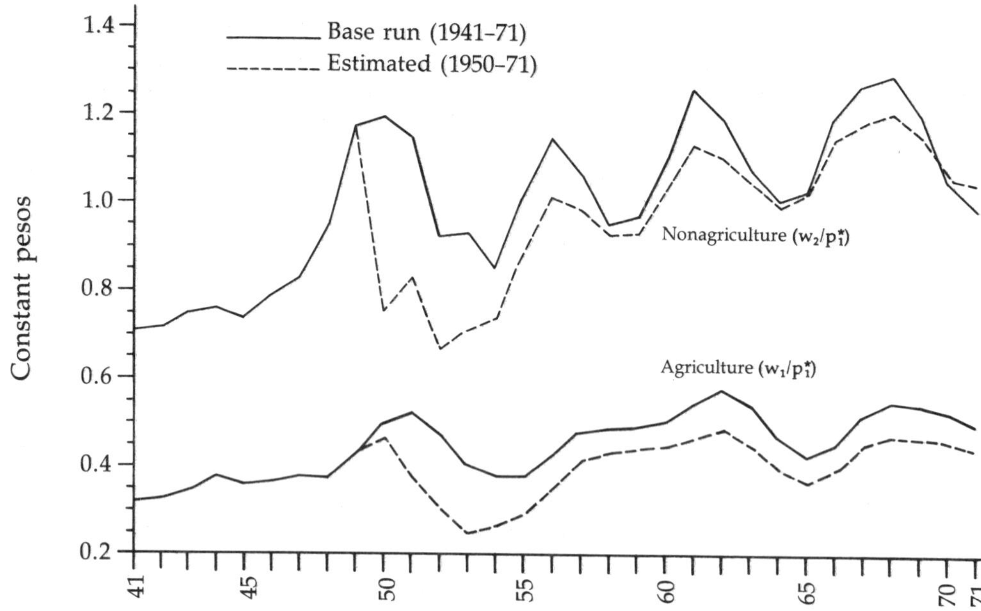

Figure 60—Effects of trade liberalization with a food subsidy on the subsidy for domestic consumption of agricultural products (t_1), 1941–71

Figure 61—Effects of trade liberalization with a food subsidy on food wages (w/p_1^*), 1941–71

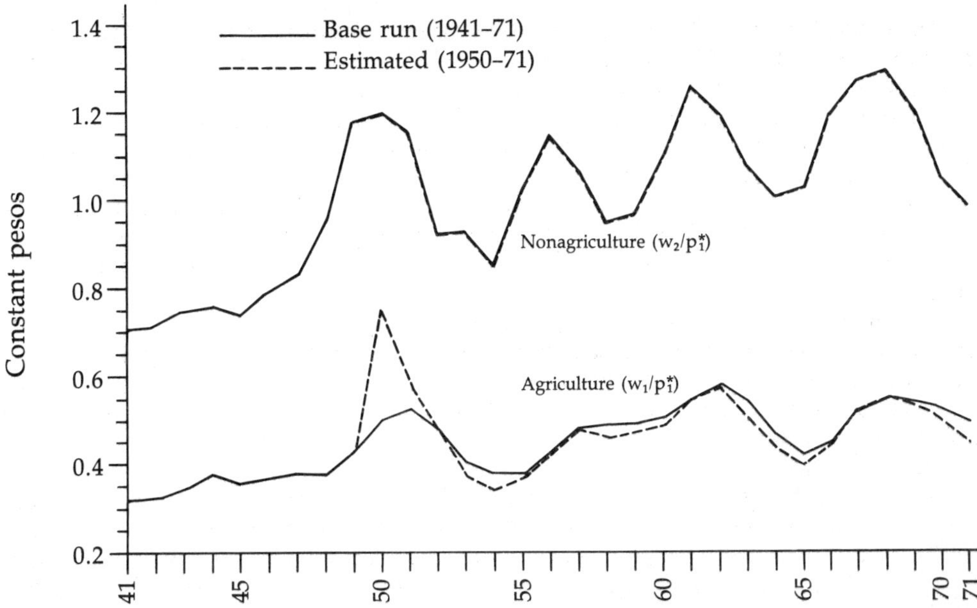

Figure 62—Effects of trade liberalization with a food subsidy on the tax rate on expenditures of nonagriculture (t_2), 1941–71

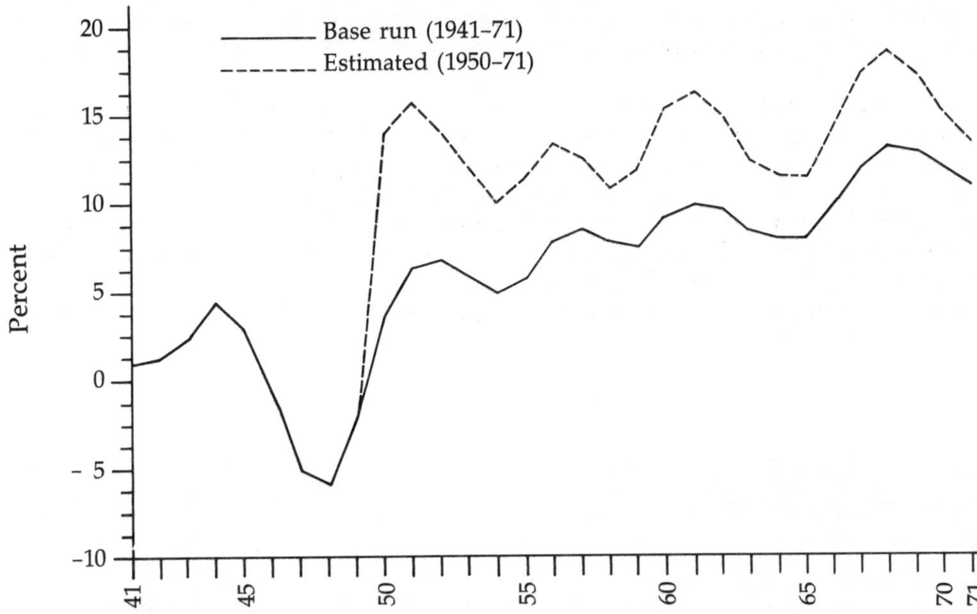

Isolating the Effects of Trade Liberalization

A question that naturally emerges from these policy simulations is how essential is trade liberalization for achieving the extra growth obtained in the second and third exercises, taking into account that, according to the first experiment, trade liberalization appears, superficially, to be costly in terms of overall growth. As Figure 41 indicates, the values of RE used in the second exercise are greater than the historical values for the first five years. It is therefore possible that the main effect of this exercise comes from this initial increase in RE. This question is dealt with by setting EC at its value in the second experiment but keeping t_x and t_m at their historical values. Domestic taxes are also kept as they were historically. This experiment thus isolates the effect of exchange rate management from that of trade liberalization.

As can be seen in Figures 64 and 65 compared with Figures 44 and 45, the growth performances of agriculture and nonagriculture are not as good as in the policy simulation that combines trade liberalization and exchange rate management. It is interesting to see that the source of the additional growth produced by the interaction of trade liberalization and exchange rate management is mainly related to the changes in factor productivities, as indicated by the factor shares.

As can be seen from the comparison of Figures 66, 67, 68, and 69 with Figures 53, 54, 55, and 56, the factor shares of capital and land in sector 1 are increased by trade liberalization, while the share of capital is reduced (and, consequently, the share of labor is increased) for nonagriculture. The higher productivity of labor in sector 2 associated with trade liberalization increases the gap between w_2 and w_1 and increases the migration out of agriculture. This can be seen in Figure 70.

The other big difference between the effects of simple exchange rate management and those of its combination with trade liberalization is in the amounts of exports and imports. These are higher under trade liberalization, as can be observed from a comparison of Figures 47 and 71.

The purpose of exchange rate management is to prevent RE from deteriorating. However, the actual choice made produced an initial increase in RE. This was done to soften the effect of trade liberalization on the tradable sector of nonagriculture. Even with this initial protection, the product price of this sector declines considerably, as can be seen from Figure 43.

It should be noted, however, that the favorable effect of trade liberalization on the economy is not the result of this protection of the tradable sector of nonagriculture. To see this another experiment is conducted where trade liberalization was introduced with RE kept exactly at its historical values. This experiment is not reported here. Its main outcome was to cause an initial decline in the production of nonagriculture. This was later reversed and the economy developed rapidly. Thus, the main effect of the exchange rate management strategy was to prevent the hardship of adjustment. The purpose of this detailed discussion is to emphasize the choices faced when implementing policies that call for large deviations in the values of exogenous variables.

Figure 63—Effects of trade liberalization with a food subsidy on per capita income and expenditures, 1941–71

Figure 64—Effects of real exchange rate management on per capita output and domestic use, agriculture, 1941–71

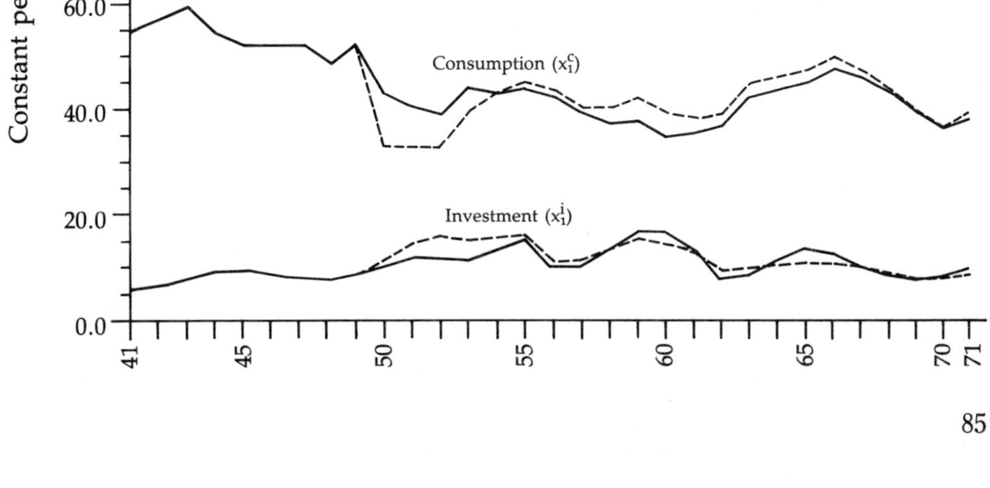

Figure 65—Effects of real exchange rate management on per capita output and utilization, nonagriculture, 1941–71

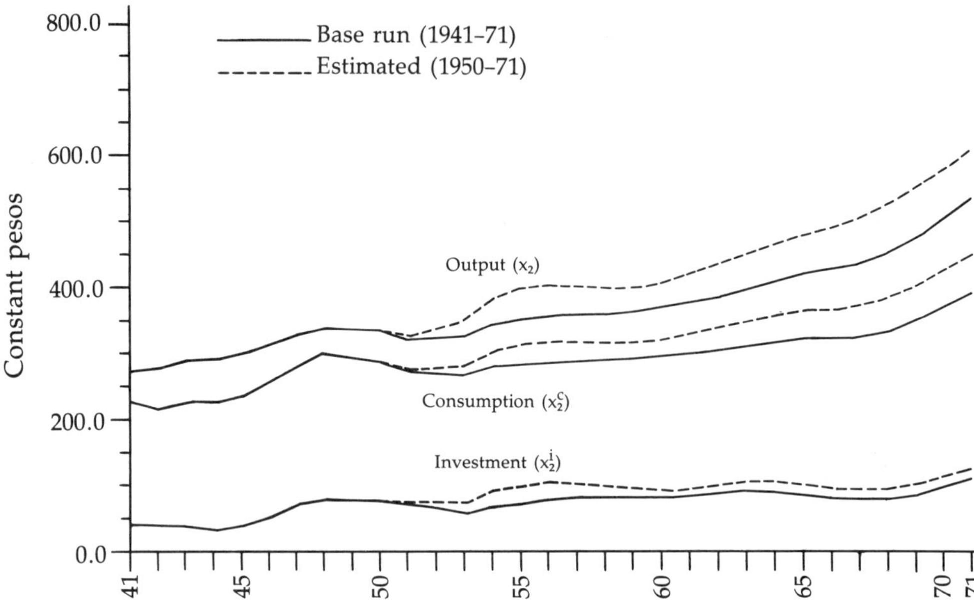

Figure 66—Effects of real exchange rate management on the share of agricultural capital originating in agriculture (S_{K11}), 1941–71

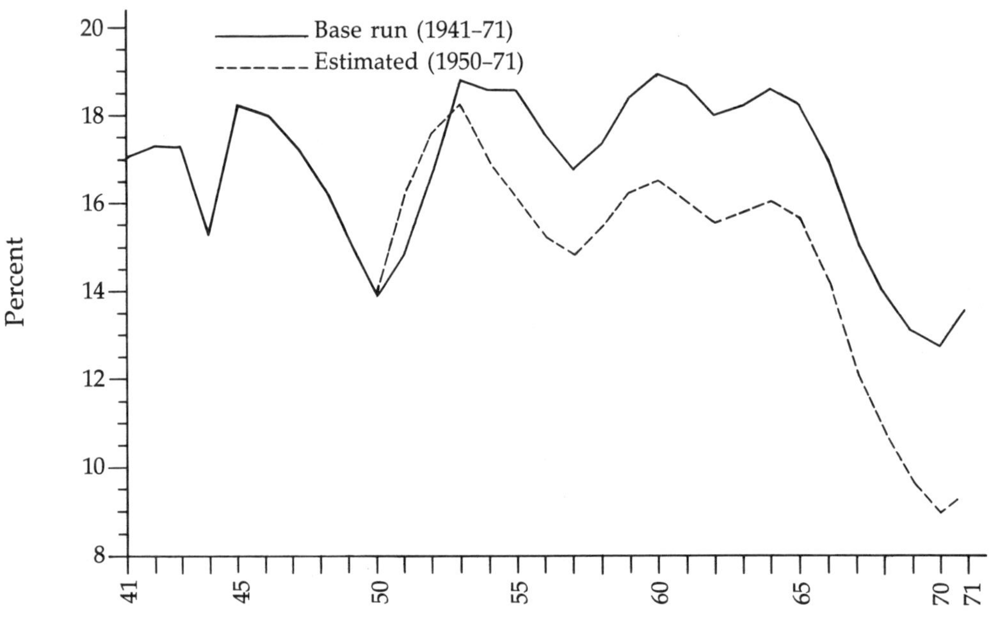

Figure 67—Effects of real exchange rate management on the share of agricultural capital originating in nonagriculture (S_{K12}), 1941–71

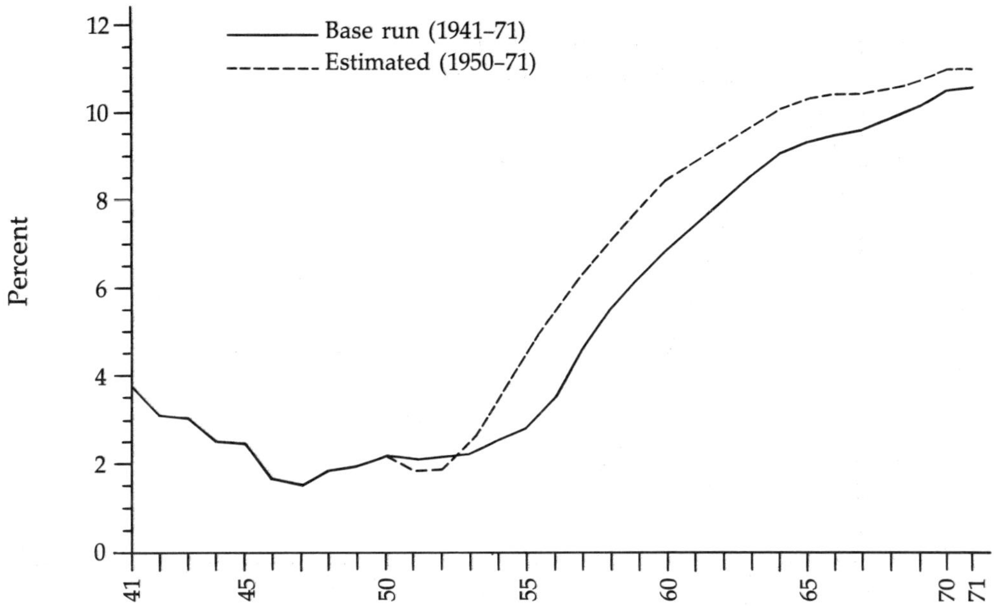

Figure 68—Effects of real exchange rate management on the share of land in agricultural output (S_A), 1941–71

Figure 69—Effects of real exchange rate management on the share of capital in nonagricultural output (S_{K2}), 1941–71

Figure 70—Effects of real exchange rate management on wage rates (w), 1941–71

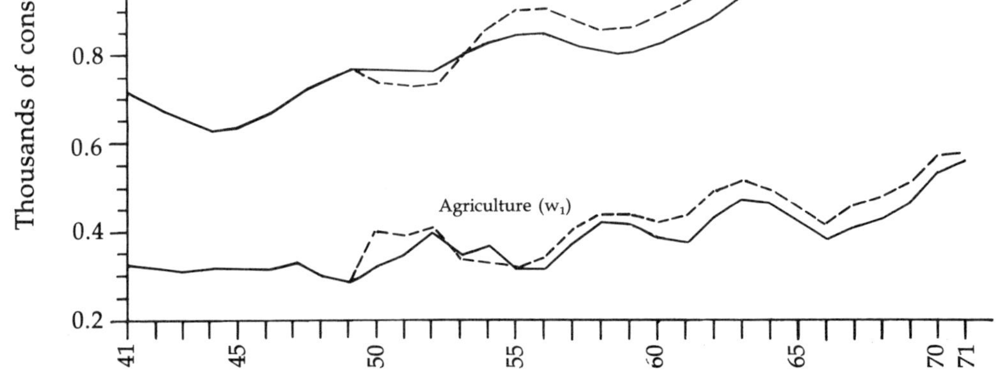

Figure 71—Effects of real exchange rate management on per capita exports (x_1^e) and imports (x_2^m), 1941–71

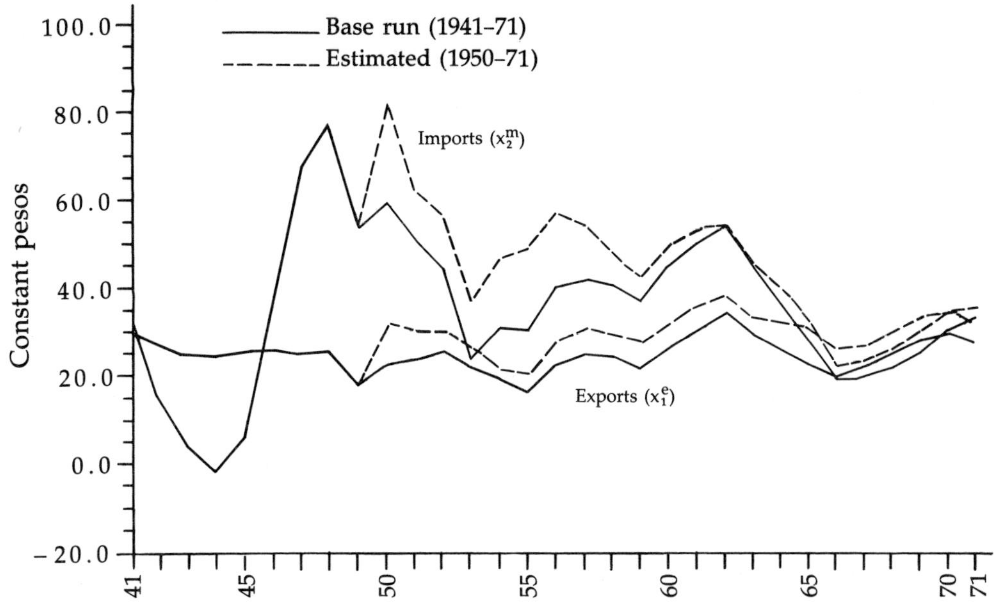

6

THE ROLE OF TECHNOLOGY, GOVERNMENT INVESTMENT, AND FOREIGN PRICES

Agricultural Productivity

An interesting result of the analysis of the previous chapter is that even though trade liberalization favored agriculture, agricultural production increased less than nonagricultural production. Thus, referring to the column in Table 3 comparing the base run with trade liberalization with exchange rate management, it can be seen that per capita agricultural production increased over the base run by 23 percent, but nonagricultural production increased 30 percent over it. The situation is somewhat reversed with a food subsidy. At the same time, the agricultural price (p_1) increased by 18 percent while the price of imported goods (p_2^{nd}) declined by 8 percent. So on the surface agricultural production could be expected to respond to trade liberalization and exchange rate management more strongly than nonagricultural production.

The growth in output can come from either an increase in resources or from an increase in productivity. The intersectoral allocation of resources responds to differential rates of returns. The rates of returns are determined by product prices and factor productivity. Table 3 indicates that in this experiment agricultural resources expanded more than nonagricultural resources. The figures for labor are an increase of 3 percent for agriculture and a decline of 1 percent for nonagriculture. The respective figures for capital are increases of 29 percent and 4 percent. In view of these figures it seems that the stronger growth of nonagricultural output can be attributed to a differential improvement in nonagricultural productivity.

In reviewing the results it should be pointed out that these are not data but simulations of hypothetical situations. Yet the results of the simulations are determined by a set of coefficients that were estimated empirically and thereby represent the past experience. It can be recalled that productivity in this model is determined endogenously in response to economic stimuli. As in any empirical analysis, the results are more pertinent, or precise, when applied to data contained in the sample domain. The results become weaker or less precise when applied to values outside the data set. This seems pertinent here. The free trade experiment produces favorable conditions for agriculture that were not observed in the past. Consequently, it is possible that the full response of productivity to such changes is underestimated. This hypothesis is substantiated by some observations on Argentine agriculture and its performance relative to postwar developments in other countries. Table 4

Table 4—Yields of selected crops in the United States and Argentina, 1948-50 and 1968-70

	United States		Argentina	
Crop	1948-50	1968-70	1948-50	1968-70
		(metric tons/hectare)		
Wheat	1.11	2.22	1.0	1.3
Corn	2.43	6.32	1.1	2.0
Sorghum	1.20	2.84	1.0[a]	1.6

Source: U.S. Department of Agriculture.

[a]The figure for sorghum is for 1958-60.

compares yields for wheat, corn, and sorghum in the United States and Argentina. It is obvious that the gap in yields between the two countries in 1968–70 is large. It partly reflects a gap that existed in 1948–50. Instead of closing, as did similar gaps for many developing countries that made serious efforts to take advantage of the green revolution, the gap for Argentina became larger. The difference between Argentina and the United States does not reflect differences in the physical environment but in practices. For instance, most of the wheat in Argentina is grown without fertilizers. This is a good indicator of the implemented agricultural technology. Some more insightful observations on Argentine agriculture were made by Lucio G. Reca, who also attributes the situation to farmers' response to prices.[28]

In making the comparison with the U.S., it is interesting to note that American farmers in general received prices greater than world prices. Thus, if farmers respond to prices, the observed differences in practices between the two countries are to be expected.

Under this hypothesis, it is reasonable to expect that under a more favorable economic environment for agriculture, Argentina would have followed other countries in adapting new techniques to increase its agricultural output. To quantify the possible effect of an augmented increase in agricultural productivity on the economy, an increase in production from a neutral technical change of 1 percent per year is introduced exogenously starting in 1950. This is a conservative estimate of what could be achieved and it is certainly not large enough to close the gap between the two countries in the period considered. This exercise is performed with trade liberalization. The results are summarized in Table 5 in the Technical Change column. The cumulative effect of the assumed technical change after 21 years is a 23 percent increase in productivity. This change moved resources into agriculture. Consequently, per capita agricultural output became 39 percent greater than in the base run. The consequent changes in the other variables offer no surprises.

The effect of the augmented agricultural productivity on nonagriculture was not as dramatic; it amounted to a 7 percent increase in per capita production and a 12.5 percent increase in per capita income. The modest response of nonagricultural output may reflect in part the fact that the model does not generate expenditure from possession of foreign assets. In this particular case, net per capita exports (−em) increased from 8.9 to 14.8. The cumulative value of the augmented possession of foreign assets is considerable. If it were allowed to generate domestic spending, nonagricultural output would have increased further.

The improvement in agricultural productivity increased the food wage without any serious cost of adjustment at the beginning of the process as it did in other experiments reviewed in Chapter 5. Thus, the combination of technical change and trade liberalization without a food subsidy should have a milder effect on the food wage than with trade liberalization alone. As explained above, the combination of the two is not an artificial construction but rather a probable outcome. It thus makes trade liberalization a more attractive policy.

Government Investment

A second scenario examined here is related to the use of the tax receipts. The model contains the realistic assumption that all taxes are spent by the government as public consumption. In view of the amounts involved, it might be asked what would have happened to the economy if a fraction of the tax revenue were invested rather than consumed. A simulation that assumes that 20 percent of the taxes collected are invested is reported in Table

[28]Lucio G. Reca, *Argentina: Country Case Study of Agricultural Prices and Subsidies,* World Bank Staff Working Paper No. 386 (Washington, D.C.: International Bank for Reconstruction and Development, 1980).

Table 5—Growth under augmented agricultural productivity and government investment, summary results for 1971

Variable	Base	TC	GIN	Ratio to Base Run TC	Ratio to Base Run GIN
y	691.718	771.062	836.150	1.12	1.21
c	478.995	524.023	572.780	1.08	1.19
i	136.555	162.227	225.763	1.19	1.65
em	−8.870	−14.832	28.975	1.67	3.27
y^t	66.703	73.504	84.974	1.10	1.27
x_1	75.759	105.281	83.461	1.39	1.10
x_1^c	38.118	54.271	49.262	1.42	1.29
x_1^i	9.886	12.060	12.758	1.22	1.29
x_1^e	28.152	38.950	21.441	1.38	0.76
x_2	537.567	575.128	653.999	1.07	1.24
x_2^c	396.462	417.369	469.593	1.05	1.18
x_2^i	114.455	135.006	192.055	1.18	1.68
x_2^m	34.066	44.124	69.495	1.29	2.04
A	27.859	28.628	28.801	1.03	1.03
L_1	1.868	1.984	1.832	1.06	0.98
L_2	7.144	7.028	7.180	0.98	1.00
K_1	6,253.73	7,957.460	8,716.870	1.27	1.39
K_2	28,165.400	29,578.700	37,253.7	1.05	1.32
K_{11}	4,199.490	4,773.180	5,178.91	1.14	1.23
K_{12}	2,130.500	3,325.670	3,699.40	1.56	1.74
S_A	0.256	0.308	0.273	1.20	1.07
S_{K11}	0.136	0.125	0.105	0.92	0.77
S_{K12}	0.106	0.117	0.123	1.67	1.16
S_{L1}	0.502	0.449	0.499	0.89	0.99
S_{K2}	0.381	0.388	0.389	1.02	1.02
S_{L2}	0.619	0.612	0.611	0.99	0.99
RE	0.756	0.762	0.763	1.00	1.00
p_2^{nd}	0.944	0.952	0.953	1.00	1.00
p_1	1.154	1.163	1.164	1.00	1.00
p^*	1.037	1.044	1.046	1.00	1.00
$1+t_1$	0.987	0.987	0.987	1.00	1.00
$1+t_2$	1.109	1.109	1.109	1.00	1.00
w_1	565.517	667.706	637.122	1.18	1.13
w_2	1,120.870	1,205.140	1,340.200	1.07	1.19
r_1	0.082	0.089	0.061	1.08	0.74
r_2	0.175	0.181	0.164	1.03	0.94
r	19.325	31.667	22.170	1.64	1.15
p_A	2.524	3.778	3.893	1.50	1.54
w_2/p_1^*	983.730	1,049.88	1,166.07	1.07	1.18

Note: The variables are defined and the sources are described in Appendix 1. TC stands for technical change. GIN stands for government investment; 20 percent of the government's revenue is invested.

5. The experiment is conducted by adding this investment to private investment and allowing the market to allocate the investment to the two sectors through the θ equation. It is obvious that such a policy would affect the economy dramatically. Per capita income would have increased in 1971 by 21 percent and consumption by 19 percent. In 1971, 17 percent more taxes would have been collected with the policy than were collected without it, and this would have resulted in the same government consumption.

All these effects seem attractive. But it should be noted that the diversion of government resources from consumption to investment produces an increment in net imports. This means that more foreign savings are called for. Alternatively, this policy could be applied with policies such as trade liberalization that reduce net imports.

Foreign Terms of Trade

As was explained in Chapter 2, the restrictive policies of foreign trade were rooted in the belief that there was a long-term deterioration of the terms of trade of export commodities. In addition it was feared that instability in world prices caused domestic instability.

It was therefore interesting to use the model to examine the possible effects of drastic changes in the terms of trade. Two experiments were conducted and are reported in Table 6. The first experiment assumed a deterioration in the terms of trade of 20 percent starting in 1950. The terms of trade affect the real exchange rate; therefore the results could be affected by the assumptions for RE. The first experiment assumed that the explanatory variables in the RE equations remained at their historical values except for the induced changes in p_1^f/p_2^f. As a result RE increased and dampened some of the deteriorating effects of the change in the terms of trade. Still, this change depressed agriculture, leading to a 16 percent decrease, relative to the base run, in the agricultural capital stock in 1971. The effect is also noticed in nonagriculture, where the capital stock decreased by 10 percent in 1971. Per capita income, evaluated in terms of the nonagricultural product, declined by 14 percent and per capita consumption declined by 12 percent. Clearly, if the real rate of exchange were not allowed to increase, the results would have been much more dramatic. The importance of this point will become clear when the effects of an improvement in the terms of trade are evaluated.

Table 6—Growth and the terms of trade, summary results for 1971

					Ratio to Base Run		
Variable	**Base**	**DTT**	**ITT**	**ITT,ERM**	**DTT**	**ITT**	**ITT,ERM**
y	691.718	597.345	626.547	896.371	0.86	0.91	1.30
c	478.955	421.157	435.127	607.885	0.88	0.91	1.27
i	136.555	109.120	123.007	186.753	0.80	0.26	0.39
em	−8.870	−5.776	−9.882	−15.143	0.65	1.11	1.71
y^t	66.703	60.900	60.741	86.483	0.91	0.91	1.30
x_1	75.759	70.812	73.492	88.355	0.93	0.97	1.17
x_1^c	38.118	28.605	27.418	43.755	0.75	0.98	1.15
x_1^i	9.886	6.613	6.951	10.275	0.67	0.70	1.04
x_1^e	28.152	35.594	29.123	34.325	1.26	1.03	1.22
x_2	537.567	455.782	480.086	685.097	0.85	0.89	1.27
x_2^c	396.462	349.448	360.074	497.235	0.88	0.91	1.25
x_2^i	114.455	91.347	105.625	156.774	0.80	0.92	1.37
x_2^m	34.066	39.721	41.404	47.543	1.17	1.22	1.40
A	27.859	27.372	27.489	29.996	0.98	0.99	1.08
L_1	1.868	2.170	1.817	1.808	1.16	0.97	0.97
L_2	7.144	6.842	7.195	7.204	0.96	1.00	1.00
K_1	6,253.73	5,235.25	5,559.22	8,401.450	0.84	0.89	1.34
K_2	28,165.400	25,270.5	25,011.1	32,964.9	0.90	0.89	1.17
K_{11}	4,199.490	3,498.11	3,636.44	4,619.28	0.83	0.87	1.10
K_{12}	2,130.500	1,754.720	2,033.21	4,794.29	0.83	0.95	2.25
S_A	0.256	0.211	0.256	0.370	0.82	1.00	1.45
S_{K11}	0.136	0.115	0.153	0.112	0.84	1.13	0.82
S_{K12}	0.106	0.088	0.101	0.122	0.83	0.95	1.15
S_{L1}	0.502	0.587	0.490	0.397	1.17	0.98	0.79
S_{K2}	0.387	0.429	0.320	0.403	1.12	0.84	1.06
S_{L2}	0.619	0.571	0.680	0.597	0.92	1.10	0.96
RE	0.756	0.933	0.637	0.771	1.23	0.84	1.02
p_2^{nd}	0.944	1.165	0.795	0.963	1.23	0.84	1.02
p_1	1.154	1.139	1.166	1.412	1.99	1.01	1.22
p^*	1.037	1.010	1.057	1.268	0.97	1.02	1.22
$1+t_1$	0.987	0.987	0.987	0.987	1.00	1.00	1.00
$1+t_2$	1.109	1.109	1.109	1.109	1.00	1.00	1.00
w_1	565.517	524.838	556.473	659.517	0.93	0.98	1.17
w_2	1,120.870	916.269	1,092.130	1,366.140	0.82	0.97	1.22
r_1	0.082	0.075	0.0942	0.083	0.91	1.15	1.01
r_2	0.175	0.186	0.147	0.202	1.06	0.84	1.15
r	19.325	14.964	19.204	37.000	0.77	0.99	1.91
p_A	2.524	2.095	2.191	5.115	0.83	0.87	2.29
w_2/p_1^*	983.730	814.875	948.585	979.898	0.83	0.96	1.00

Note: The variables are defined and the sources are described in Appendix 1. DTT stands for determination of the terms of trade, ITT for improvement of the terms of trade, and ERM for exchange rate management.

The first experiment is of interest for another reason as well. The analysis of the trade liberalization with exchange rate management results shows a large increase of agricultural exports. This result was obtained under the small country assumption. Suppose that this assumption is changed and increased exports cause a fall in the price of the agricultural product. Would such an outcome still produce a net gain? To answer this, the experiment assuming a deterioration of the terms of trade can be compared with the experiment assuming trade liberalization with exchange rate management. The net effect is still positive. This comparison gives a lower bound on the gain from trade liberalization and exchange rate management without the small country assumption, because the expected deterioration of the agricultural price caused by augmented agricultural exports is likely to be well below the 20 percent assumed for the experiment, assuming that the terms of trade deteriorate.

The improvement of 20 percent in the terms of trade was evaluated under two alternatives. First, RE was allowed to fall. Second, compensatory policies were implemented that prevented RE from falling. The results differ substantially, as Table 6 shows. In the first case, RE declined in year 21 of the experiment to 0.84 compared to the base run. Consequently, per capita agricultural output declined relative to the base run. The decline in nonagriculture was somewhat larger, as expected. The overall performance of the economy, measured in terms of nonagriculture, was worse than in the base run. Domestic production gave way to imports with the per capita imports of nonagriculture increasing by 22 percent.

The implementation of exchange rate management policies to prevent the drastic reduction in RE changes the results.[29] In this experiment, a 20 percent improvement in the foreign terms of trade leads, after 21 years, to a 30 percent increase in per capita income. This increase comes from increases in per capita production of 17 percent for agriculture and 27 percent for nonagriculture as well as from improvements in agricultural prices. The differential effect on agriculture is reflected in the growth of its capital stock, 34 percent, compared to 17 percent in nonagriculture. Perhaps the best indication of the improvement in agricultural conditions is reflected in the doubling of the price of land. This, however, partly reflects the estimated structure of production.

What emerges from these experiments is that even though changes in the foreign terms of trade affect the domestic economy, the range of those effects depends strongly on the domestic policies adopted. The exercises show that an improvement in the terms of trade tends to be more than neutralized by a deterioration induced in the real exchange rate and that an active domestic macro policy is called for if full advantage is to be taken of the improved terms of trade. On the other hand it is shown that a deterioration of the terms of trade has less depressing effects than if a compensatory increase in the real exchange rate, such as the one shown by the exchange rate equation, were not present.

---

[29]The RE was prevented from falling by assuming an active policy that affected the growth in domestic credit (EC).

7

THE PRODUCTION FUNCTIONS

The approach of this analysis is considerably different, both in concept and in practice, from other approaches used in the empirical analysis of production. This deviation is not related specifically to the analysis of the Argentine data. It is of a general nature and a detailed discussion of it will divert the report from its main course. For that reason, only a brief explanation is given here of the approach and the technique used in order to prepare the ground for the presentation of the results. The relationships of this analysis to the literature are discussed in the last section of this chapter.

The Formulation

The point of departure is the distinction made between two concepts, technique and technology. A technique is identified with a micro production function. Technology is viewed as the collection of all techniques. Technological change is defined as a change in the collection. The economic agents choose the techniques to be implemented in accordance with their constraints and the values of the exogenous variables, to be referred to as the state variables, denoted by the vector z. Observed data consist of the true output vector y, the available (not necessarily implemented) input vector x, and the state variables z. It is assumed that, aside from a stochastic disturbance, a functional relationship exists:

$$F(y,x,z) = 0. \tag{7.1}$$

As it stands, this formulation is general enough to be indisputable, for the zs have not yet been defined. Thus the specification of the zs is an important element of the model. To elaborate on the scope of the algebraic specification for any empirical work, it is noted that F by itself has no direct or obvious relationship to the micro production functions. It is, however, desirable to postulate that for any given value of z, F maintains the essential properties of a production function. However, because z changes over time, there is no reason to expect that $H(y,x) = 0$ behaves like a production function. But this is the functional relationship that is usually estimated as a production function.

When competitive conditions are maintained, the price ratios represent, aside from stochastic variations, the first derivatives of the function evaluated for a given z. That seems to exhaust the information one can infer about the technological relationships. In general, the econometrics of production deal with inferences based on observations of inputs, outputs, and their relative prices. The main point here is that such an approach may yield erroneous results in that it ignores the continuous shifts among techniques made by firms. Furthermore, the zs are expected to vary widely. Therefore, the main changes that take place over time are changes in inputs and outputs, generated by movements across functions rather than along a particular function.

To illustrate the specification for empirical application of this framework, a simple process is considered that looks like a Cobb-Douglas production function with constant returns to scale

$$\ln x = \Gamma(z) + \beta(z) \ln k + u, \tag{7.2}$$

where x is the average labor productivity, k is the capital-labor ratio, $\Gamma(z)$ is the intercept, and $\beta(z)$ is the production elasticity for capital. The dependence of Γ and β on the zs are also written in a linear-in-parameters form:

$$\Gamma = \pi_{00} + \pi_{01}z_1 + w_0, \tag{7.3}$$

and

$$\beta = \pi_{10} + \pi_{11}z_1 + w_1. \tag{7.4}$$

Combining equations (7.2)-(7.4) gives

$$\ln x = \pi_{00} + \pi_{10}\ln k + \pi_{11}z_1 \ln k + \pi_{01}z_1 + \epsilon, \tag{7.5}$$

where $\epsilon = u + w_0 + w_1 \ln k$. Thus it is easily recognized that when $z_1 = 0$, equation (7.5) is a Cobb-Douglas function. If instead of thinking of z_1 as a state variable it is made equal to ln k, a translog-like function is obtained. This similarity to the translog function is algebraic in nature and as such it is used below. The difference between the two formulations is in the presence and nature of the zs, and this difference is substantive indeed.

When the function has several inputs and several state variables, equation (7.5) is likely to contain an uncomfortably large number of variables for a direct estimation.[30] Alternatively, equation (7.4) can be estimated by regressing the capital share on the state variable, using the competitive conditions. Such a procedure will generate a time series of β estimates, which are introduced into equation (7.2). Subsequently, $\ln x - \beta \ln k$ is used to estimate the coefficients of Γ as given in equation (7.3). This estimation of Γ and the coefficients of the β equation can be made simultaneously.

The problem with indirect estimation using first-order conditions is that the estimates are biased when systematic differences exist between the production elasticities and the factor shares. This problem, which is usually ignored, can be handled within the present formulation by allowing for the discrepancy between the factor share and the production elasticity. To do this, ln k is added as an additional variable to equation (7.4) with a coefficient π_{1k}. Let S_k be the share of capital in total output, then

$$S_k = \pi_{10} + \pi_{11}z_1 + \pi_{1k}\ln k + w_1. \tag{7.6}$$

For reasons that will shortly become clear, equation (7.2) is rewritten:

$$\ln x = \Gamma + (S_k - \pi_{0k}\ln k)\ln k + u. \tag{7.7}$$

The model now consists of equations (7.3), (7.6), and (7.7). Now the production elasticity of capital is given by:

$$\begin{aligned}(\partial \ln x/\partial \ln k) \equiv \beta &= (S_K - \pi_{0k}\ln k) + \ln k\,(\pi_{1k} - \pi_{0k}) \\ &= S_K + (\pi_{1k} - 2\pi_{0k})\ln k \\ &= \pi_{10} + \pi_{11}z_1 + 2(\pi_{1k} - \pi_{0k})\ln k. \end{aligned} \tag{7.8}$$

[30]One way to overcome this difficulty is to impose zero restrictions using the principal component procedure. See Yair Mundlak and R. Hellinghausen, "Intercountry Comparison of Agricultural Productivity—Another View," *American Journal of Agricultural Economics* 64 (November 1982).

There are several cases of interest. One is when $\pi_{1k} = \pi_{0k}$. In this case the variable $(\ln k)^2$ does not appear in the production function because

$$S_k - \pi_{0k} \ln k = \pi_{10} + \pi_{11} z_1.$$

If also $\pi_{1k} \neq 0$, then there will be a discrepancy between the factor share (S_k) and the production elasticity (β), which is equal to $\pi_{1k} \ln k$. Thus, estimating the coefficients of the production functions solely from the first-order conditions may lead to the erroneous conclusion that the production function contains a quadratic term $(\ln k)^2$, when it actually does not.

Also of interest is when $\pi_{1k} = 2\pi_{0k}$. In this case the production function contains the quadratic term $(\ln k)^2$, and there is no discrepancy between the factor share and the production elasticity. If $\pi_{11} = \pi_{01} = 0$ as well, the function reduces to a production function similar to a translog.

In all other cases the production function contains the quadratic term, and there is a discrepancy between the factor share and the production elasticity.

Empirical Results

The empirical application of the model requires the specification of the state variables. Some general directions can be drawn from the literature, as the discussion later in this chapter indicates. In what follows the variables actually used in the analysis are listed with a short explanation that can be related to the later discussion. Assuming constant returns to scale, the production function is written as $x_2 = f(k_2, z)$, where x_2 is the average labor productivity, k_2 is the capital-labor ratio, and z is the vector of state variables. In line with the discussion, the function is:

$$\ln x_2 = \Gamma(\ ) + S_k \ln k_2 + \text{error},$$

where ( ) denotes the arguments of the function to be described. The state variables are:

K/N = per capita overall reproducible physical capital in the economy at the beginning of the year. This is the measure used for overall capital abundance. Any choice of techniques is constrained by the existing capital stock.[31]

I_2/L_2 = gross investment divided by the labor force in nonagriculture. This variable represents the embodied improvement in productivity, the effect of capital deepening, and the effect of expectations about the economic environment.

r_2 = the average rate of return on capital in nonagriculture lagged one year.

w_2 = the average nonagricultural wage rate lagged one year.

p_2^{nd} = the price of nonagriculture imported goods.

The capital share and the rate of return were derived by using national accounts data on wage income and capital stock,

$$S_k = (X_2 - w_2 L_2)/X_2,$$

where p_2X_2 is value output in nonagriculture. By assumption,

$$r_2 = (X_2/K_2)\, S_k.$$

[31]This is derived from the analysis in Y. Danin and Yair Mundlak, *Introduction of Techniques and Capital Accumulation,* Working Paper No. 7909 (Rehovot: Center for Agricultural Economic Research, 1979).

Capital accumulation in the economy (represented here by K/N), investment, and the rate of return are expected to be positively related to productivity. Wage rates are likely to have a suppressive effect. However, the rate of return is measured as a residual and as such it reflects actual changes in the wage rates. This makes the role of wages as an additional variable unclear. Wage rates are included in the analysis in order to gain some empirical evidence on this point. Wages and the rate of return are lagged one year. Therefore they represent current conditions without being affected by developments during the year itself. Their values also influence expectations. No analysis is made to separate the expected from the current conditions over and above what is conveyed by the investment variable. The real price of tradables, p_2^{nd}, represents the demand for their domestic production and as such is likely to be positively related to productivity.

The analysis begins with the estimation of the capital share equation, with the results, using annual data, appearing in column 1 of Table 7. Throughout, the estimation involved the elimination of the statistical null component of the design matrix using a significance level of 0.1.[32] The share equation is regressed on four state variables and one input ($\ln k_2$)—five variables altogether. The statistical rank is 3, indicating a redundancy. The partial effects of investment and K/N on the share of capital are in opposite directions to that of the rate of return. Investment and K/N increase the labor share, whereas r increases the share of capital. This result may represent short-term effects, so that an increase in r has the immediate effect of increasing capital utilization, thereby increasing the share of capital. On the other hand, new investment and capital accumulation appear to be labor using. These as well as other findings will have to be substantiated in further analysis.

Table 7—Nonagricultural production function, annual data, 1940-72

Variable	Share of Capital (S_K)	Level (Γ)	Elasticity
R^2	0.818	0.994	. . .
Statistical rank	3	5	. . .
Constant	−0.324	−1.824	. . .
	(3.3)	(1.9)	
Logarithm			
K/N	−0.1377	1.690	0.582
	(1.5)	(13.4)	(28)
I_2/L_2	−0.0033	0.167	0.131
	(0.1)	(3.9)	(281)
$r_2(t-1)$	0.1026	−0.684	0.143
	(9.8)	(16.0)	(9)
p_2^{nd}	0.1595	−1.261	0.024
	(10.5)	(24.8)	(1)
k_2	0.2314	−0.123[a]	0.244
	(3.3)	(19.2)	(4.4)

Notes: Figures in parentheses in the first two columns are the t-ratios obtained from the individual regressions. The elasticities are with respect to each of the variables. They vary with the observations. The ratios reported for the elasticities are arithmetic means and the figures in parentheses indicate the ratios of means to their standard deviations. K/N is the per capita overall reproducible physical capital in the economy at the beginning of the year. I_2/L_2 is gross investment divided by the labor force in nonagriculture. $r_2(t-1)$ is the average rate of return on capital in nonagriculture lagged one year. p_2^{nd} is the price of nonagriculture imported goods. k_2 is the capital-labor ratio for nonagriculture.

[a]This is the coefficient of $(\ln k_2)^2$ rather than of $\ln k_2$.

[32]The procedure of estimation is explained in Mundlak, "On the Concept of Non-Significant Functions."

The share equation is used to estimate the annual values of the capital share, S_k. These values were then introduced into the original equation to obtain the residual $\ln x_2 - S_k \ln k_2 = \Gamma^e$, which constituted the dependent variable for estimating the coefficients of the level, or Γ equation. The results appear in the second column of Table 7. Here again, the statistical rank is smaller than the algebraic rank, but the redundancy cannot be identified with any single variable used in the regression. The signed effect of state variables on the level of the function (Γ) is different from their signed effect on the factor share. The net effects of the state variables on productivity are obtained by computing the elasticities of average productivities with respect to the state variables. These elasticities vary with the values of the variables. The averages and ratios of averages to standard deviations appear in the last column of Table 7. The results indicate that, as expected, an increase in productivity is positively related to all four state variables.

The effects of the inputs, in this case the capital/labor ratios, are given by the coefficients of the last row. The quadratic term is empirically relevant. Furthermore, k is positively related to the share of capital. This is consistent with an elasticity of substitution larger than unity.[33] This means that there is a distinction between the effect of investment, which shifts the production function as if technical change were labor-augmenting, and the effect of the capital-labor ratio. The net effect of such a shift and an elasticity of substitution larger than 1 is to decrease the share of capital.

The production elasticity is obtained by differentiating the function, noting that

$$\partial \ln x_2 / \partial \ln k_2 = S_K + \ln k_2 (\partial S_K / \partial \ln k_2) + (\partial \ln \Gamma / \partial \ln k_2).$$

Using the results in Table 7, the average of the production elasticity is 0.244 as compared with a capital share of 0.354, indicating qualitatively an overpayment to capital.

The analysis was repeated after adding the wage rate to the state variables. This was done under the constraint that the production elasticity of capital equals the capital share. The results are summarized under equation (2) in Table 8. Equation (1) of the table is the summary of the results reported in Table 7. The R^2 in each case measures the fit of the final estimated production function. Comparing the results of equations (1) and (2), no qualitative changes are evident, except that an elasticity for the wage rate is obtained.

The results for annual data are reported here so that they can be compared with those obtained for moving averages. The latter are reported under equations (3) and (4) of Table 8. Equation (4) repeats the calculations of equation (2). Equation (3) repeats equation (4) without constraining the capital elasticity to equal the capital share. The results are qualitatively similar. It appears that all the state variables were positively related to changes in productivity.

Figures 72 and 73 plot the values computed from the first regression. It is clear from Figure 73 that the factor shares varied considerably over the sample period. The present analysis indicates clearly that such variations cannot be accounted for by the inputs alone. They reflect changes in the state variables.

In the simulation it was desirable to maintain a recursive system and to avoid the use of current investment as a state variable. Instead, a value for I_2/L_2, lagged one year, was used.

[33] Let the ratio of factor shares be $\phi(k) \equiv S_L/S_K = wL/rK = \omega/k$, where $\omega = w/r$ and $k = K/L$. Let σ be the elasticity of substitution and differentiate to obtain:

$$\phi'(k) = \partial \ln \omega / \partial \ln k - 1 = 1/\sigma - 1 \gtrless 0 \leftrightarrow \sigma \lessgtr 1.$$

$\phi'(k) > 0$ implies an increase in S_L and a decline in S_K. Consequently, an increase in the capital share caused by an increase in k indicates that $\sigma > 1$.

Table 8—Summary results of the nonagricultural production function, 1940-72

	Equation			
Variable	**1 (AN)**	**2 (AN)**	**3 (MA)**	**4 (MA)**
R^2	0.955	0.954	0.983	0.983
D.W.	1.472	1.434	0.72	0.663
Statistical rank				
S_K	3	1	3	3
Γ	5	5	5	5
Elasticity				
K/N	0.582	0.446	0.340	0.515
I_2/L_2	0.131	0.140	0.075	0.100
$r_2(t-1)$	0.143	0.163	0.238	0.193
p_2^{nd}	0.024	0.017	0.056	0.060
$w_2(t-1)$	. . .	0.069	0.342	0.183
k_2	0.244	0.377[a]	0.239	0.377[a]

Notes: R^2 was computed from $R^2 = 1 - [\Sigma(\text{residuals})^2/SS_t]$, where the residuals were computed from the production function after introducing the estimates for S_K (the share of capital) and Γ (which stands for level). The denominator is the total sum of squares of the dependent variables. The D.W. statistic was computed from the same residuals. AN refers to annual data; MA is the moving average. K/N is the per capita overall reproducible physical capital in the economy at the beginning of the year. I_2/L_2 is gross investment divided by the labor force in nonagriculture. $r_2(t-1)$ is the average rate of return on capital in nonagriculture lagged one year. p_2^{nd} is the price of nonagricultural imported products deflated by the price of nonagricultural products produced domestically. $w_2(t-1)$ is the nonagricultural wage rate lagged one year. k_2 is the capital-labor ratio for nonagriculture.

[a]This regression was obtained by restricting the elasticity with respect to capital to equal the capital share.

The equation actually used in the simulation is reported in Chapter 4. It was obtained by a procedure that differs somewhat from that described above. The difference is not significant enough to be discussed here.[34] Also, to decrease the degree of serial correlation present in the moving average regressions, the final equation also includes a lagged dependent variable.

Next, the production function for agriculture was estimated, using three-year moving averages. The production function was assumed to have constant returns to scale in labor, capital, and land. The function is written as $x_1 = f_1(a, k_1, z)$, where x_1 is the average labor productivity, a is the land-labor ratio, k_1 is the capital-labor ratio, and z represents the vector of state variables.

The function to be estimated is:

$$\ln x_1 = \Gamma(\ ) + S_A(\ )\ln a + S_K(\ )\ln k_1 + \text{error},$$

where S_A is the share of the land.

The factor shares and the rate of return are obtained by using the available data on agricultural wage income, capital stock, and land prices. The share of nonwage income in agriculture is the sum of the shares of land and capital. The share of land can be written as $S_A = RA/X_1p_1$, where R is the rent on land. The rent is not observed, but it can be detected from land prices by assuming that the rate of return in agriculture is the same for land and reproducible capital. Thus, $R = p_A r_1/p_1^*$, so that

$$S_A + S_K \equiv (p_1X_1 - w_1L_1)/p_1X_1 = (r_1p_A A/p_1^* + r_1K_1)/p_1X_1.$$

[34]Basically, the function was obtained by first running a regression on the state variables alone, extracting the significant principal components, and then recomputing the regression with those principal components and the inputs.

Figure 72—Share of capital in nonagricultural output (S_{K2}), 1940–72

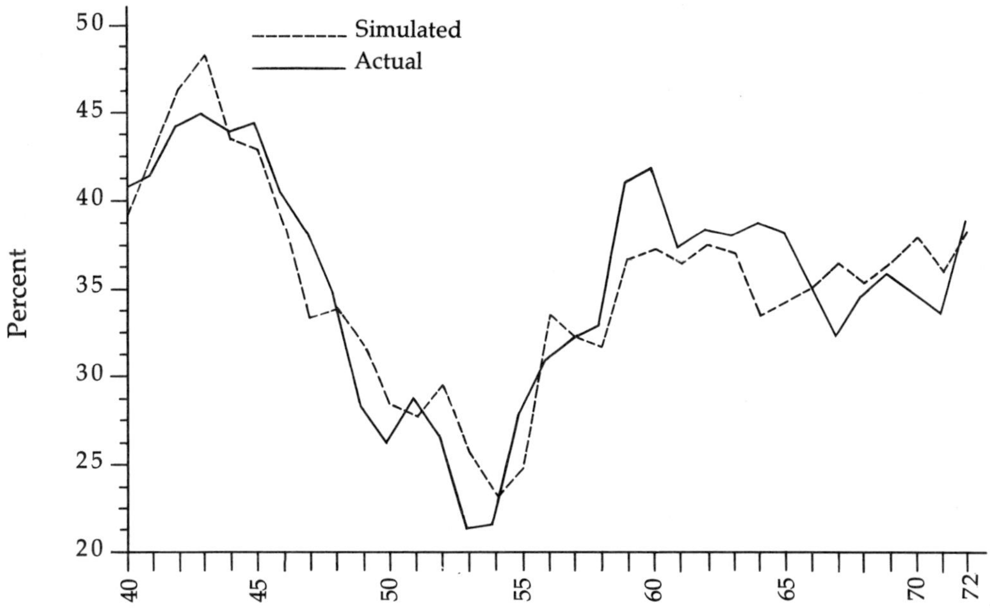

Figure 73—Log of labor productivity in nonagriculture ($\ln X_2/L_2$), 1940–72

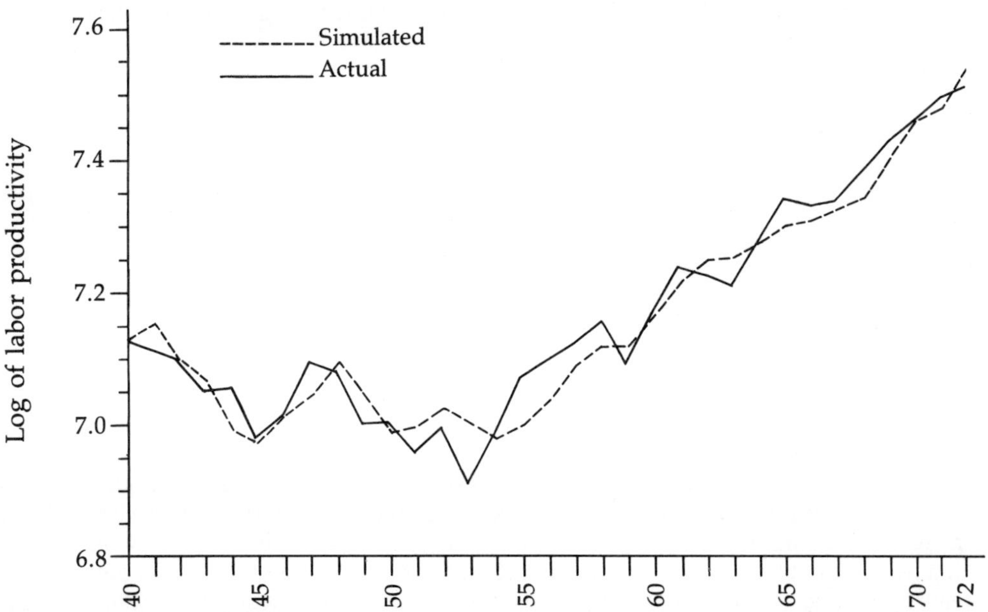

From this one can obtain

$$r_1 = (S_A + S_K)\, p_1 X_1 / (p_A A / p_I^* + K_1).$$

Having derived r_1, it is now possible to differentiate between S_A and S_K.

The state variables for sector 1 (K/N, I_1/L_1, r_1) are similar to those used for sector 2. In addition, the price of land, p_A, and the nonagricultural wage rate, w_2, are used. The wage rate for nonagriculture is used for a variety of reasons. The nonagricultural wage rates appear to be more accurate. In part, this may be because agricultural wages in a given year may be affected by productivity in that year. In bad years agricultural labor may share part of the burden. Agricultural wages will then act as a rate of return and not as an input cost. In addition, the nonagricultural wage rate is the alternative wage for agricultural labor. It is positively correlated with the agricultural wage rate, and thus it conveys the pertinent information: the higher the w_2, the larger the share of labor in agriculture.

The rate of return, the wage rate, and the price of land are lagged one year. The estimation procedure is the same as that used for nonagriculture. The results for the initial run are reported in Table 9. The algebraic rank of each of the three equations is 7; thus the results, with a statistical rank of 4, indicate three redundancies for the share equations and one for the level equation. Subsequently, some state variables are eliminated. In interpreting the results, it may be more meaningful to look at land and capital as an aggregate against labor and to pay less attention to the differences between land and capital. An increase in the intensity of capital and land increases their share. This is consistent with an elasticity of substitution of capital and land for labor larger than 1. Taking this result as given, the column S_L is obtained by adding the coefficients of S_A and S_K and reversing the sign. Thus, except for wages, all the state variables decrease the labor share. With an elasticity of substitution larger than 1, that means that their effect is similar to that of capital-augmenting technical change. Note that this result differs from that obtained for sector 2 where investment had the effect of augmenting labor.

The elasticities of the inputs indicate a sum of about 0.8, leaving the production elasticity of labor at 0.2. The averages of the actual factor shares are $S_L = 0.52$, $S_A = 0.27$, and $S_K = 0.21$. It appears that there is a substantial gap between the production elasticities and the factor shares and that agricultural labor is overpaid. It is interesting to examine the origin of this result in terms of the regression coefficients of Table 9. By differentiation, the land elasticity is

$$E_A = S_A + \ln a[0.2142 - 2(0.0936)] + 0.0172 \ln k_1.$$

Evaluating this expression at the simple mean values of $\ln A$ and $\ln k_1$, it appears that the terms involving $\ln A$ and $\ln k_1$ contribute 0.073 and 0.131 respectively to the difference, $E_A - S_A$. This is approximately the difference between the average share and the average elasticity. Therefore, the difference is largely from having the quadratic terms of the inputs, or simply the translog extensions. The result for the difference, $E_K - S_K$, is qualitatively similar, with each of the two terms contributing about 0.055 to the difference. Indeed, when the analysis is carried out without the quadratic inputs, the discrepancies between the shares and the elasticities are negligible. So if the quadratic terms are to be added, it is inappropriate to impose the fulfillment of the first-order conditions on the data.

The next set of computations involves gradually omitting some of the state variables. The results are reported in Table 10. Equation (1) is reported in detail in Table 9. Equation (2) is obtained by omitting the wage rate. There is some compensation in the average elasticities of the remaining state variables, but no qualitative changes occur. Equation (3) is obtained by eliminating the price of land as well as the wage rate. The main effect is a considerable reduction in the elasticity of K/N. Equation (4) is obtained by omitting K/N rather than p_A.

Table 9—Agricultural production function, 1940-72

Variable	Share of Land (S_A)	Share of Capital (S_K)	Level (Γ)	Share of Labor (S_L)[a]	Elasticity
R^2	0.846	0.868	0.994	...	...
Statistical rank	4	4	6	...	...
Constant	1.2209	−1.1068	5.813	...	...
Logarithm					
K/N	−0.0313 (2.5)	0.3403 (4.8)	−2.0862 (1.7)	−0.3090	0.4264 (3.2)
I_1/L_1	0.0045 (1.9)	0.0060 (6.3)	0.0544 (3.4)	−0.0105	0.0039 (1.4)
r_1 (t−1)	0.0888 (4.8)	0.0621 (4.8)	−0.5820 (21.9)	−0.1509	0.1314 (4.0)
w_2 (t−1)	−0.1928 (5.0)	−0.2351 (4.5)	2.1796 (21.2)	0.4279	−0.1344 (1.2)
p_A (t−1)	0.0904 (4.1)	−0.0874 (3.5)	0.2907 (5.6)	−0.0030	−0.1323 (4.7)
a	0.2142 (3.7)	0.0172 (0.5)	−0.0936[b] (5.2)	...	0.469 (8.5)
k_1	0.0211 (6.9)	0.0844 (2.3)	−0.0387[b] (9.4)	...	0.328 (7.6)

Notes: The data are three-year moving averages. Figures in parentheses in the first three columns are the t-ratios obtained from the individual regressions. The elasticities are with respect to each of the variables. They vary with the observations. The ratios reported for the elasticities are arithmetic means and the figures in parentheses indicate the ratios of means to their standard deviations. K/N is the per capita overall reproducible physical capital in the economy at the beginning of the year. I_1/L_1 is gross investment divided by the labor force in agriculture. r_1 is the average rate of return on capital in agriculture. w_2 is the nonagricultural wage rate. p_A is the price of land. a is cultivated land − labor ratio. k_1 is the capital-labor ratio for agriculture. (t − 1) implies that the variable is lagged one year.

[a]The share of labor was derived from S_A and S_K.

[b]This is the coefficient of $(\ln k_1)^2$ rather than of $\ln k_1$.

The outcome is a positive average elasticity for the price of land. It can then be inferred that the price of land adjusts itself to changes in the overall productivity that occur due to overall capital accumulation in the economy. However, when both variables are included as state variables, the negative overall effect of the price of land can be attributed to factors that affect the price of land but are not related to overall capital accumulation in the economy. In that case the price of land has the same effect as the price of an input. It is suggested, however, that this result be considered preliminary and analyzed further.

One possibility is to use a more refined assumption when deriving r_1. In the foregoing analysis, the computation of land and capital shares was done without making an allowance for depreciation on physical capital and land appreciation. This can be corrected by redefining the relationship between r_1 and R:

$$r_1 = R\, p_1^*/p_A + E(\hat{p}_A) + \Delta,$$

where $E(\hat{p}_A)$ is the expected rate of land appreciation and Δ is the depreciation rate. The average rate of p_A for the period as a whole is 0.035 and this figure is used as the expected value. For depreciation, the actual values used in the construction of the national accounts are used. Here the overall series of p_A is also adjusted so that in 1978 it is equal to the average value of land obtained from the property tax authorities. Column N1 in Table 10 reports the results for the set of variables used in equation 1. It is clear that the net effect is to increase somewhat the numerical values of the elasticities with respect to p_A and w_2. At the same time,

Table 10—Summary results of the agricultural production function, 1940-72

Variable	Equation 1	2	3	4	N1
R^2	. . .	0.983	0.980	0.971	0.987
Statistical rank					
S_a	4	5	4	2	4
S_K	4	2	2	2	2
Γ	6	5	4	2	7
Elasticity					
K/N	0.426 (3.2)	0.322 (20.1)	0.180 (13.3)	. . .	0.408 (11.6)
I_1/L_1	0.004 (1.4)	0.018 (4.5)	0.011 (1.9)	0.024 (4.8)	0.003 (0.4)
r_1 (t−1)	0.131 (4.0)	0.127 (3.2)	0.121 (2.8)	0.110 (2.7)	0.225 (7.0)
w_2 (t−1)	−0.134 (1.2)	. . .	. . .	. . .	−0.199 (3.8)
p_A (t−1)	−0.132 (4.7)	−0.098 (4.7)	. . .	0.065 (4.2)	−0.154 (10.2)
A	0.469 (8.5)	0.554 (9.7)	0.467 (8.6)	0.454 (8.3)	0.411 (6.8)
K_1	0.328 (7.6)	0.254 (7.2)	0.265 (7.3)	0.261 (7.3)	0.382 (7.9)
A+K	0.787	0.808	0.732	0.715	0.793

Notes: The data are three-year moving averages. Figures in parentheses are the t-ratios obtained from the individual regressions. The results of equation (N1) were obtained from modified data as explained in the text. S_A is the share of land; S_K is the share of capital; Γ stands for level. K/N is per capita overall reproducible physical capital in the economy at the beginning of the year. I_1/L_1 is gross investment divided by the labor force in agriculture. r_1 is the average rate of return on capital in agriculture; w_2 is the nonagricultural wage rate. p_A is the price of land. A is cultivated land and K_1 is capital. (t−1) implies that the variable is lagged one year.

there has also been an increase in the elasticity with respect to r_1. Otherwise, there are no important qualitative changes. This leaves the conclusion drawn about the effect of the price of land unchanged. The plots of the estimated equations reported in Table 9 appear in Figures 74, 75, and 76.

In the model, the agricultural capital stock is disaggregated according to the sector of origin. For consistency, the agricultural production function can also be expressed in terms of the two types of capital stock. Such an extension implies two factor share equations for the two types of capital. The equation used in the simulation is reported in Chapter 4. The detailed results appear in Table 11.

Estimating the Production Function

In this section of the paper, the approach used to estimate the production function is discussed so that it can be placed properly in relation to other work in this area. Those readers more interested in the results of the model may wish to proceed directly to Chapter 8.

In economic thinking, the performance of the economy largely depends on the nature of the technology used. However, determining the role of technology is not a simple matter, as the voluminous work on the subject attests. The difficulty arises basically because technology is not an observable quantity but an abstract concept. The dominant approach in economics has been to identify technology with a production function and technological change with

Figure 74—Log of labor productivity in agriculture ($\ln X_1/L_1$), 1940–72

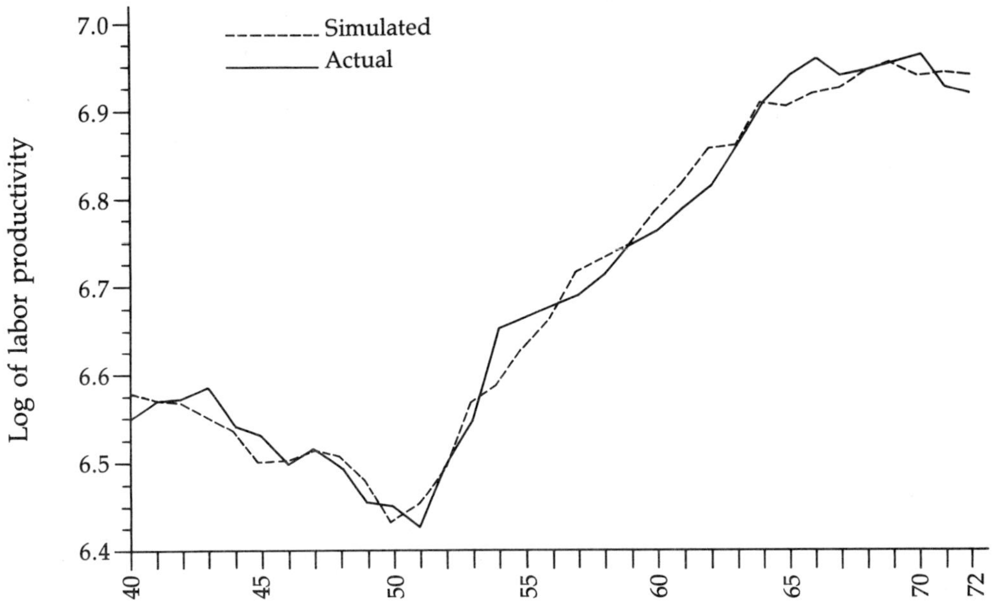

Figure 75—Share of land in agricultural production (S_A), 1940–72

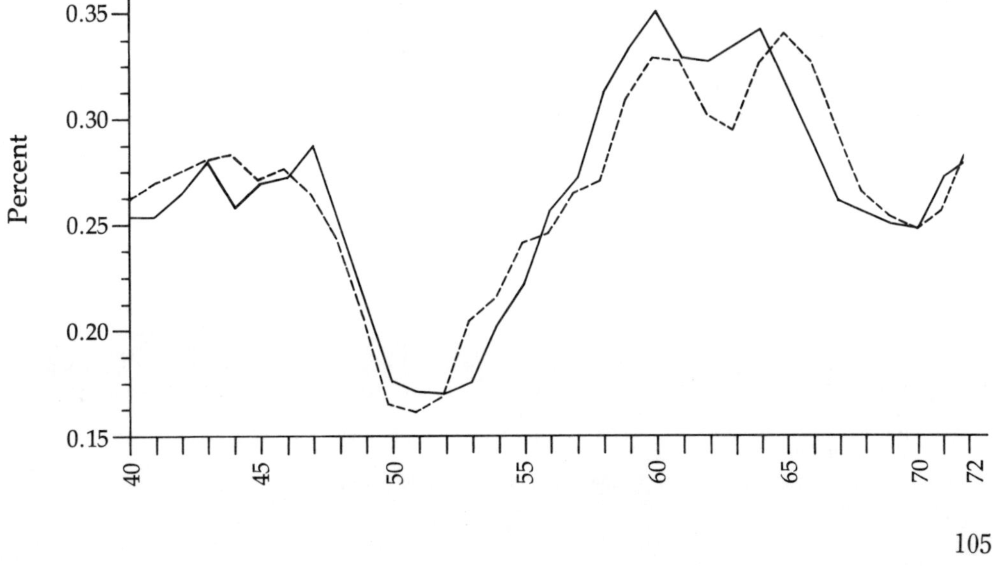

Figure 76—Share of capital in agricultural production (S_K), 1940-72

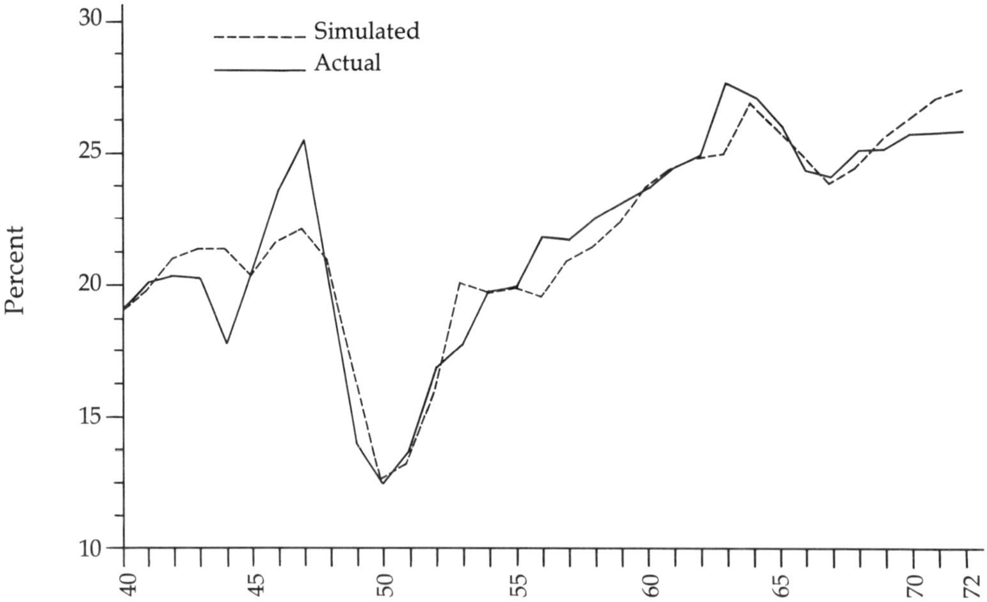

Table 11—Agricultural production function with disaggregated capital, 1940-72

Variable	Share of Land (S_A)	Share of Capital: Agriculture (S_{K11})	Share of Capital: Nonagriculture (S_{K12})	Level (Γ)	Elasticity
R^2	0.719	0.626	0.969	0.992	. . .
Statistical rank	3	2	3	3	. . .
Constant	0.5094	−0.0017	−0.3694	4.4901	. . .
Logarithm					
I_1/L_1	0.0432	0.0085	−0.0143	−0.0778	0.0184
	(2.5)	(2.8)	(3.6)	(15.0)	(2.5)
$r_1(t-1)$	0.1129	0.0799	0.0094	−0.8327	0.1148
	(4.7)	(6.6)	(4.0)	(42.8)	(3.0)
$p_A(t-1)$	0.1276	−0.0409	−0.0066	−0.0464	−0.0418
	(2.7)	(3.0)	(0.6)	(2.2)	(4.6)
a	0.2154	0.1094	−0.0565	−0.1540[a]	−0.4922
	(3.3)	(3.9)	(3.2)	(18.1)	(11.2)
k_{11}	−0.0742	0.0120	0.0641	−0.0118[a]	−0.2525
	(1.8)	(2.5)	(7.0)	(20.9)	(5.0)
k_{12}	−0.0402	−0.0070	0.0342	−0.0015[a]	−0.0738
	(1.9)	(3.7)	(7.4)	(4.9)	(1.4)

Notes: The R^2 for the final ln K_1/L_1 is 0.983. The data are three-year moving averages. Figures in parentheses in the first four columns are the t-ratios obtained from the individual regressions. The elasticities are with respect to each of the variables. They vary with the observations. The ratios reported for the elasticities are arithmetic means and the figures in parentheses indicate the ratios of means to their standard deviations. I_1/L_1 is the gross investment divided by the labor force in agriculture. r_1 is the average rate of return on capital in agriculture. p_A is the price of land; a^1 is the ratio of cultivated land to labor. k_{11} is the ratio of agricultural capital originating in agriculture to labor; and k_{12} is the ratio of agricultural capital originating in nonagriculture to labor. $(t-1)$ implies that the variable is lagged one year.

[a]This is the coefficient of $(\ln a)^2$ rather than of ln a, and similarly for k_{11} and k_{12}.

shifts in production functions. The concept of a production function is borrowed from the sciences, where input-output relationships are generated by what are thought to be well-described processes. As such, production functions describe some laws of nature.

Agricultural production functions have empirical applications that are close in spirit to this concept of production functions.[35] Examples from agriculture were suggestive in the early days of economic theory when agriculture accounted for a large part of total output. However, this universality diminished as time passed, and it became desirable to find a way to apply the concept to nonbiological processes. This led to "engineering production functions."[36] In the words of Solow:

> The pure theory of production is fundamentally microeconomic in character; it deals with physically identifiable inputs and outputs. In the classroom one usually says that the economic theory of production takes for granted the 'engineering' relationships between inputs and outputs and goes on from there. By contrast, much (thought not quite all) of the recent interest in the theory of production has been macroeconomic in character. Since the 'inputs' and 'outputs' are statistical aggregates like 'labor,' and 'plant,' 'equipment,' 'durable manufactures,' there is no possibility of finding engineering relationships. Econometric methods have to do duty instead. Still, it remains an intriguing idea to deduce economically useful production functions from raw technological information.[37]

The role Solow attributes to econometric analysis is narrow and basically impossible to implement. First, an ideal aggregation of inputs and outputs depends on prices and requires a knowledge of production functions, the very thing one wants to estimate with the aggregated variables. Second, the micro functions change with time and therefore affect the relationships between the aggregate inputs and outputs. Thus, strictly speaking, there are no pure engineering-type relationships that can be revealed by econometrics. In fact, Solow himself does not really believe in it. He says, "If aggregation is inevitable, relax and enjoy it."

This problem has not been solved. In general, work on production functions deals with a search for algebraic relationships that make economic sense and can be fitted to data. The estimation is conducted under the basic but tacit assumption that all observations come from the same aggregate relationship, which is allowed to change in one way or another over time.[38] New developments largely fall within the same conceptual framework.

This chapter departs from earlier work in the way it conceives technology.[39] The technology of the economy at any one time is characterized by the collection of all possible techniques. The techniques are micro production functions. Broadly speaking, they are not necessarily the same as engineering production functions in that they are allowed to be affected by the management or entrepreneurial capacity of the firms. At any one time, firms

---

[35]For a discussion of agricultural production functions see Earl O. Heady and John Dillon, *Agricultural Production Functions* (Ames, Iowa: Iowa State University Press, 1961).

[36]See H. B. Chenery, "Engineering Production Functions," *Quarterly Journal of Economics* 63 (November 1949): 507–531.

[37]Robert M. Solow, "Some Recent Developments in the Theory of Production," in *The Theory and Empirical Analysis of Production,* ed. Murray Brown, Studies in Wealth and Income, vol. 31 (New York: National Bureau of Economic Research, 1967), p. 26.

[38]That work alone is very rich. See for instance M. Fuss, D. McFadden, and Yair Mundlak, "Survey of Functional Forms in Economic Analysis of Production," in *Production Economics: A Dual Approach to Theory and Applications,* ed. M. Fuss and D. McFadden (New York: Elsevier/North Holland, 1978).

[39]See Yair Mundlak, *Cross-Country Comparison of Agricultural Productivity,* Working Paper No. 8105 (Rehovot: Center for Agricultural Economic Research, 1980).

choose techniques that are appropriate considering the constraints they face and the values of the pertinent economic variables, such as expected prices. The net outcome is a set of values for the inputs implemented and the outputs produced at that time. Time series of such observations seem to have all the data needed for fitting a production function. However, a function fitted in this way may convey little information or may be erroneous.

To illustrate this point, two production functions, F_1 and F_2, are presented in Figure 77. Economic forces place the economy at point A in one period (say the first) and at point B in the other. A locus of these points provides the data for the estimation of the aggregate production function. However, this function, though generated by perfectly legitimate micro functions, is a convex rather than a concave function of the inputs. Convex functions are familiar in the literature on empirical production functions. In the early days, when a Cobb-Douglas function could be presented without apologies, it took the form of increasing returns to scale. More recently, when functions are allowed to be more flexible—for example, in the case of the translog function—convexity can be obtained using constant returns to scale, and indeed empirical analysis has shown that to be a possible outcome. This is a troublesome result, for one cannot assume the fulfillment of the first-order conditions for cost minimization, which are needed to estimate the function.

In puzzling over this example, one may decide to seek more information about how points A and B were formulated. This is the essence of the present approach. It concentrates on the choice of techniques made in the economy in each period. As the choice depends on the collection of techniques available, their constraints, and the exogenous variables, the framework can be applied to short- as well as long-run variations. Short-run variations are primarily changes that occur because of changes in the exogenous variables; the collection of techniques and the constraints are fairly constant. Such changes usually reflect changes in the economic environment. They may take place with any technology. They are transitory in nature compared with the more basic changes that occur following changes in the available collection of techniques or in the constraints. By their nature, transitory variations in outputs

Figure 77—Production function

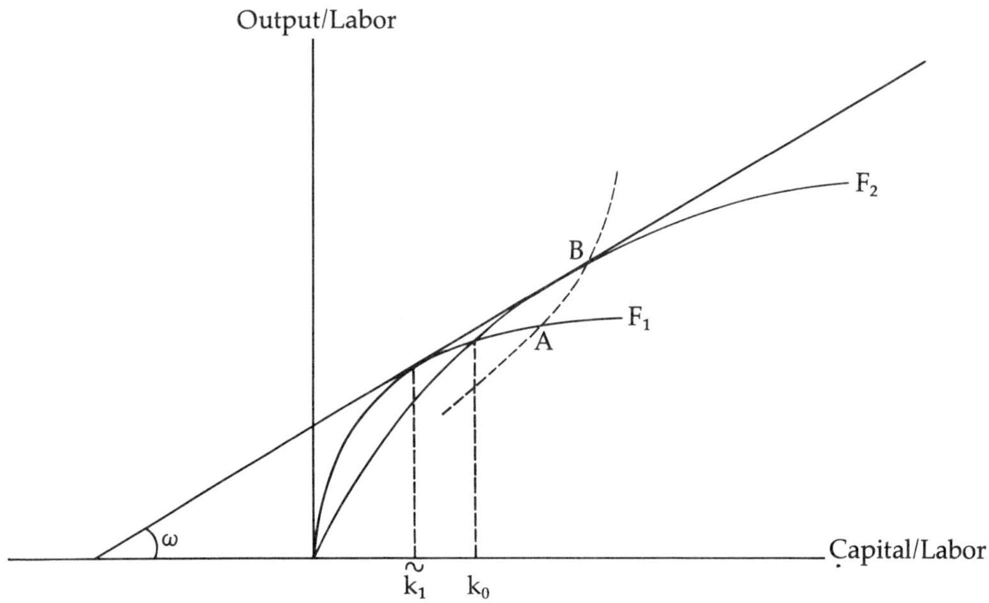

are not reflected in corresponding changes in contracted inputs, such as plant size or the core labor force. Usually the data for empirical analysis report the available inputs rather than the implemented inputs. Thus, underutilization of available inputs affects their productivity.

The approach proposed in this chapter is formulated for empirical analysis. The formulation requires an explicit specification of the state variables.

The State Variables

At any one time, more than one technique is used in production. That is true for any economy that produces more than one product, if a technique is identified with a production function. Although this assertion seems trivial, it conveys pertinent information about the coexistence of techniques. Another example of coexistence of techniques becomes obvious when production functions are identified with firms. If firms differ in efficiencies ("management" or "firm effects"), then the coexistence of firms implies the coexistence of techniques. But the coexistence of techniques is not limited to cases that are obvious and yet somewhat remote from the common concept of a production function. Techniques also coexist in the production of a well-défined product and sometimes within a given homogeneous, simple firm. For instance, in the rice-growing countries of Asia, rainfed and irrigated varieties are sometimes found in the same district or even on the same farm. This situation is far more complex for the production functions of large modern firms: what, for instance, is the production function of General Motors?

None of this is new; it is well-known that the economy consists of a collection of micro production functions. However, the major attempts to relate micro functions to a macro function have viewed the problem as one of aggregation.[40] Such efforts have tried to establish the conditions for viewing the macro function as a well-defined analytic function, keeping the main features of micro functions. The basic premise is that the collection of the implemented micro functions to be aggregated is given. This study questions that premise. It considers the implemented functions to be endogenous to the economic system. So it cannot be assumed—it is meaningless to assume—that they are given.

What then determines which techniques are implemented? In terms of Figure 77, under what conditions do F_1 and F_2 coexist and what determines the shift from F_1 and F_2? F_2 dominates F_1 for $k > k_0$. F_2 may be a new technique, so that when F_1 was selected, F_2 did not exist. If implementing the new technique requires some specific equipment, the technique is viewed as embodied in that equipment. This situation was analyzed by Solow in his discussion of embodied technological change.[41] Under his framework, F_2 can be implemented only by the introduction of a new "machine." So the pace of adoption of F_2 depends on the rate of gross investment, whereas the rate of disappearance of F_1 depends on the rate of obsolescence generated by the increase in wages caused by the introduction of advanced techniques (machines) and by the rate of investment. In this case, the replacement of the old technique by the new technique is gradual, leading to a coexistence of various techniques (machines of various vintages). It is important to note that the process takes place even if there is no net

---

[40]For a somewhat different approach, see H. S. Houthakker, "The Pareto Distribution and the Cobb-Douglas Production Function in Activity Analysis," *Review of Economic Studies* 23 (No. 1, 1955): 27–31. A recent treatment along this line is given in W. Hilderbrand, "Short-Run Production Functions Based on Micro Data," *Econometrica* 49 (September 1981): 1095–1125. In these studies, short-run production functions are viewed as being of the fixed coefficient type and the aggregates are obtained from the distribution of firms. In these terms the approach adopted here does not require fixed coefficient production functions and it emphasizes the dependence of the distribution of techniques on the state variables which, in part, are endogenous to the economic system.

[41]Robert M. Solow, *Capital Theory and the Rate of Return* (Amsterdam: North Holland Publishing Company, 1963).

investment and the only investment is that of replacement. Of course, the larger the investment, the faster the shift to the advanced technique.

Solow's framework does not cover those important cases where the new techniques are not embodied in specific capital goods, but their introduction still depends on investment—to be more specific, on net investment. As shown in Figure 77, for low values of k ($k < k_0$), F_1 dominates F_2. Thus the choice of techniques depends on resource availability or, alternatively, on the wage-rental ratio (ω). This approach can be outlined as follows.[42] Assume production functions with constant returns to scale in capital and labor. Draw the unit isoquants of two available techniques, F_1 and F_2 (Figure 78), and note that there exists a wage-rental ratio, $\tilde{\omega}$, at which the cost of production is the same for the two techniques. When $\omega < \tilde{\omega}$, technique 1 dominates technique 2; the converse is true when $\omega > \tilde{\omega}$. Thus, for $\omega \neq \tilde{\omega}$, the choice of a technique is determined by the existing wage-rental ratio.

The capital-intensive technique is selected when the wage-rental ratio is high, as expected. But what happens when $\omega = \tilde{\omega}$? For the economy at large, the choice depends on the available capital-labor ratio, k. The ratio at which each of the two techniques is implemented is determined so that labor and capital are employed fully. That is, let $k_1(\tilde{\omega}) \equiv \tilde{k}_1$ and $k_2(\tilde{\omega}) \equiv \tilde{k}_2$ be the capital-labor ratios of techniques 1 and 2 corresponding to ω, and let k be the capital-labor ratio available for the two techniques. Then the proportion of the labor force that will be allocated to technique 1, l, is determined by the equation:

$$l\tilde{k}_1 + (1 - l)\tilde{k}_2 = k.$$

Hence,

$$(\partial l/\partial k)\,|\,_{\tilde{\omega}} < 0,$$

and, as long as the two techniques coexist, the rate at which the capital-intensive technique, F_2, is shifted depends on capital accumulation. The analysis carries over to an equilibrium economy.[43] This analysis, which may be deceptively simple, leads to three important conclusions.

First, the availability of two techniques and the possibility of activating them both simultaneously, as indicated by a movement along the market line tangent to the two techniques, represents a superior alternative to the use of one technique alone. Said differently, the coexistence of techniques is superior to a selection of a point on the envelope, obtained by joining the efficient point of the individual isoquants.

Second, with well-behaved production functions, there is always a wage-rental ratio that sustains more than one technique in the sense that ω sustained F_1 and F_2 in the foregoing examples, or, if that is not the case, relatively small variations in ω will result in a value that sustains more than one technique. The reason is related to the simple proposition stated above, that in the process of capital accumulation it becomes profitable to employ capital-intensive techniques. Thus producers of new techniques, anticipating this outcome, will concentrate their production in that direction, for that is where the demand is.

Lastly, the new technique need not necessarily be embodied in a particular capital good (machine). What restricts its implementation is the availability of capital. Thus, unlike Solow's machines, the technique could be implemented immediately without waiting for the quasi-rent of the old machines to disappear. That is, the introduction of the new technique

[42] Danin and Mundlak, "Introduction of Techniques."

[43] Ibid.

Figure 78—Unit output isoquants

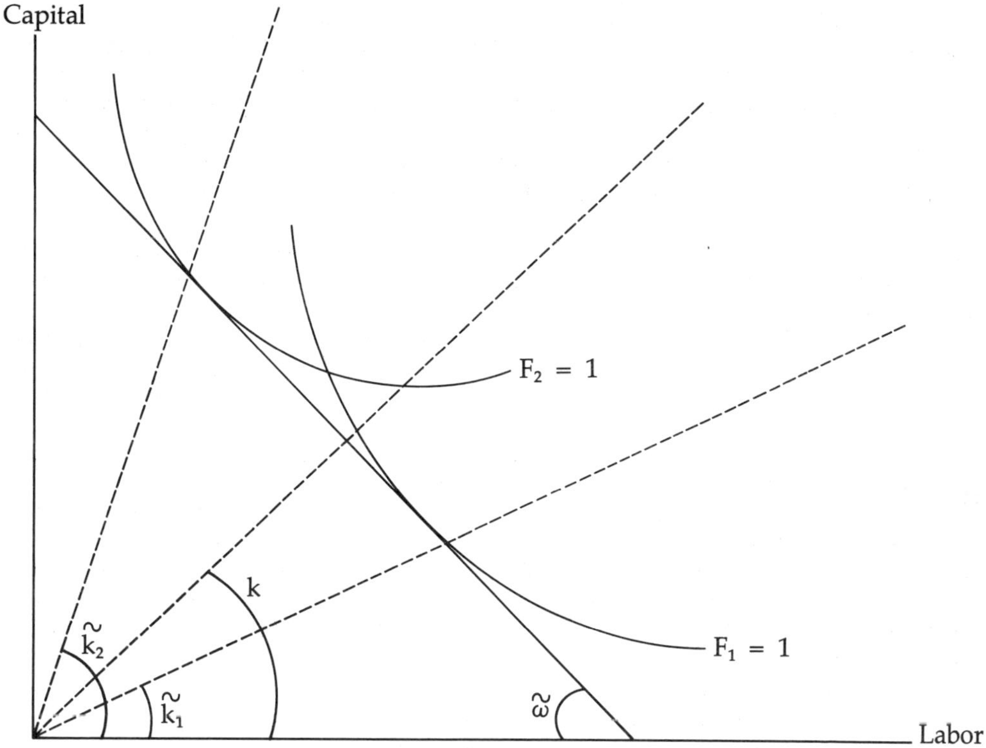

need not be hindered by committed capital. However, unlike the Solow model, the implementation of the new technique requires net capital accumulation.

An example of such techniques is provided by the high-yielding grain varieties. There is no commitment in the form of old machines that could interfere with the introduction of such varieties. However, the potential of such varieties is reached under irrigation, with heavy doses of fertilizers, insecticides, and the like. All these inputs represent capital inputs. But in addition to these, the new technique requires better knowledge, which is generated through education, extension, and research, or, in short, human capital, to be implemented successfully.[44] Being capital, its quantity at any one time is limited. Therefore, advancing the new technique requires that this capital as well as the physical component of the technology be augmented.

Turning to the empirical implications of the discussion, an increase in productivity due to an increase in investment is consistent with the two approaches under consideration. In the first model, based on Solow, investment is the carrier of the new technique. In the second model, based on the Danin-Mundlak study, investment represents the augmentation of capital stock. Note, however, that this approach does not exclude the possibility that existing capital is committed, so that the shift to the new technique is affected by gross rather than net investment. Because of this, in an empirical analysis gross investment as a state variable may represent more than the embodiment component.

---

[44] T. W. Schultz, *Transforming Traditional Agriculture* (New Haven, Conn.: Yale University Press, 1964).

The main emphasis so far has been on capital accumulation. It should be noted, however, that the techniques that are actually implemented also depend on the wage-rental ratio. That means that in the decision to implement new techniques, their rates of return have to be determined. When the techniques produce a homogeneous product, the rate of return of a new technique evaluated at a given wage rate is determined by the production function that describes the technique. Since the technique is new, it may be superior and yet firms may be unaware of it or uncertain about its performance. This is basically the approach followed by Griliches in his study of the diffusion of hybrid corn.[45] After a time, more observations will be generated on the new technique and the uncertainty about it will be reduced.

The speed of the shift to the new technique also depends on the difference in the rates of return of the new and the old techniques. With any amount of uncertainty, the larger the difference, the faster will be the shift. When output is not homogeneous, the output of each technique receives a different price. An increase in the price of the product associated with the new technique will increase its rate of return and will therefore increase the speed of its adoption. This statement can also be applied to several inputs. This discussion emphasizes the diffusion process and explains why the response to the introduction of a new technique takes time.

Another, related, possibility that yields a different result is that each technique is optimal under a different price regime. Because prices follow a stochastic process, it is possible that the optimum strategy is to have a portfolio of techniques. In some ways the handling of the choice of assets and of production theory are asymmetrical. The first allows risk considerations, in addition to expected income, to enter the decision. On the other hand, modern production theory, particularly its econometric aspects, assumes a single criterion—that of profit maximization. This approach may be extremely misleading in the interpretation of data.[46]

This discussion on the choice of technique places a natural emphasis on what is usually considered to be technical progress. It relates such progress to investment, capital abundance, and a favorable, or profitable, economic environment, all of which can be approximated by measurable economic variables. It thus replaces the time trend variable, which is used in empirical analysis to monitor technical changes.

So far it has been assumed that the collection of available techniques is given, and this does not change in the empirical analysis. However, it is evident that the generation of new techniques is capital-intensive and is carried out under both production and market uncertainty. As such, it is also expected to be positively related to the accumulation of capital and favorable economic conditions. In that sense, any empirical analysis that establishes such relationships basically summarizes market observations, and those in turn represent supply and demand conditions. But an available technique is defined loosely. The basic knowledge available at any time makes it possible to generate more techniques than those actually observed. Thus the available techniques already represent some economic decisions, which reflect certain expectations about demand. But demand depends on the state variables. Consequently, the available techniques, representing supply, depend on the expected values of the state variables.

It is simpler to deal with a country that is not at the frontier of knowledge or technology generation. Such a country has access to the international pool of techniques. For instance, there is not much difference between countries in the techniques used in oil drilling and

---

[45] Zvi Griliches, "Hybrid Corn: An Exploration in the Economics of Technological Change," *Econometrica* 25 (October 1957): 501–522.

[46] Yair Mundlak and Z. Volcani, "Correspondence of Efficiency Frontier as a Generalization of the Cost Function," *International Economic Review* 14 (February 1973): 223–233.

pumping or in the airline industry, but there are wide differences in other industries. That means that the difference between countries is in implementation and not in availability. This argument was used in a study based on comparisons between countries.[47] Its relevance here is to emphasize the importance of state variables in determining the techniques to be chosen for implementation from a large collection of available techniques.

This framework can also be applied to short-run choices of techniques. For the short run, the pool of techniques and resources is constant. Thus the emphasis is largely on the selection of committed techniques. The distinction between short and long runs (in this context, as in many others) is conceptual, and it is made to allow for proper interpretation of the results. In reality, any decision by an economic agent takes place at a given time and place, and so may reflect short- or long-run considerations, or both.

The short-run analysis deals basically with variations in economic conditions that affect profitability but are not fully reflected in the quantity of contracted resources. This is explained by setup costs. Firms may not expect current conditions to last long enough to justify the changes in inputs that would be necessary if these conditions were to last. This does not imply that changes do not occur. They do occur but not to the same extent as if the current conditions were considered permanent. This seems to be a trivial point to emphasize. Yet this is exactly the point that is ignored in current empirical work using the duality between production and profit (or cost) functions. It is mentioned here because it affects the measurement of productivity by relating output to contracted (hired) resources and not to implemented resources. The repercussions need not be the same for all resources, because the cost of adjustment is not the same. Consequently, for the production function, such short-term variations need not be neutral in nature.

Turning to the state variables for the short-run variations, any short-run response function by definition should include the variables that represent the short-run constraints. For firms or industries, these variables can be located in a natural way; for instance, the size of a farm or the extent of an irrigation system can be determined. For the economy at large, or for large sectors, the constraints are those faced by the economy and may not differ from those dictating long-run choices.

Aside from the constraints, there are variables describing the economic environment, namely prices, including factor prices and rates of return. Short-run decisions are dictated by current prices, whereas long-run decisions are determined by expected prices. The measurement of expected prices is not unique. For the present analysis, there are two major alternatives: first, to follow the mainstream of the literature and define some process based on the interpretation of past or future performance and, second, to try to determine the expectations of the firms from their behavior and search for variables that reveal those expectations. A natural variable for this purpose is investment. It is likely that, other things being equal, large investment reflects favorable economic conditions and the converse is true for small investment. With this interpretation, the effect of investment on the choice of technique and therefore on productivity reflects in part expectations about the performance of the economy. There may be other variables serving the same purpose.

Relationships to Other Studies

This approach differs in some important ways from alternative ones. From the conventional viewpoint, the equation appears to be a mixture of a production function and a supply function. This should come as no surprise, as the function was originally formulated to be $F(y,x,z) = 0$. Once z includes prices, this mixture can be obtained. Because changes in

[47] Mundlak and Hellinghausen, "Intercountry Comparison of Agricultural Productivity."

techniques are allowed for, the response of y to z is not exactly what one would expect from a given supply function. To some extent, this feature is also part of the conventional approach using supply functions of different runs. Whatever approach, the response is for given resources, and therefore it is a short-run supply response. To obtain a long-run response, the changes in resources in response to changes in prices are studied. This is done within a more comprehensive framework that specifies a hierarchy of responses, recognizing that different inputs adjust to market forces at different speeds. In that it follows the framework for the analysis of behavioral functions, which avoids imposing an arbitrary exogenous response pattern on variables that are endogenous within the economic system.[48]

Alternatively (and this is the point of departure of this work) by holding the state variables constant, the function can be viewed as a production function. That is, for any given size of the state variables, the function expresses output as a function of inputs. The function is increasing monotonically with the inputs having positive marginal productivities. The test for competitive conditions using the Argentine data leads to the conclusion that the first-order conditions for profit maximization are not maintained in the particular sample under investigation. Therefore, for that sample it would be inappropriate to use a dual function, such as profit or cost, for estimating the production function. This is an empirical finding for this particular sample and has no general validity. However, the findings emerge from a framework that allows discrepancies in the factor markets to be detected. The same cannot be said for the approaches that use dual functions outright without tests or, for that matter, for estimates based on the fulfillment of the first-order conditions. Those two possibilities cover a substantial portion of existing work in the econometrics of production functions.

As has been postulated, most of the variations in inputs and outputs are in response to changes in state variables, and they can be thought of as being generated by alternating techniques rather than along a single technique. Therefore, only some of the existing variations contain information about a given production function. When only small variations take place in a given function, then the function may well be approximated by simple functional forms. The applications used here allow for quadratic terms, which are mostly supported by the data. It may well be that in other applications, a Cobb-Douglas function, perhaps with a few quadratic terms added, may suffice. The direction, however, is toward simple approximations, rather than those based on high-order polynomials or their equivalents.

In this formulation, the first-order conditions express factor shares as functions of inputs and prices. This is in contrast to the formulation generated by the translog function, where the factor shares are expressed as functions of the inputs alone. Alternatively, when one starts with translog profit or cost functions and differentiates for prices, the outcome expresses factor shares as functions of prices alone. This approach was used recently by Jorgenson and Fraumeni to study technical change.[49] Their study uses duality conditions without an empirical justification and allows technology to be monitored by a time variable.

The present framework deviates from another approach used in empirical studies of production, the efficiency frontier.[50] The premise of that approach is that a production function is the efficiency frontier of the feasible set, and therefore all deviations from the

[48] Mundlak, "Long-Run Coefficients and Distributed Lag Analysis."

[49] D. W. Jorgenson and B. M. Fraumeni, *Substitution and Technical Change in Production,* Discussion Paper No. 752 (Cambridge, Mass.: Harvard Institute of Economic Research, 1980).

[50] See, for instance, the *Journal of Econometrics* of May 1980 for a discussion of this approach.

functions are one-sided and fall in the feasible set. The present framework suggests that the relevant efficiency frontier is endogenous to the system.

Points that are considered inefficient may well be efficient, considering the relevant constraints. The application of the present approach in another study illustrates this point.[51] A combination of cross-country and time-series data is used to infer resource productivity in agriculture. The comparison between countries makes it easier to see the prominence of the initial endowments of the primary resources, namely land, labor, and capital. These variables are used as state variables instead of their prices, which are largely unavailable. In addition, the choice of techniques is also dictated by such physical conditions as climate. Measures reflecting the importance of the physical environment are thus included among the state variables. Neglecting these factors could be extremely misleading in choosing feasible sets and efficiency frontiers.

To summarize, this work is based on the assumption that at any one time the economy has a large collection of techniques for production. Each technique is identified with a production function. Output is obtained by implementing a subset of the set of available techniques. The subset is determined by several constraints and prices, referred to as state variables. These variables include contracted or committed capital, overall capital stock, the rate of capital accumulation, product and factor prices, and expectations of those prices. Changes in these variables cause changes in the implemented subset. Thus, observed outputs and inputs are generated through several techniques and do not convey the correct information about the existing technology. To correct for this shortcoming, allowance should be made for the effect of the state variables.

This approach has several repercussions. First, it provides more accurate information about the production process. Second, it may lead to a different approach in the empirical analysis of production. Third, it endogenizes factor productivity (or technical change in common usage) and enriches considerably the empirical analysis of growth.

---

[51] Mundlak and Hellinghausen, "Intercountry Comparison of Agricultural Productivity."

8

THE EXPENDITURE SYSTEM

The expenditure system is described in Chapters 3 and 4. In order to implement the system in the model, it is necessary to estimate the consumption and demand functions, and the investment and allocation of investment functions. The empirical equations that were finally selected for the analysis were presented in Chapter 4. This chapter considers the specification of those equations, dwelling in somewhat more detail on subjects already discussed. Some results are presented, using single-equation least-square estimates to supplement the discussion of specification with the information contained in the data. Finally, results of simultaneous equation estimation are presented.

Consumption

A reason for estimating the consumption function is obvious from the role it plays in the model. However, there is another reason as well. The literature on growth and distribution often contains the classical assumption that rates of saving out of nonwage income are high but that there is no saving out of wage income. This assumption has been adopted by many students of the Argentine economy.[52] In general, however, the assumption is made without the necessary empirical support and verification. To overcome this deficiency, saving behavior by factor income is examined. The subject is also broadened to deal with differential saving rates by sectors.

In any given sector, the saving rate can be expressed as a weighted average of the saving rates of wage and nonwage incomes. Thus sectoral differences in the saving rates may arise from either differences in the saving rates of the wage and nonwage incomes or from differences in the weights; those are the factor shares.

Agricultural income in general and in Argentina in particular varies more than nonagricultural income. Therefore one would expect higher saving rates in agricultural income. As most of the variability is absorbed by nonwage income, the rate of saving of this source should be relatively high.

According to economic thinking, savings absorb most of the fluctuations in current income. Under this assumption, it may be more appropriate statistically to obtain saving rates from estimates of consumption rates. As the necessary data on consumption are available, the consumption function can be estimated. The saving function is then obtained as a residual. This is the procedure followed here.

The direct way to estimate the consumption function for different income sources is to use observations on consumption by income sources. Such observations do not exist for this study. Therefore, an indirect approach is adopted. Assume, for simplicity, that there are two types of income, wage, y^w, and nonwage, y^{nw}. Let the consumption functions of these two sources take the form of $c^j = c_j y^j + u^j$, where c_j is the consumption coefficient and u^j is a

[52] See Diaz Alejandro, *Essays on the Economic History of the Argentine Republic;* and Rinaldo A. Colomé, "'Excedente Financiero' del Sector Agropecuario Argentino: Reflexiones en Torno de un Trabajo Anterior y Nueva Estimación," *Desarrollo Económico* 18 (Julio-Septiembre 1978): 275–282.

disturbance. Because total consumption is the sum of consumption generated by the two sources of income, $c = c^w + c^{nw}$ can be written:

$$c = c_w y^w + c_{nw} y^{nw} + u. \quad (8.1)$$

Such an equation can be estimated by using data on overall consumption and the two sources of income. Now the same approach is extended to include more sources of income. It can also be extended by allowing each of the consumption coefficients, now constant, to vary. This possibility is not pursued here. The analysis estimates the consumption function, differentiating income by sectors and factors, which results in four sources altogether. As will be shown later, there is no significant difference between the consumption coefficients of wage and nonwage income in nonagriculture. Therefore, three sources—wages and nonwages in agriculture and average income in nonagriculture—are dealt with first. Income is taken to be factor payments in factor prices. As shown below, wage income in agriculture behaves like income from nonagriculture.

No attempt is made to differentiate between the behavior of consumers in rural and urban areas. Although this would be interesting to investigate, this is not crucial for this study. Furthermore, the issue is not as simple as it may seem. First, not all consumers can be classified as clearly rural or urban. Second, because there is continuous intersectoral migration, a question arises about how long it takes to change the consumption behavior of a migrant. Third, what determines consumer behavior? Is it social and cultural environment or economic environment? Basically, the main weight in this study is given to the latter. If agricultural income becomes less stable, it should affect the consumption behavior of its recipients according to the relative weight it has in their total income. Instability will have a different quantitative effect on a rural family receiving all its income from farming than on a rural family receiving part of its income from nonagricultural sources. It is, therefore, not just a question of how to proceed with the analysis without direct observations on consumption according to the classification of consumers. The approach adopted here may simply be more meaningful. Basically, this also holds true for the classification of wage and nonwage earners. In this case there is a large group that enjoys both kinds of income.

The consumption function should actually be expressed in terms of the permanent components of the income sources. Agricultural nonwage income fluctuates the most because it depends on international prices and on weather conditions in addition to the sources of variation common to other sources of income.

Generally in empirical studies, the effect of permanent income on consumption is derived by using the observed values of income and consumption. It is not often that one can approximate permanent income by directly using wealth variables. But agriculture's output depends on a specific factor, land. The value of land should serve as a good measure of the present value of the expected flow of nonwage income from agriculture, and therefore it represents the main component of agricultural physical wealth. Thus the marginal propensity to consume out of the permanent component of agricultural nonwage income should be related to the rate of interest in agriculture multiplied by land values.

Fortunately, a recent monograph provides a time series of land prices based on actual transactions. If these prices are known, it is possible to approximate agricultural wealth by the product of land prices and the area of cultivated land. To derive permanent income, one would need data on the rates of interest applied to agriculture. Such data are not readily available, and it is better not to contaminate the data with assumptions before the calculation. Therefore, the wealth variable is used directly in the consumption function instead of derived permanent income. The coefficient of this variable derived from the regression should provide an approximation of the average rate of return in agriculture.

There is no natural variable representing the wealth of the other components. Wages are not much of a problem because the transitory component is relatively small. Still, the situation may differ between the sectors because agricultural wage income might be affected by the fluctuations of total agricultural income. Consequently, income derived from agricultural wages might be more susceptible to irregularity in the transitory component than nonagricultural wages.

In overcoming the errors generated by the presence of transitory income in the observed values, it is possible to express permanent income as a weighted geometric average of past observed values. If properly substituted, that approach leads to the inclusion of the lagged value of the dependent variable, c_{t-1}, in the regression.[53] This happens when only one source of income is considered. Extending this to more than one source requires an assumption that the income sources have the same first-degree, distributed lag pattern between their permanent components and their lagged values. Under this assumption, an aggregate consumption function can be constructed where the consumption rates for the permanent components are obtained by using a correction factor based on the coefficient of c_{t-1}.

The presence of a transitory component in observed income may also lead to a simultaneity problem in the estimation. This is partly due to the method used to construct the data. The consumption variable may actually include changes in agricultural inventories. It is possible that agricultural wages and changes in inventories are both affected by agricultural income. In that case, the agricultural wage variable will be correlated with the disturbance in the consumption function. The problems created by the transitory components are often overcome by using instrumental variables that are correlated with permanent income and are not correlated with the transitory income. To deal with agricultural wage income, the correlation of agricultural wages with nonagricultural wages is used. Consequently the variable w_2L_1/N is used as an instrument in addition to lagged values of agricultural wage income. For nonagricultural income, lagged values of the same variables are used as instruments.

The main results of the empirical analysis are summarized as follows:

1. No substantive differences are observed between the estimates derived by instrumental variables and those of ordinary least squares.
2. There is no difference between the marginal propensities to consume of wage and nonwage income in nonagriculture.
3. When agricultural income is decomposed to wage and current nonwage income, the marginal propensity to consume of wage income is larger than 1, whereas that of nonwage income is negative.
4. When land value replaces current agricultural nonwage income as a measure of agricultural wealth, the marginal propensity to consume of wages becomes close to that of nonagricultural income, and the marginal propensity to consume of wealth is positive and significantly different from zero.
5. When the equation is estimated by allowing for a first-order serial correlation, the lagged consumption variable disappears; that is, its coefficient is not different from zero.

The final outcome of this exercise can be given in terms of the following equation:

$$c^p = \underset{(3.6)}{62.1} + \underset{(2.9)}{0.106}\, p_A A/N + \underset{(15.8)}{0.66}\,(x_2 + w_1 L_1/N);$$

$R_2 = 0.9959$, D.W. $= 1.53$, $\rho = 0.823$;

where c^p is per capita private consumption, $p_A A/N$ is per capita land value, $x_2 + w_1 L_1/N$ is

[53]Marc Nerlove, *Distributed Lags and Demand Analysis for Agricultural and Other Commodities* (Washington, D.C.: U.S. Department of Agriculture, 1958).

per capita private income excluding agricultural nonwage income, and ρ is the estimated first-order correlation coefficient.

The consumption variable that is used in this analysis was obtained net of indirect taxes for both domestic and foreign trade. It is assumed that all indirect taxes are used for government consumption. The analysis is repeated, adding per capita indirect taxes to the dependent variable and also including them as an explanatory variable. The results thus obtained reflect a unity marginal propensity to consume out of indirect taxes.

Note that the marginal propensities to consume are for gross rather than net income. In order to derive those coefficients for disposable income, it is necessary to subtract from the gross income figure the value of direct personal taxes and corporate taxes. The resulting coefficients will be somewhat higher than those above.

The results indicate a propensity to consume out of land wealth of about 11 percent. Presumably, this figure is equal to the rate of return from production plus the rate of appreciation less the tax rate on land. The actual rate of appreciation for the period under consideration is obtained from a semilogarithmic regression of the price of land on time. The result for the period 1946–72 is

$$\ln p_A = -0.417 + 0.042t;$$

$R^2 = 0.871.$

Thus land prices appreciated during the period 1946–72 at an average annual rate of about 4.2 percent. Assuming that the appreciation of land values was fully anticipated, the returns from agricultural production net of taxes were on average about 6.4 percent. To obtain the gross returns, it is necessary to add land taxes, which at that time were relatively high. As an indication, a value of 2 percent might be used.[54]

There are two qualifications to this calculation. First, there are other forms of wealth that should have been taken into account. By ignoring them, this coefficient of land value may be somewhat inflated. If so, the calculation suggests an upper boundary. Second, as explained in Chapter 7, the land values calculated may be low. The consumption function is not recalculated for this new series. Nevertheless, it is believed that the present calculation offers some economic insight into the results.

Demand

The complete demand system of private consumption as postulated in Chapter 3 consists of the following equations:

$$x_1^c = D_1 (p^*, c^p), \tag{8.2}$$

$$x_2^{c,p} = D_2 (p^*, c^p), \tag{8.3}$$

$$c^p = c (y^p), \tag{8.4}$$

and

$$c^p = p_1^* x_1^c + p_2^* x_2^{c,p}, \tag{8.5}$$

[54]See Reca, *Argentina: Country Case Study of Agricultural Prices and Subsidies.*

where p_j^* denotes the market price of the jth commodity and $p^* = p_1^*/p_2^*$. Equation (8.2) expresses per capita consumption of the agricultural product, x_1^c, as a function of the price ratio and per capita private consumption. Equation (8.3) expresses per capita private consumption of nonagricultural products, $x_2^{c,p}$. Equation (8.4) gives the consumption function, where per capita private consumption is expressed as a function of the sources of permanent income. This is the function that was estimated in the previous section. Finally, equation (8.5) states the consumption identity. The system then consists of two independent equations and an identity. Once the consumption function is estimated, any one of the two demand equations can be estimated.

The agricultural products considered here are basically measured at the farm gate. All the inputs required to transform the product into a consumer product are included in the nonagricultural product. Consequently agricultural consumption constitutes less than 10 percent of total consumption.

In the actual estimation of the demand equations, additional variables were included, as can be seen in Table 12. The table reports empirical results for the $x_2^{c,p}$ equation, or simply for the private demand for nonagricultural products. The table also reports two versions of the same formulation, where the second equation is obtained by allowing for a first-order serial correlation. As a result the second lag of the dependent variable becomes statistically irrelevant, and is therefore omitted. Equation 2 is estimated in linear form because there was not much difference between the functional forms, and the linear form makes it more convenient to use the results.

The income coefficient is 0.608. To obtain the "long-run" effect, the coefficient is divided by (1 − 0.188), where 0.188 is the coefficient of the dependent variable lagged one year. The result is 0.749.

The relevant price in the demand equation is the ratio of the market prices of the two sets of products. However, recall that the market price of nonagricultural products is a weighted

Table 12—Private per capita demand for nonagricultural products, 1946-72

	Equation	
Variable	1	2[a]
R^2	0.9971	0.996
D.W.	1.54	1.74
ρ	. . .	0.547
Constant	16.5 (1.1)	12.1 (0.5)
c^p	0.587 (14.2)	0.608 (10.6)
p^*	22.2 (3.1)	36.7 (3.1)
ω	234.8 (7.4)	296.6 (8.1)
p_1x_1/x	−158.6 (2.8)	−245.9 (2.5)
$x_2^{c,p}(t-1)$	0.407 (4.8)	0.188 (3.0)
$x_2^{c,p}(t-2)$	−0.198 (3.3)	. . .

Notes: The figures in parentheses are t-ratios. ρ is an estimate of the first-order autocorrelation coefficient. c^p is per capita private consumption; p^* is the market price of agriculture relative to nonagriculture (p_1^*/p_2^*); ω is the share of imports in the total supply of nonagriculture; p_1x_1/x is the share of agricultural income in total income in factor prices; $x_2^{c,p}(t-i)$ is per capita private consumption of the nonagricultural product lagged i years.

[a]This equation allows for a first-order serial correlation.

average of the domestic and foreign products, the weight being the share of imports in the total utilization of x_2. As import is an endogenous variable in the model, it is desirable to add the weight as an additional variable. Consequently the coefficient 36.7 is the response to price, holding the share of imports in total availability constant. The sign of the coefficient is as expected. The higher the relative price of agricultural products, the higher the demand for nonagricultural products. The next variable is the weight. The larger the share of imports, with p^* held constant, the larger the demand for x_2.

The variable $p_1 x_1 / x$ represents the share of agricultural income in total income in factor prices. The coefficient of the variable has a negative sign. This can be interpreted as a lower demand coefficient for x_2 related to income generated in agriculture. The result may also reflect the effect of the transitory nature of agricultural profits discussed in the section on consumption. No effort is made to differentiate between these two effects. Another interpretation of this result is that this variable represents the availability of agricultural products. In a year of shortages (a low value for the variable) there were restrictions on food sales, which forced a shift to nonfood consumption.

A similar equation is estimated for agricultural products, but the signs of the price and the income coefficients are reversed. The hypothesis is that such results are due to changes in inventories. The basic data on agricultural consumption are obtained as a residual after total output is subtracted from the quantities used for export and farm investment. As such, the resulting variable actually includes consumption as well as changes in inventories. In view of the sizes of the variables in question, such changes can be large. This is particularly true for the war years when exports declined and inventories piled up.

To verify the hypothesis with respect to the effect of inventories, variables are sought that are likely to be correlated with changes in inventories. Two variables are particularly pertinent, agricultural output and exports. Output is likely to be positively correlated with inventory and agricultural exports negatively correlated. With the addition of these two variables, the price coefficient becomes negative and the consumption coefficient becomes positive.

The basic premise of the analysis is that demand-consumption relationships are given by equations (8.2)-(8.5) presented above. The consumption function and the demand for nonagricultural products behave empirically according to expectations, and they fit quite well. Thus there is no reason to assume that the demand for agricultural products behaves differently, so that the poor empirical performance of that equation can be attributed to the nature of the data.

Another possibility for obtaining the demand equation for the agricultural product is simply to use the system of equations to derive x_1^c from the consumption identity, using the estimated values for x_2^c. The discrepancy between the values of x_1^c computed this way and the actual values can then be attributed to changes in inventories. From this, the missing variable, changes in inventory, can be measured. Using this variable, a new variable is constructed, x_1^c less changes in per capita inventories, to be denoted as x_1^d. A new consumption variable is also constructed that fulfills the following consumption identity, $c^* = p_1^* x_1^d + p_2^* x_2^c$. The difference between c and c^* is in the value of the change in per capita inventories of the agricultural product. The demand equation is then recomputed, using x_1^d and c^*. The results are satisfactory in that the price and income coefficients have the right signs and are important statistically.

The same procedure could be repeated to recompute the demand for x_2. This is not done. It seems evident from this exercise that the utilization of the consumption system provides satisfactory results. The system is then estimated by full information maximum likelihood (FIML), which confirms the assertion about the utilization of the system as a whole. The system is later expanded to include the investment equation. Only the final results of the FIML estimates are presented, following the discussion on investment.

Investment

The empirical analysis of investment behavior is a widely discussed subject.[55] The approach taken here emphasizes the importance of the expected rate of return in the determination of overall investment. The implementation of this approach requires data on the expected returns and cost of investment funds, which are not available. However, some indirect representation of the expected returns can be constructed with the available data, which are used conventionally in investment studies.

Clearly, more favorable values for the expected rate of return are likely to result in higher investment. However, the actual effect of the rate of return depends on the prevailing excess capacity. An expected high rate of return is likely to have a different effect on investment when a large excess capacity exists than when existing capital is fully utilized. One possible measure for taking into account the combined effect of the expected rate of return and the degree of utilization is given by the capital-output ratio (K/X). An increase in output, holding K constant, may signal an increase in activity and consequently an improvement in the rate of return. However, looking at the capital-output ratio, the existence of excess capacity will be taken into account in determining the size of investment.

For any constant amount of capital stock, the capital-output ratio is proportional to the reciprocal of output. Consequently, a change in output, when output is relatively high, is going to have a smaller effect on the ratio than if it occurred around the average value of output. Thus, this measure discounts the effects of an expansion of output occurring at low capital-output ratios. This imposes a strong restriction on the information contained in output variations. It is therefore desirable to submit such a restriction to empirical determination. This is done by introducing another variable, a change in output, ΔX. A change in output will then affect the capital-output ratio.

A direct observation of the ex post rate of return is obtained from the nonwage income. This variable was introduced as such and also as a rate of return on the existing capital stock.

Finally, when examining gross investment, the size of investment is expected to be positively related to the stock of capital, simply because of the maintenance or replacement requirement. Another variable, investment lagged one period, is also introduced. The results for the moving averages of the variables in question are reported in Table 13. The dependent variable is the overall gross investment in equations (1) and (2) of the table and per capita gross investment in equation (3).

All the equations indicate clearly a negative relationship between investment and the capital-output ratio and a positive relationship with the change in output. Whereas lagged investment is important empirically, the importance of the rate of return is only marginal, with the current rate more relevant than the lagged rate. The stock of capital did not prove to be significant by itself and for this reason is not included. Part of its effect may actually be captured by the capital-output ratio.

Because the model is fitted to the period 1946–72, the equation is also estimated for this period. It is calculated on a per capita basis to be in line with the rest of the expenditure system. The result is equation (3) in Table 13, which does not differ in substance from equation (1).

Estimation of Simultaneous Equations

The empirical equations discussed above were estimated simultaneously, taking into

[55] A recent survey of the literature can be found in S. J. Nickell, *The Investment Decisions of Firms* (Cambridge: Cambridge University Press, 1978).

Table 13—Investment function, 1940-72

Variable	Equation 1[a]	2[a]	3[b]
Period	1940-72	1940-72	1946-72
R^2	0.992	0.992	0.974
D.W.	1.27	1.28	1.1
Constant	421.6 (1.6)	459.7 (1.6)	65.8 (2.3)
K/X	−216.2 (2.6)	−211.1 (2.4)	−27.1 (2.5)
ΔX	0.428 (5.5)	0.467 (6.2)	0.416 (6.1)
r	1,477.0 (1.8)	. . .	67.7
r(t−1)	. . .	1,141.0 (1.44)	. . .
I(t−1)	0.914 (29.1)	0.902 (29.0)	0.876 (21.8)

Notes: The figures in parentheses are t-ratios. K/X is the ratio of capital to output. ΔX is the change in output. r is the rate of return; r(t−1) is the lagged rate of return. I(t−1) is lagged investment.

[a]In this equation, the variables are total values.

[b]In this equation, the variables are per capita values.

account the identities of the model. All the equations were written in a linear form, using the FIML method and allowing for a first-order serial correlation. The empirical equations, estimated for 1946–72, and identities are given below. The numbers in parentheses are the ratios of the coefficients to the standard errors.

Investment:

$$i = \underset{(5.7)}{-27.7}\,(K/X) + \underset{(11.2)}{0.491}\,[x(t) - x(t-1)] + \underset{(27.0)}{0.866}\,i(t-1);$$

$$\rho = \underset{(1.8)}{0.202}.$$

Private consumption:

$$c^p = \underset{(2.3)}{8.5} + \underset{(1.9)}{0.0459}\,(p_A A) + \underset{(18.6)}{0.704}\,(x_1 + w_1 L_1/N);$$

$$\rho = \underset{(16.0)}{0.846}.$$

Demand:

$$x_2^{c,p} = \underset{(0.6)}{4.8} + \underset{(15.7)}{0.603}\,c^p + \underset{(3.7)}{29.251}\,p^* + \underset{(159.8)}{295.1}\,\omega - \underset{(3.6)}{237}\,(p_1 x_1/x) + \underset{(4.5)}{0.221}\,x_2^{c,p}(t-1);$$

$$\rho = \underset{(4.7)}{0.407}.$$

Demand identity:

$$x_1^c = (c^p - x_2^c p_2^*)/p_1^*.$$

Agricultural capital goods:

$$x_1^i = \theta\lambda \, i/p^*.$$

Nonagricultural capital goods:

$$x_2^i = [(1 - \theta) + \theta(1 - \lambda)] \, i/p^*.$$

Imports:

$$x_2^m = -x_2 + x_2^c + y^t/p_2^* + x_2^i.$$

Taxes:

$$y^t = t_1 p_1 (x_1 - x^e) - t_x p_1^e x_1^e + t_2 x_2 + t_m p_2^e x_2^m.$$

Exports:

$$x_1^e = x_1 - x_1^c - x_1^i.$$

And the market price ratio:

$$p = [1 - \omega(t-1)](1 + t_2) + \omega(t-1) \, p_2^{nd}.$$

This is basically the same system given in Chapter 3, equations (3.44)-(3.50), with a few modifications. To simplify the analysis, the weight used in p^*, $\omega = x^m_2/(x_2 + x^m_2)$ is imposed exogenously. The investment allocation functions, θ and λ, which are discussed below, are made exogenous here to reduce the size of the problem.

There are two changes from the OLS estimates discussed above. First, the coefficient of land wealth in the consumption function declines to about 4.6 percent, about half what it was before. Second, the coefficient of the rate of return in the investment function becomes insignificantly different from zero and therefore is not included in the equation. These results are used in the simulator in fitting the model.

Intersectoral Allocation of Investment

The allocation of capital to alternative uses is implemented primarily through decisions on new investment. In general, existing capital has little flexibility in changing from one line of production to another. This is particularly true when intersectoral allocation of capital is considered. Thus the annual expansion of the capital stock in a given sector is limited by the size of the gross domestic investment. The actual allocation depends on profitability conditions as evaluated through expectations of future economic conditions.

In formulating the framework for the empirical analysis it may be convenient to begin with a simplified and somewhat restricted case, where the amount of investment is identical to the amount of depreciated capital. In addition, the size and composition of the labor force remain constant, the rates of depreciation are the same in the two sectors, and the economy is in equilibrium. In this case there should be no tendency to change the intersectoral composition of capital. Therefore the composition of investment is the same as that of the capital stock.

Let $\theta = I_1/I$, and $\Delta =$ the rate of depreciation, then $I_1 = \Delta K_1$, $I_2 = \Delta K_2$, and $\theta^K = K_1/(K_1 + K_2)$. Under this specific assumption, $\theta^K = \theta$, hence the elasticity of θ with respect to θ^K is unitary. Said differently, a unitary elasticity reflects the tendency to preserve the capital composition. This holds true independent of the actual capital composition that the economy maintains at any particular moment.

Deviations from any of these assumptions will affect the composition of investment. This point can be discussed with the aid of the competitive transformation curve, as drawn in Figure 79. True, under imperfect factor markets, where factor prices between sectors are not the same, the feasible production set is a subset of the competitive set. Its frontier will differ from that of the competitive transformation curve. Yet, qualitatively, the results obtained for the competitive case remain unchanged. Let point A be the initial equilibrium point and assume constant returns to scale. Doubling the amount of resources in the economy will leave the transformation curve unchanged; point A remains the equilibrium point.

Alternatively, when capital accumulation exceeds population growth, a new transformation curve is obtained, reflecting expansion. The maintenance of the initial composition of production, as indicated by point B, may not be consistent with demand. In that event assume point C, rather than point B, to be the equilibrium point. The production plan of point C is obtained by moving resources from agriculture in a relative or absolute sense, depending on whether C reflects a decline in agricultural output. In any case, the share of agriculture in total resources is smaller at C than at A.

What signals actually promote the intersectoral mobility of resources? Labor migration is dealt with in a separate section, whereas this section is devoted to investment decisions. For both, market prices are important. Yet there are some intrinsic differences between the two markets because movements of funds do not require the same personal considerations as movements of labor. Consequently an excess supply of funds in any particular sector can, in principle, be cleared quickly by moving it to the other sector, but an excess supply of labor takes longer to correct. Therefore intersectoral differential rates of return may converge faster toward their equilibrium or quasiequilibrium values. In an extreme case, mobility is instantaneous and one may find only small variations in the rates of return across sectors. Yet the economy may develop along its equilibrium path, which goes through points A and C in Figure 79.

Instantaneous adjustment is characterized by intersectoral equality in the rates of return. Since point C is not identical to point B, there will be changes in the equilibrium composition of investment. In this case a nonunity elasticity of θ with respect to θ^K may be found. More specifically, when the share of agriculture in the total capital stock is declining, it can be accomplished only by a decline in θ, so that at point t, $\theta(t) < \theta^K(t)$. It seems therefore that the less the economy relies on price signals to adjust the composition of the capital stock to its equilibrium level, the further away the elasticity will be from unity. Again, a value of unity for that elasticity implies that if it were not for the price signals, the economy would not have changed the composition of its investment.

There are no direct measurements of the sectoral rates of return, nor are there measurements of anticipation of such variations. Therefore a series of pertinent variables is considered. The first variable is the ratio of the actual average productivities of capital in the two sectors. It is possible to use the ratio of marginal productivities, where the marginal productivity is obtained by dividing the sectoral nonwage income by the value of its capital stock. The average productivity seems to have performed better in the empirical analysis.

The relative profitability of agricultural investment is affected by the relative cost of labor in the two sectors. The higher the labor cost in agriculture relative to the other sector, the less profitable agricultural investment becomes, compared to nonagricultural investment. The

Figure 79—Competitive transformation curve

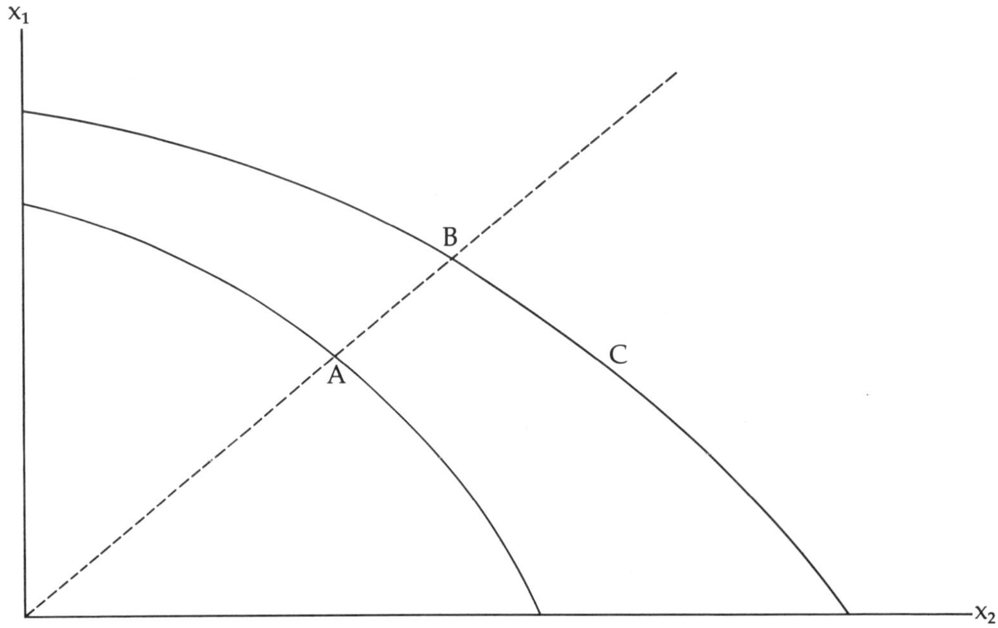

Note: x_1 is agricultural output per capita; x_2 is nonagricultural output per capita.

profitability of agricultural investment is also affected by subsidized credit under a program implemented by the central bank. So a variable representing the relative importance of credit is introduced.

The expectation of the future profitability of agriculture is represented by the price of land. It is expected that higher prices for land should be associated with a larger share of agriculture in total investment.

Finally, it sometimes takes several years for agricultural investment to be completed. For example, investment in orchards, once started, continues for several years. The duration of the investment in pasture is shorter. Introducing lagged values of the dependent variable into the regression partially adjusts for this.

The empirical analysis consists of fitting a regression with $\ln\theta$, as the dependent variable, and the natural logs of the variables as explanatory variables. The relative rate of return is measured by the ratio of average productivities,

$$\delta_r = (X_2/K_2)/(p_1X_1/K_1).$$

The analysis is conducted for the three-year moving-average data used in the simulator. The results are reported in Table 14.

Equation (1) in Table 14 indicates that the two leading variables, δ_r and θ^K, are not significantly different from zero. The introduction of credit changes matters for θ^K, but not for δ_r, as can be seen in equation (2). The results change considerably with the introduction of the real price of land, which serves as an expectation variable. Clearly, higher land prices are associated with a larger share of agriculture in total investment. Adding the ratio of wage rates leads to equation (4), which shows that a larger intersectoral wage differential increases the share of agriculture in total investment.

Table 14—Intersectoral allocation of investment, 1945-72

Variable	Equation 1	2	3	4	5
R^2	0.879	0.944	0.962	0.975	...
D.W.	1.60	1.51	1.82	2.65	...
Constant	−0.385 (0.9)	−1.146 (3.5)	−1.503 (5.0)	−2.288 (6.7)	−1.294 (4.3)
θ^K	0.079 (0.3)	0.603 (2.7)	0.587 (3.1)	0.869 (4.9)	0.539 (3.7)
δ_r	−0.051 (0.9)	−0.064 (1.4)	−0.189 (3.4)	−0.273 (5.2)	−0.605 (5.6)
Agricultural credit	...	0.316 (5.0)	0.322 (6.0)	0.434 (7.8)	0.297 (6.4)
p_A	...	...	0.220 (3.1)	0.292 (4.7)	0.291 (6.0)
w_2/w_1	...	...	...	0.746 (3.3)	...
Dependent Variables					
Lagged 1 year $\theta(t-1)$	1.466 (9.3)	0.882 (5.6)	0.712 (5.0)	0.760 (6.8)	0.721 (7.0)
Lagged 2 years $\theta(t-2)$	−0.791 (5.6)	−0.579 (5.4)	−0.469 (4.9)	−0.662 (6.7)	−0.446 (6.5)
Long run factor	...	...	0.78	0.96	0.74

Notes: Figures in parentheses are t-ratios. θ^K is the composition of capital. δ_r stands for differential returns. p_A is the price of land. w_2/w_1 is the ratio of wages in nonagriculture to wages in agriculture.

In all cases the lagged values of θ are important. The cumulative effect of the lag values is reported in the table.[56] Applying this to the coefficient of θ^K gives the effect of the capital composition. The result is 0.78 for equation (3) and 0.96 for equation (4). Thus, if the result of equation (4) is accepted, it implies that there is no autonomous change in the composition of investment anticipating the equilibrium.

Equation (3) was estimated again, simultaneously with the equation discussed in the next section. The results appear as equation (5) of Table 14. Although equation (4) is more complete, equation (5) was used in the simulator for technical reasons and can be removed in future applications.

The Allocation of Agricultural Investment

Agricultural investment consists of investments that originate in agriculture, mainly livestock, and items purchased from nonagriculture, such as machines and structures. The decomposition of agricultural investment into these two components is inspired by the structure of the model; they add to the aggregate demand for the sectoral outputs. The underlying assumption is that the composition of investment is largely determined by relative

[56] For example, for equation (3) it is obtained from

$$(1 - 0.712 + 0.469)^{-1} = 1.321.$$

To obtain the long-run coefficient, θ^k is $1.321 \times 0.587 = 0.78$.

prices. However, the actual direction of the effect of relative prices cannot be postulated beforehand. Agricultural investment that originates in agriculture is an intermediate product. When the price of the agricultural product goes up, there is an increase in demand for the intermediate product due to the product expansion effect. At the same time, if output can also be increased by several inputs that are substitutes, then an increase in the price of the agricultural product would cause a substitution effect disfavoring the intermediate product. It remains for the empirical analysis to determine the net effect of a change in the price of an intermediate input for the sample uner consideration.

The empirical analysis consists of regressing λ, the share of total agricultural investment originating in agriculture, on relative prices and related variables. The explanatory variables are chosen because agricultural output consists of two major components, livestock and crops. Investment in cattle is an input for livestock and generally has little effect on the output of crops. An increase in the price of cattle relative to the price of crops, p_{LS}/p_C, has a positive supply response on livestock. Investment in livestock is the most important component of investment that originates in Argentine agriculture. In livestock production there are no important substitutes for the size of the herd and it is therefore expected that the expansion effect will dominate the substitution effect. Consequently, an increase in the price of livestock is likely to affect λ positively. On the other hand, conditions favorable to crop production for which the supply response of crops will be positive will encourage investment of nonagricultural origin and thus decrease λ.

As in the allocation of overall investment, price effects can be expected to measure deviations from normal or permanent positions measured by the ratio of the components of λ in the capital stock. A larger share of livestock in the total stock of capital will require a larger share of livestock in investment to maintain the same composition of capital stock.

Livestock production is subject to wide fluctuations. These, in turn, lead to fluctuations in λ. Consequently the analysis of the determinants of λ can be used to illustrate the possible effects of working with moving averages on the empirical results.

The analysis consisted of regressing ln λ on its various determinants, all in ln form. The results are summarized in Table 15, with equation (1) reporting the results for the annual data. In this regression the coefficients of capital composition (K_{11}/K_1) and of p_{LS}/p_C, current and lagged one year, are significant and have the expected signs. In addition to those variables, the regression includes the price of the agricultural products lagged one year, $p_1(t-1)$, the price of land, p_A, and the dependent variable lagged one and two years. Those coefficients are imprecise in that their t-ratios are small. It can then be concluded that the price information contained in p_{LS}/p_C exhausts the information contained in p_1.

Equation (2) repeats equation (1) with moving average data. As expected, an autoregression is produced by the moving average, leading to a statistically significant coefficient for the dependent variable lagged one year. As a result, the fit of the equation improves somewhat. The resulting changes in the other coefficients are a decline in the coefficient of K_{11}/K_1 and a substitution of $p_1(t-1)$ for $p_{LS}/p_C(t-1)$ as the significant variable. It thus appears that the three variables are substituting for each other. However, it can be said categorically that the role of the price variables in explaining the variations in λ is not less important in the equation with the annual data. In fact, the opposite is true. Thus it would be incorrect to attribute the significance of the results of the empirical analysis to the use of moving average data. It appears that the conclusions drawn from the two regressions are somewhat different. A closer analysis indicates that the substantive information of the two regressions is not that much different. To see this, the cumulative effect of a once-and-for-all change in the explanatory variable is completed. The results, presented at the lower part of the table, indicate that the coefficients of the composition of capital in the two equations are close. There are wider differences in the coefficients of prices, which may suggest that p_1 is dominated by the price of crops, p_C, the denominator of the price ratio p_{LS}/p_C. For that reason it has a negative coefficient. Under this interpretation, the effects of p_{LS}/p_C and p_1 can

Table 15—Allocation of agricultural investment, 1942-72

Variable	Equation 1	2	3	4	5	6
Period	1942-72	1942-72	1942-72	1946-72	1946-72	1946-72
Data	Annual	MAV	MAV	MAV	MAV	MAV
Method	OLS	OLS	OLS	OLS	FIML	OLS
Dependent variable	λ	λ	λ	λ	λ	λ^*
R^2	0.880	0.944	0.920	0.900	...	0.95
D.W.	...	...	2.12	2.18	...	1.72
K_{11}/K_1	1.923	1.181	0.660	0.906	0.808	−3.130
	(5.3)	(2.8)	(2.4)	(3.1)	(2.9)	(4.1)
$p_1(t-1)$	−0.071	−1.045	−0.913	−0.779	−0.620	1.975
	(0.2)	(2.4)	(3.4)	(2.9)	(3.3)	(2.8)
$p_{LS}/p_C(t)$	0.461	0.458	...	...	...	...
	(2.5)	(1.9)				
$p_{LS}/p_C(t-1)$	0.633	−0.033	...	...	...	...
	(2.7)	(0.1)				
p_A	−0.065	0.252	...	...	...	...
	(0.3)	(1.1)				
$\lambda(t-1)$	0.113	0.739	1.155	1.00	1.080	−2.605
	(0.6)	(3.2)	(7.6)	(6.1)	(7.9)	(5.9)
$\lambda(t-2)$	0.048	−0.213	−0.654	−0.651	−0.621	1.812
	(0.3)	(1.0)	(4.1)	(4.2)	(5.2)	(4.4)
Dummy 1962	...	...	...	...	...	2.451
						(8.0)
Constant	0.309	...	−0.196	−0.214	−0.163	−0.212
			(2.8)	(3.1)	(3.1)	(1.2)
Cumulative multiplier	1.173	2.110	2.0	1.596	1.848	...
K_{11}/K_1	2.26	2.49	1.32	1.39	1.49	...
Combined price effect	1.37	3.10	1.830	1.197	1.146	...

Notes: The numbers in parentheses are t-ratios. MAV stands for moving average. The two methods used were ordinary least squares (OLS) and full-information maximum likelihood (FIML). λ is the share of total agricultural investment originating in agriculture. K_{11}/K_1 is capital composition. $p_1(t-1)$ is the price of agricultural products lagged one year. p_{LS}/p_C is the ratio of the price of cattle to the price of crops. p_A is the price of land. All variables in the regression are of logarithmic form. The multiplier is obtained from $[1 - \text{coefficient } \lambda(t-1) - \text{coefficient } \lambda(t-2)]^{-1}$. The cumulative coefficient of capital composition is obtained by multiplying the regression coefficient of that variable by the multiplier. The cumulative combined price effect is obtained by adding the coefficients of p_{LS}/p_C, current and lagged, and of $p_1(t-1)$ with sign reversed and then multiplying the result by the multiplier.

be combined by adding their coefficients. The results are 1.37 for the annual regression and 3.1 for the moving average regression.

Equation (3) repeats equation (2) but with only one price, $p_1(t-1)$. The combined long-run price coefficient is now 1.83, much closer to the value of equation (1). Equation (3) also displays a more distinct lag structure with significant two-year lagged dependent variables.

The simulation of the model begins in 1946. Consequently, equation (3) is recomputed for the period 1946–72. The results appear in equation (4). The result is a still weaker price effect, 1.2. The same equation was reestimated simultaneously with the θ equation. The result appears in the table under equation (5) with only small changes from those for equation (4).

To conclude the review of the five regressions, it is clear that the economic information contained in the moving average equations is basically the same as that obtained from the annual equation; it only appears in a different form. The analysis indicates that the composition of investment is affected by the prices and the composition of the capital stock.

For the simulation, it was desirable to introduce a lower boundary on λ. That was done by generalizing the functional form of λ by defining a new dependent variable $\lambda^* = [1/(\lambda - 0.27)] - 1$. As λ approaches 0.27, λ^* approaches infinity. Or, writing $\lambda = [1/(\lambda^* + 1)] + 0.27$. As λ^* becomes large in absolute value, λ approaches 0.27. The result of the regression with λ^* as the dependent variable, but with $\lambda(t - 1)$ and $\lambda(t - 2)$ as the lagged variables, are reported as equation (6) in Table 15. It appears that the results of this equation are comparable to those of equation (4). This regression was actually used in the simulation.

9

OTHER EMPIRICAL RELATIONSHIPS

Labor Migration

The analysis of intersectoral labor migration starts with the framework outlined in an earlier study and applies it as follows.[57]

It is postulated that the rate of intersectoral labor migration depends on the difference between labor income in the two sectors. The higher the labor income in nonagriculture compared with that in agriculture, the higher the rate of migration from agriculture. The rate of migration is measured as the percentage of the agricultural labor force that migrates to nonagriculture in a given year. This rate depends not only on the differential income in the two sectors but also on the relative size of the labor forces. The larger the nonagricultural labor force relative to that of agriculture, the larger the rate of migration generated by a given income differential. This outcome arises from several effects. The larger the agricultural labor force, the larger the absolute migration that is generated by any given income differential. Such a migration may have a depressing effect on labor income in nonagriculture. Thus the size of this effect is likely to be inversely related to the size of the nonagricultural labor force.

This line of reasoning calls for incorporating the size of the labor force in the two sectors into the migration equation. However, constant returns to scale with respect to the size of the country should be maintained. That is, doubling the size of the labor force in the country without changing its sectoral composition should leave the functional relationship between the rate of migration and the differential income unchanged.[58] These considerations are accommodated by an equation of the form:

$$\ln(m + c_0) = \beta_0 + \beta_1 \ln(\delta - c_1) + \beta_2 \ln(RL) + \beta_3 z + u; \qquad \textbf{(9.1)}$$

$u \sim N(0,\sigma_u^2)$.

δ is a measure of intersectoral income differential; RL is the ratio of the labor force in the two sectors; $RL = L_2/L_1$, where L_j is the labor force of sector j, and $j = 1,2$; z stands for other variables that might be included in the migration equation that are not discussed here; and u is the random disturbance distributed as specified above. The β coefficients are unknown constants to be estimated. Finally, the constants c_0 and c_1 need some explanation. The constant c_0 is introduced in order to accommodate observations with negative migration, that is, with migration into agriculture. In this sense the equation accommodates migration in both directions. The term c_1 represents that value of δ at which migration becomes zero. Positive migration is expected as long as $\delta > c_1$[59]

To estimate an equation like equation (9.1) requires a knowledge of m. This variable is not observed but can be constructed from the data on the labor force. Unfortunately, there is

[57]Yair Mundlak, *Intersectoral Factor Mobility and Economic Growth.*

[58]The formulation allows for empirical testing of this relationship.

[59]In the empirical analysis there is a point of discontinuity at $\delta = c_1$. For $\delta < c_1$, the variable should be redefined as $c_1 - \delta$.

no consistent time series on agricultural labor available that covers the whole period under investigation. A series is constructed from four sources.

The first is the census data reports on the main occupations of people. They are available for 1914, 1947, 1960, and 1970. The report for 1980 is now being prepared.

The second is a series of five-year averages beginning with 1900-04 and ending with 1950-54, prepared by the Economic Commission for Latin America (ECLA) in connection with their study of the economic development of Argentina.[60]

The third is a series of annual figures for the period 1946-61 prepared by the Consejo Nacional de Desarrollo (CONADE), the Interamerican Development Bank (IDB), and the ECLA in connection with their study of income distribution.[61] This series (the CIE series) looks much like an annual interpretation of the ECLA data for the overlapping period. Its definition of agricultural labor includes family wage earners. However, it differs somewhat from the definition used in the census data.

Lastly, the central bank (CB) published an annual series for the period 1950-73. Their data, based on social security data, report the number of wage earners but do not cover family labor of farm owners.[62]

To obtain a series for the period under consideration, the CIE series has to be linked with that of the CB. This is first done for 1951-54. Because the coverage of the two series is different, there is a jump in those years. In addition, the CB series has a much larger variance, which may be due to the exclusion of family labor. The analysis is first conducted with this simple linked series, using dummy variables for the linkage years, to obtain estimates of the migration equation. However, the two series are somewhat different, which creates difficulties when using the migration equation in the simulator. As a consequence another procedure is used. The CIE data are smooth whereas those of the CB are not. To generate uniformity, the CB data are fitted with a second degree polynomial on time for the period 1953-73. The difference between the fitted data and the CIE data is calculated for the period 1953-61. A trend line is then obtained for this difference and extrapolated to 1973. The values thus obtained are added to the CIE series to extend it to 1973. The final outcome is consistent with the census data, although there are still some differences reflecting the difference in definitions.

Once a series on the labor force is available, migration is computed under the assumption that the natural rate of growth of the agricultural labor force ($\hat{L}_1$) is equal to that of the total labor force ($\hat{N}$). The migration of labor out of agriculture expressed as a proportion of the agricultural labor force is then given by $m = \hat{N} - \hat{L}_1$. In computing the series for m, the rate of growth of the population is used for $\hat{N}$. Table 16 gives selected empirical results for the first data linkage procedure, before the CB data were smoothed.

The measure used for the sectoral income differential, δ, is the ratio of the average labor productivities in the two sectors, each measured in current prices. This variable is expected to be highly correlated with the ratio of per capita permanent consumption in the two sectors, each measured in current prices. However, the value of δ at which migration disappears is determined empirically by the estimated value of c_1. The joint estimation of c_0,c_1, and the βs in the migration equation requires a nonlinear method. Equation (1) in the table gives the results of such an estimation. It is interesting to note that the value obtained for c_1 is 0.965,

---

[60]United Nations Economic Commission for Latin America, *El Desarrollo Económico de la Argentina* (New York: United Nations, June 30, 1958).

[61]Argentina, Consejo Nacional de Desarrollo y Naciones Unidas, Comision Económica para America Latina, *Distribución del Ingreso y Cuentas Nacionales en la Argentina* (Buenos Aires: CONADE, 1965).

[62]Banco Central de la República Argentina, *Sistema de Cuentas del Producto e Ingreso de la Argentina,* vol. 2 (Buenos Aires: BCRA, 1975).

Table 16—Labor migration equations, using unsmoothed data, 1940-73

Regression Number	R^2	c_0	c_1	Intercept	Variables δ-c_1	RL	SE	D.W.	$E_{m/\delta}$
1	0.560	0.306 (11.3)	0.965 (1.78)	−1.205 (38.0)	0.073 (2.6)	0.097 (3.5)	0.021	1.97	3.46
2	0.653	0.23	0.85	−1.526 (27.0)	0.114 (1.8)	0.130 (2.3)	0.083	1.91	3.71
3	0.701	0.23	0.85	−1.554 (16.0)	0.166 (1.2)	0.155 (1.7)	0.081	1.94	5.40
4	0.830	0.10	1.30	−2.359 (25.0)	0.165 (3.2)	0.320 (2.9)	0.164	1.84	4.15

Sources: Calculated from data in Argentina, Consejo Nacional de Desarrollo y Naciones Unidas, Comision Económica para America Latina, *Distribución del Ingreso y Cuentas Nacionales en la Argentina* (Buenos Aires: CONADE, 1965); United Nations Economic Commission for Latin America, *El Desarrollo Económico de la Argentina* (New York: United Nations, June 30, 1958); and Banco Central de la República Argentina, *Sistema de Cuentas del Producto e Ingreso de la Argentina,* vol. 2 Buenos Aires: BCRA, 1975).

Notes: c_0, c_1 are constants as defined by the equation; $\delta - c_1$ is the natural log of a measure of differential returns minus c_1. RL is the natural log of the ratio of the labor force in nonagriculture to that in agriculture; SE is the standard error of the residual; and $E_{m/\delta}$ is the elasticity of migration with respect to δ, computed at $\delta = 2$ and $m = 0.013$. The numbers in parentheses are t-ratios. Equation (1) gives the results of a nonlinear equation where c_0 and c_1 are estimated together with the remaining coefficients. Equation (3) was estimated by allowing for polynomial distributed lags (fifth degree). The coefficient of $\delta - c_1$ (0.166) is the cumulative effect of all the six $(\delta - c)(t-i)$ variables.

which is close to 1. That is to say, migration will have stopped when the average productivities in the two sectors are equal. The corresponding value of c_0 is 0.306. This is somewhat higher than in other studies. It is, therefore, of some interest to explore the sensitivity of the results to changes in the values of these coefficients. This is done by iterating on c_0 and c_1. As the values of c_0 and c_1 are changed, the regression coefficients change accordingly. However, the resulting changes in the regression coefficients may simply be a result of a change in units.

To examine this possibility, the elasticity of m with respect to δ is computed. The results are reported in the $E_{m/\delta}$ column of Table 16.[63] The elasticities are computed for the mean value of m and for $\delta = 2$, which is close to its mean value. Thus the elasticity obtained from the nonlinear regression is 3.46. The other regressions that were experimented with produced elasticities somewhat higher, up to 4.15 except for equation (3). It does appear that migration responded positively to variations in the income differential.

It is likely that migration responds to an income differential of several years. To accommodate such a possibility, regressions are computed with lagged values of δ. Equation (3) is obtained by allowing for five lagged values of δ in addition to the current value. The coefficient 0.166 is the sum of the individual coefficients. It is somewhat higher than the coefficient of equation (2) that was computed with the same values of c_0 and c_1 but with only one value of δ. That difference explains the larger value that is obtained for the elasticity in equation (3). However, it should be noted that the difference in the coefficients is not statistically significant; thus there is no evidence that adding the lag values introduces any additional information.

The results with the smoothed data are somewhat different in several respects: first, better results are obtained when the income differential is measured by wage differentials rather than by the average productivities; second, the ratio of the labor force is not statistically significant. Instead, unemployment is an important variable. The variable referred to as

[63] By chain differentiation,

$$E_{m/\delta} = \beta_1 \, \delta(m + c_0)/(\delta - c_1)m.$$

unemployment also includes changes in the participation rate. Its construction is explained in the next section.

These deviations from the previous results are attributed to the smoothing of the data. It should be noted that the migration is largely of wage earners and not of farm owners, as the number of farms did not decline. This may partly explain the variability of the CB data. By smoothing it, part of the economic response may have been wiped out, although it yields a more coherent series for the rest of the analysis. The equation for one choice of variables and c_0 and c_1 is:

$$\ln(m + 0.06) = \underset{(2.06)}{-\,0.259} + \underset{(2.1)}{0.079} \ln(\delta_w - 1.25) \underset{(5.4)}{-\,0.127} \ln UN(t-1) + 0.873 \ln(m + 0.06)(t-1); \quad (9.2)$$

$R^2 = 0.964$, D. W. $= 1.1$, $E_{m/\delta_w} = 4.4$.

The same equation, when computed by allowing for the first-order serial correlation, gives similar coefficients. Thus equation (9.2) is used for further computation. Note that the migration elasticity of δ_w, the ratio of wage rates (w_2/w_1), is within the range of results reported in Table 16. It is computed at the mean value, $\delta_w = 2.09$. Thus, the economic response is still about the same size as that obtained for the first series.

Instead of the ratio of the labor force, the unemployment variable is now used, which indicates that unemployment deters migration. When the income differential is measured by the ratio of average labor productivities computed using the labor force, the effect of unemployment is accounted for. The reason is that the average productivity is obtained by dividing output by the total labor force rather than by employment.

Unemployment

Unemployment is generally neglected in studies of growth. They focus more on multiplication of output; reducing unemployment may have a relatively small effect on output. However, the empirical study of growth is based on actual data. There are not two sets of data, one for growth and one for short-term macro variations. Therefore in dealing with the data it is important to consider their determinants, even though some of those determinants are not of immediate interest for this study. For example, the discussion in the previous section showed that labor migration is affected by unemployment. So the process of resource allocation and its dependence on exogenous factors may be understood better if unemployment is made endogenous in the analysis. This will be done in future analyses, but an empirical analysis of unemployment will be needed. The results of such an analysis reported here reveal some effects that affect the interpretation of the performance of the model.

To study unemployment, observations of that variable would have been used. But as was indicated in the previous section, such data were not available. Instead, a measure was derived that combines unemployment and changes in the participation rate. To be specific, if $e = L/N$ is the employment rate, $un = UN/N$, the unemployment rate, and pr, the participation rate of the population in the labor force, then $e = pr - un$. The observations here are of e. Instead of working with e, the difference $u = \bar{e} - e(t)$ is observed where $\bar{e}$ is the highest value over the sample period. Thus $u = \bar{e} - pr + un$, and changes in this measure of unemployment, u, are positively related to changes in unemployment proper, un, and inversely related to changes in the participation rate, pr.

At any one time, employment is assumed to depend on the demand for labor at the going wages. As unemployment occurs mainly in nonagriculture, two sources are considered for the demand for labor: the traded and nontraded sectors. The demand of the traded sector is here represented by the price of imports, p_2^{nd} and the demand of the nontraded sector is given by the tax divided by the wage rate, y^t / w_2. An increase in either of these variables should reduce the rate of un. The quantity of labor demanded also depends on the wage rate. However, the wage rate also affects the participation rate. An increase in the wage rate increases pr and un. These two variables appear with different signs in the definition of u. Consequently the net effect of the wage rate on u can only be determined empirically.

The variables in the analysis are logarithms. Because un had a value of zero in 1950, the dependent variable is taken as ln(u + 0.03). The result for the period 1946-72 is:

$$\ln(u + 0.03) = \underset{(0.3)}{-0.027} + \underset{(27.3)}{1.001} \ln(u + 0.03)(t-1)$$

$$\qquad - \underset{(3.5)}{1.675} \ln[w_2(t-1)/w_2(t-2)] - \underset{(5.1)}{0.644} \ln p_2^{nd};$$

$R^2 = 0.970$, D.W. = 2.22.

The coefficient of the lagged dependent variable is 1. Thus the equation explains the rate of change in unemployment in terms of the rate of change in wages with a constant that depends on p_2^{nd}. For $p_2^{nd} = 1$, the rate of change of unemployment depends only on the rate of changes of wages, which have an elasticity of 1.675. The negative sign of this coefficient indicates a dominant effect of the response of the participation rate.

The role of p_2^{nd} is interesting. First, an increase in p_2^{nd} implies an increase in the demand for labor and, therefore, a fall in unemployment. Note that the ratio of per capita taxes to wages, assumed to represent government demand, is not significant and is not included in the equation. Second, recall that p_2^{nd} is deflated by the price index of the domestic nonagricultural product. Thus, if the price ratio is 1, changes in unemployment will be determined only by changes in wages. If p_2^{nd} is larger than 1, there will be a tendency for unemployment to decline and, vice versa, for p_2^{nd} to be less than 1. The average value for p_2^{nd} for the period 1940-72 was 0.96 and the standard deviation was 0.2. As p_2^{nd} is determined by the rate of exchange, it is clear that during that period an increase in the real rate of exchange was associated with a decrease in unemployment and an increase in the participation rate in nonagriculture.

The Land Equation

In 1941 the area under cultivation was 27.05 million hectares. It fell to 24.59 million hectares in 1950 due to the decline in trade during the war and the Peronist policy toward agriculture after. Thereafter, the area increased with some mild fluctuations and reached 30.1 million hectares in 1969. It decreased somewhat in the next two years. To what extent were these changes in cultivated land (A) a response to economic forces? The margin for the decision in land utilization is between natural pasture (not reported under cultivated land) and crops. In this decision the price ratio of livestock to crops (p_{LS}/p_C) is important. In view of the dynamic nature of livestock enterprises, this variable is introduced with several lags. In addition, the price of land (p_A) affects how much new land is brought under cultivation. The empirical results are reported in Table 17.

The coefficients of the price ratio p_{LS}/p_C alternate signs but their net sum is low, − 0.05 for the first equation and − 0.03 for the second. To obtain the long-run effect of changes in

Table 17—Land response, 1946-72

Variable	Equation 1	Equation 2
R^2	0.942	0.922
D.W.	2.39	2.56
Constant	0.529 (1.4)	1.000 (2.6)
A(t − 1)	1.329 (8.3)	1.372 (7.6)
A(t − 2)	−0.490 (2.5)	−0.678 (3.4)
$p_A(t-2)$	0.017 (0.71)	0.047 (2.1)
$p_{LS}/p_C(t)$	−0.142 (2.6)	−0.213 (4.1)
$p_{LS}/p_C(t-1)$	0.264 (2.9)	0.348 (3.7)
$p_{LS}/p_C(t-2)$	−0.281 (3.2)	−0.270 (2.7)
$p_{LS}/p_C(t-3)$	0.247 (3.3)	0.105 (1.9)
$p_{LS}/p_C(t-4)$	−0.138 (2.5)	

Notes: All the variables are logarithms. The numbers in parentheses are absolute values of t-ratios. A stands for area, either lagged one year (t − 1) or two (t − 2). p_A (t − 2) is the price of land lagged two years. p_{LS}/p_C is the ratio of the price of livestock to the price of crops, either current (t) or lagged (t − i) years.

prices, the coefficients of A(t − 1) and A(t − 2) are subtracted from 1 and the reciprocal is taken. That gives a coefficient of 6.2 for equation (1) and 3.3 for equation (2). Consequently, the long-run price elasticities of the area response to changes in this price ratio are − 0.31 for equation (1) and − 0.1 for equation (2). The values of both are small. The main effects of changes in the price ratios are on the annual pattern of land utilization rather than on the long-run values. The difference between the two equations is in the value of the coefficient of the price of land. The elimination of the price ratio lagged four years makes the coefficient of the price of land lagged two years empirically relevant. The long-run effect of the price of land using equation (2) is 0.047 × 3.3 = 0.16. Thus there appears to be a trade-off in the accountability for area response between the price of land and the number of lagged terms introduced for the price ratio of livestock to crops. Equation (1) is used in the simulation.

Real Rate of Exchange

The present model has no explicit formulation of the nontradable sector that permits the price ratio of tradables to nontradables, which is simply the real rate of exchange, RE, to be determined directly. Yet this variable is of extreme importance in studying the past performance of the economy and its response to simulated changes in the exogenous variables. For that matter, an empirical analysis is conducted whereby variations in the RE are related directly to their exogenous determinants.

In a small, moneyless economy, the real rate of exchange depends on foreign prices and on tariffs and export taxes used in the home country. A reduction in the tax on exports (t_x) increases the domestic price of the exported commodity, increases the incentive for producing exportables, reduces their domestic consumption, and thereby leads to an increase in exports. This change requires a shift of resources to the exporting sector. Resources mobilized from the production of nontradables decrease their output, thus leading to excess demand, an increase in their prices, and a decrease in the real exchange rate.

A reduction in the import tariff (t_m) will lower the domestic price of the imported good. Following the preceding argument with respect to a decline in t_x, this change will result in excess supply of nontradables, decrease their price, and consequently increase the real exchange rate.

A change in the terms of trade generates an income, or wealth, effect and a substitution effect. The net effect on net exports is not uniquely signed and has to be determined empirically.[64] When the effect is to reduce net exports, resources will move out of the export sector, in part to the nontraded sector. Such a movement can be prevented by increasing the returns to resources in the traded sector relative to those in the nontraded. That means an increase in the real exchange rate.

Although a nonmonetary model is dealt with here, an empirical analysis of the rate of exchange should take into account that the observations were actually generated in a monetary economy. An expansion in the domestic supply of money in excess of the increased demand for it increases the prices of the domestically produced goods and thereby causes a decline in the real exchange rate. This yields an equation where the real rate of exchange is expressed in terms of three variables. The first is the commercial policy of the country, represented by $1 + t_m$ and $1 + t_x$. The computations of t_m and t_x are explained in Appendix 1. The values obtained for these variables represent not only the official quotations but also the effects of such other variables as subsidized credit, import or export quotas, and the multiple exchange rate regime. The second is the foreign terms of trade, measured as the price ratio of foreign prices of agriculture to nonagriculture (p_1^f/p_2^f). The last is the monetary changes, summarized as the expansion of domestic credit, expressed as a proportion of the money supply at the end of the previous period less the rate of growth of national income (EC). The effect of these variables may last for more than one period, either for technical reasons related to the time required to respond to the changes or to the effect on expectations of information already received. This variable is measured in natural units whereas the others are in logarithms.

The dependent variable in the analysis is the real exchange rate corrected for foreign inflation. It is the product of the nominal exchange rate and an index of foreign prices, deflated by the price of domestic nonagricultural products. The index of foreign prices is simply a weighted average of p_1^f and p_2^f, where the weights are the shares of exports and imports in total trade. The empirical results appear in Table 18.

Equation (1) in the table contains only real variables, which all have the expected signs. The only variable that is only marginally significant is $1 + t_m$. The monetary variable EC is introduced in equation (2). It is not significant, and its introduction reduces the significance of $1 + t_m$. The net effect of all the foreign prices is given at the bottom of the table and it is negative.

Equation (3) introduces the ratio of net imports to the money supply, lagged one year, $EM/M_3(t - 1)$. This introduction increases the t-ratio of $1 + t_m$ to an acceptable value. Finally, adding EC to equation (3) slightly improves its t-ratio compared to equation (2) but does not make it relevant empirically. It still has the right sign, as can be seen in equation (4). This equation is used in the simulation whenever an instrument is needed to affect the rate of exchange.

The addition of EM/M_3 to the equation algebraically reduces the coefficient of $1 + t_m$. This indicates a negative correlation between $1 + t_m$, net imports, and $EM/M_3(t - 1)$. This

[64] L. Svensson and A. Razin, *The Terms of Trade, Spending and the Current Account: The Harberger-Larsen-Metzler Effect,* Seminar Paper No. 170 (Stockholm: Institute for International Economic Studies, University of Stockholm, 1981).

Table 18—Real exchange rate, 1946-72

Variable	Equation 1	2	3	4
R^2	0.94	0.95	0.96	0.96
D.W.	2.22	2.16	2.44	2.36
Constant	0.033	0.028	0.031	0.024
	(1.1)	(0.9)	(1.12)	(0.9)
$1-t_x$	−0.702	−0.694	−0.647	−0.635
	(6.9)	(6.9)	(6.9)	(7.0)
$1+t_m$	−0.254	−0.097	−0.505	−0.337
	(1.6)	(0.5)	(2.9)	(1.7)
p_1^f/p_2^f	0.683	−0.525	0.691	0.511
	(4.5)	(2.7)	(5.1)	(3.0)
$p_1^f/p_1^f(t-1)$	−1.296	−1.165	−1.208	−1.054
	(8.4)	(6.3)	(8.5)	(6.3)
$p_1^f/p_2^f(t-3)$	0.604	0.581	0.522	0.491
	(3.5)	(3.4)	(3.3)	(3.2)
$p_1^f/p_2^f(t-4)$	−0.467	0.484	−0.374	−0.388
	(3.6)	(3.8)	(3.1)	(3.3)
Net price effect	−0.476	−0.543	−0.369	−0.44
EC(t−1)	...	−0.206	...	−0.236
		(1.22)		(1.6)
EM/M3(t−1)	...	...	−0.448	−0.469
			(2.47)	(2.7)

Notes: All variables, except EC and EM/M3, are logarithms. The numbers in parentheses are the absolute values of t-ratios. t_x is the tax on exports; t_m is the import tariff. p_1^f/p_2^f is foreign terms of trade, which is lagged (t − i) years. EC(t − 1) is the rate of growth of real domestic credit lagged one year. EM/M3(t − 1) is the ratio of net imports to the money supply lagged one year.

relationship may be explained by imperfections in the market. Because imports were regulated during most of the period under study, it is possible that importers took advantage of periods with liberal trade policies to overstock, thereby depressing the domestic prices of imported goods in later periods. That reduced t_m, which is a realized variable rather than an official quotation. It also decreased the demand for foreign exchange in subsequent periods, thereby reducing the real exchange rate. The results are in general agreement with the findings for quarterly data obtained by Cavallo for the period.[65]

[65] Domingo F. Cavallo, "El Saldo de la Balanza Comercial y Tipo de Cambio Real," *Ensayos Económicos* 16 (Diciembre 1980).

APPENDIX 1:

THE BASIC DATA AND THE DEFINITIONS AND DERIVATIONS OF THE VARIABLES

The Variables

This appendix presents a list of all the variables, their definitions and their derivations from the basic data and, in Tables 19 to 31, presents the annual data as reported in the original source. The per capita values are determined from the moving averages of the actual values. This procedure is followed for each algebraic transformation of the variables. As shown in Chapter 3, the model determines prices up to p_2^d, the price of the nonagricultural product produced domestically. Thereafter all value variables are reported as ratios to p_2^d. Actually, they are deflated by the implicit price index of nonagricultural products produced domestically. Aggregates, unless otherwise indicated, are value aggregates. Quantity flow variables are Xs, with the superscript identifying the sector. Lowercase letters represent per capita variables, whereas uppercase letters indicate total values.

Both sectors export and import. However, agriculture usually exports, and nonagriculture usually imports. Consequently, sectoral exports and imports refer to net values unless problems arise. It is also assumed that the foreign price for each sector's output moves at the same rate for exported and imported goods.

The list follows.

Commodity Flows

x_1 = per capita output originating in agriculture. It is determined as X_1/N, where X_1 is agricultural gross domestic product at factor cost (Table 19) and N is total population in millions of inhabitants (Table 25).

x_2 = per capita output originating in nonagriculture, determined as X_2/N where X_2 is nonagricultural gross domestic product at factor cost (Table 19).

x_1^e = per capita net exports from agriculture, determined as $(PX_1 - PM_1)/[p_1^f(NREX)N]$, where PX_1 and PM_1 are exports and imports of agricultural products at current prices (Table 29), p_1^f is the foreign price of the aggregate agricultural product, and NREX is the nominal rate of exchange (Table 27).

x_2^m = per capita net imports of nonagricultural goods and services, determined as $(PM_2 - PX_2)/[p^f(NREX)N]$, where PM_2 and PX_2 are imports and exports of nonagricultural goods and services at current prices. They are determined as the difference between the total values and those of sector 1 as reported above. The totals are reported in Table 22. p^f is the foreign price of nonagricultural goods; it is obtained as explained below.

x_1^i = per capita investment from agriculture, determined as $PI_{11}/Np_1^*p_2^d$, where PI_{11} is agricultural gross domestic investment at current prices originating in agriculture (Table 23); p_1^* is the market price of agricultural output.

x^i_2 = per capita investment from nonagriculture, determined as $(PI_{12} + PI_2)/Np^*_2p^d_2$, where PI_{12} is agricultural domestic investment at current prices originating in nonagriculture and PI_2 is nonagricultural gross domestic investment at current prices (Table 23); p^*_2 is the market price of nonagricultural products, and it is defined below.

x^c_1 = per capita consumption of agricultural products, determined as $x_1 - x^i_1 - x^e_1$, which is the identity in equation (3.1).

x^c_2 = per capita consumption of nonagricultural agricultural products derived from identity (3.2): $x^c_2 = x_2 - x^i_2 + x^m_2$.

Prices

p^f_1 = the foreign price of agricultural exports in foreign currency. It is an index with a base of 1960 = 1/(1 − 0.317) = 1.466, where 0.317 is the effective rate of taxation on agricultural value added estimate for 1960. The computation of p^f_1 is explained below.

p^f_2 = the foreign price of nonagricultural imports in foreign currency. It is an index with a base of 1960 = 1/(1 + 0.099) = 0.91, where 0.099 is the effective rate of protection on nonagricultural value added, estimated for 1960. The computation of p^f_2 is also explained below.

p^f = aggregate foreign price, obtained as a weighted average of p^f_1 and p^f_2: $p^f = (p^f_1x^e_1 + p^f_2x^m_2)/(x^e_1 + x^m_2)$.

p^d_2 = the domestic price of nonagricultural products produced domestically. It is obtained as an implicit price deflator of the GDP generated in sector 2 by dividing GDP at current prices (Table 20) by GDP at constant prices (Table 19). It is used as a numeraire in the analysis. All prices reported here are deflated by p^d_2.

RE = the real exchange rate. It is an index with a base of 1960 = 1.0. It is determined by transforming the series on the nominal exchange rate (NRE) (Table 27) into an index and deflating it by p^d_2.

p^e_1 = the foreign price of agricultural exports in domestic currency, determined as p^f_1 RE.

p^e_2 = the foreign price of nonagricultural imports in domestic currency, determined as p^f_2 RE.

p_1 = the price of agricultural products. The implicit price deflator of agricultural GDP at factor cost is deflated by p^d_2. The implicit price is obtained by dividing GDP at current prices (Table 20) by GDP at constant prices (Table 19).

p^{nd}_2 = the price of nonagricultural imported products deflated by p^d_2 (Table 26).

p_2 = the price of nonagricultural goods obtained as $(x_2 + p^{nd}_2 x^m_2)/(x_2 + x^m_2)$.

t_x = the effective tax on agricultural value added. It is estimated for 1969 using the work of Berlinsky and Schydlowsky.[66] For the other years it is obtained from $t_x = 1 - p_1/p^e_1$.

[66] J. Berlinsky and D. M. Schydlowsky, "Incentives for Industrialization in Argentina," in *Development Strategies in Semi-Industrialized Countries,* ed. B. Balassa (Washington, D.C.: The World Bank, forthcoming).

t_m = the effective tariff on nonagricultural value added. For 1969 it is obtained from Berlinsky and Schydlowsky[67] and for the other years from $t_m = p_2^{nd} / p_2^e - 1$.

t_1 = the rate of indirect taxation on agricultural products consumed domestically. It is computed from $t_1 = (T_1 - t_x p_1^e x_1^e)/(x_1 - x_1^e)\, p_1$, where T_1 is the total indirect tax on agricultural products (Table 28).

t_2 = the rate of indirect taxation on nonagricultural products. It is computed from $(T_2 - t_m\, p_2^e x_2^m)/x_2$, where T_2 is the total indirect tax on nonagricultural products. It is obtained as a difference between total indirect revenue and T_1 (Table 28).

p_1^* = the market price of agricultural products. It is obtained from $p_1(1 + t_1)$.

p_2^* = the market price of nonagricultural products. It is equal to $[x_2(1 + t_2) + p_2^{nd} x_2^m]/(x_2 + x_2^m)$.

p^* = the price ratio p_1^*/p_2^*.

p_A = the price of land deflated by p_2^d and reported as an index, with 1935 = 1.0 (Table 31). The index is multiplied by 107, which is an estimated value for the price in pesos of a hectare in 1940.

p_{LS} = the price of livestock deflated by p_2^d (Table 31).

p_C = the price of crops deflated by p_2^d (Table 31).

w_1 = the agricultural wage rate in pesos per worker per year. It is determined from the average nominal wage in agriculture (Table 26) deflated by p_2^d.

w_2 = the nonagricultural wage rate in pesos per worker per year determined by dividing the nominal wage rate in nonagriculture (Table 26) by p_2^d.

r_1 = the real rate of return on capital in agriculture. It is obtained under the assumption that the price of land is equal to the ratio of rent to the rate of return obtained on investments in reproducible capital. It is computed from $p_1^*(p_1 X_1 - w_1 L_1)/(K_1 + p_A A) = r_1$, where L_1, K_1, and A are the agricultural labor force, agricultural capital stock, and cultivated land respectively. These variables are described below.

r_2 = the rate of return on capital in nonagriculture. It is computed from $(X_2 - w_2 L_2)/K_2$.

R = rent per hectare of land, and it is determined as $p_A r_1/p_1^*$.

Value of Flows and Derived Ratios

All value flows are deflated by p_2^d.

y^t = per capita indirect taxes obtained from $t_1 p_1(x_1 - x_1^e) + t_x x_1^e p_1^e + t_2 x_2 + t_m p_2^e x_2^m$.

[67] Ibid.

x = per capita income at factor cost, equal to $p_1 x_1 + x_2$.

y = per capita income in market prices, equal to $p_1 x_1 + x_2 + y^t$.

i = per capita investment: $i = (I_{11} + I_{12} + I_2)/N$.

i_1 = per capita investment in agriculture: $i_1 = (I_{11} + I_{12})/N$.

i_2 = per capita investment in nonagriculture (Table 23).

θ = the share of agriculture in total investment: $\theta = i_1/i$.

λ = the proportion of agricultural investment originating in agriculture: $\lambda = x_1^i p_1^* / i_1$.

em = per capita savings originating abroad (foreign savings). It is obtained from $x_2^m p_2^e - x_1^e p_1^e$.

c = per capita consumption, equal to $c = y + em - i$.

s_d = per capita domestic savings, equal to $y - c$.

c^p = per capita private consumption, obtained from $c - y^t$.

Resources

N = total population (Table 25).

L_1 = the agricultural labor force in millions of workers (Table 25).

L_2 = the nonagricultural labor force in millions of workers (Table 25).

L = the overall labor force, equal to $L_1 + L_2$.

m = the migration from agriculture expressed as a proportion of L_1: $m = \hat{N} - \hat{L}_1$. In applying this formula it is assumed that all unemployment and changes in the participation rate take place in sector 2.

UN = a calculated measure of unemployment and reduction in the participation rate, reported in millions of workers. It is computed by taking the year with the highest ratio of L/N and projecting it to the other years by applying the rate of population growth. The difference between L and the computed value thus described gives the measure. In symbols: $UN = 0.4237N - L$.

K_{11} = the agricultural capital stock originating in agriculture, evaluated in agricultural prices (Table 24).

K_{12} = the agricultural capital stock originating in nonagriculture, evaluated in nonagricultural prices (Tables 24).

K_1 = overall agricultural capital stock, evaluated in agricultural prices; it is equal to $K_{11} + (K_{12}/p^*)$.

K_1^N = the overall agricultural capital stock, evaluated in nonagricultural prices: $K_1^N = K_1 p^*$

K_2 = the capital stock in nonagriculture (Table 24).

A = cultivated land in millions of hectares (Table 24).

Other Variables

CRED = the share of agriculture in banking credit (Table 30).

EC = expansion of domestic credit as a proportion of the quantity of money in the previous period, less the inflation rate and less the real growth of the economy in the previous period. Domestic credit and M_3 are taken from Table 30.

M_3 = the quantity of money, including all kinds of bank deposits (Table 30).

δ_r = the ratio of average capital productivities in the two sectors: $\delta_r = (X_2/K_2)/(X_1 p_1/K_1)$.

To help determine the order of magnitudes, Appendix 2 contains a table with averages, standard deviations, coefficients of variation, and the minimum and maximum values of the variables during the period 1940-72, with the corresponding years and average rates of growth of the variables computed from a regression of the natural log of the variable on time.

Derivation of p_1^f and p_2^f

There is no data series for the foreign prices of agricultural and nonagricultural products. The available data report import and export goods in current dollars (Table 27) and in constant prices (Table 21). That allows the foreign export prices (p_x^f) and import prices (p_m^f) to be determined. The export data contain some nonagricultural products whereas the import data contain some agricultural products. It is therefore necessary to derive the sectoral foreign prices. The identities expressing imports and exports in current prices in terms of their sectoral composition are used. Thus,

$$PM = PM_1 + PM_2,$$

and

$$PX = PX_1 + PX_2.$$

Deflating by the implicit price indexes and imposing the assumption that for each sector the foreign price of imports is equal to the foreign price of exports,

$$PM/p_m^f = PM_1/p_1^f + PM_2/p_2^f,$$

and

$$PX/p_x^f = PX_1/p_1^f + PX_2/p_2^f,$$

where p_1^f and p_2^f are indexes with base 1960 = 1. The result is a system of two equations in terms of the two unknowns, p_1^f and p_2^f.

Note that this system expresses the overall import and export price indexes as harmonic means of their sectoral components:

$$p_m^f = [(1/p_1^f)(PM_1/PM) + (1/p_2^f)(PM_2/PM)]^{-1},$$

and

$$p_x^f = [(1/p_1^f)(PX_1/PX) + (1/p_2^f)(PX_2/PX)]^{-1}.$$

Solving the system for the two unknowns gives:

$$p_1^f = [(PX_1/PX) - (PM_1/PM)]/[1 - (PM_1/PM)/p_x^f - (1 - PX_1/PX)/p_m^f],$$

and

$$p_2^f = [(PX_1/PX) - (PM_1/PM)]/[1 - (PM_1/PM)/p_m^f - (1 - PX_1/PX)/p_x^f].$$

Recall that the sectoral prices are defined as

$$p_1 = p_1^f RE(1 + t_x),$$

and

$$p_2^{nd} = p_2^f RE(1 + t_m).$$

There are independent readings on p_1, p_2^{nd}, and RE, whereas p_1^f and p_2^f are now derived. All these variables were indexes with base 1960 = 1. Therefore, the only unknowns are t_x and t_m, which can now be solved with the available data.

In a detailed study, Berlinsky and Schydlowsky obtained values for t_m and for t_x for 1968.[68] Their estimates of the effective rates of protection for that year are: agriculture, − 0.114; mining and energy, 0.257; and manufacturing, 0.767. Assuming that protection is negligible for the other sectors of the economy (which are mainly nontraded services), the above values are averaged, using the 1969 value-added figures as weights, to yield an estimate of the effective rate of protection for nonagriculture. The result is 0.282.

With these results, the value of p_1^f and p_2^f can now be adjusted:

$$p_{1.69}^f = p_{1.69}/R_{69}^E (1 - 0.114),$$

and

$$p_{2.69}^f = p_{2.69}^{nd}/R_{69}^E (1 + 0.282).$$

Next, the whole series of p_1^f and p_2^f is reconstructed using the indexes p_1^f and p_2^f and the benchmark values of $p_{1.69}^f$ and $p_{2.69}^f$.

It is interesting to note that Reca calculated the tax rates on the main agricultural

[68] Ibid.

Table 19—Gross domestic product at factor cost and constant 1960 prices, 1939-73

Year	Agriculture	Nonagriculture	Total
		(million pesos)	
1939	1,230.4	3,816.4	5,046.8
1940	1,192.7	3,754.2	4,946.9
1941	1,344.1	3,830.6	5,174.7
1942	1,346.3	4,066.0	5,412.3
1943	1,265.3	4,178.1	5,443.4
1944	1,462.9	4,506.9	5,969.8
1945	1,243.6	4,447.8	5,691.4
1946	1,301.6	4,876.6	6,178.2
1947	1,414.1	5,633.8	7,047.9
1948	1,354.3	5,780.8	7,135.1
1949	1,234.5	5,566.6	6,801.1
1950	1,242.8	5,657.6	6,900.4
1951	1,327.5	5,840.6	7,168.1
1952	1,138.4	5,665.0	6,803.4
1953	1,488.4	5,683.9	7,172.3
1954	1,479.9	5,984.9	7,464.8
1955	1,540.9	6,454.7	7,995.6
1956	1,470.5	6,747.3	8,217.8
1957	1,463.3	7,175.9	8,639.2
1958	1,527.0	7,640.7	9,167.7
1959	1,511.5	7,065.3	8,576.8
1960	1,536.6	7,712.8	9,249.4
1961	1,526.6	8,381.9	9,908.5
1962	1,588.4	8,159.4	9,747.8
1963	1,619.2	7,895.1	9,514.3
1964	1,732.2	8,766.4	10,498.6
1965	1,834.9	9,622.9	11,457.8
1966	1,766.3	9,763.3	11,529.6
1967	1,842.1	9,998.2	11,840.3
1968	1,742.1	10,603.0	12,345.1
1969	1,837.6	11,566.1	13,403.7
1970	1,940.6	12,180.6	14,121.2
1971	1,842.8	12,957.4	14,800.2
1972	1,697.8	13,566.6	15,264.4
1973	1,983.6	14,212.6	16,196.2

Sources and Notes: For the period 1950-73 the series were taken from Banco Central de la República Argentina (BCRA), *Sistema de Cuentas del Producto e Ingreso de la Argentina,* vol. 2 (Buenos Aires: BCRA, 1975).

For the period 1935-49, the basic data were originally published by the Secretaría de Asuntos Económicos and were reproduced in BCRA, *Sistema de Cuentas,* vol. 3.

To match the series, figures from the Secretaría de Asuntos Económicos were transformed into indexes with base 1950 = 100 and applied to the figures for 1950 from the BCRA. The matching was done at the highest level of disaggregation that was available and the aggregates were obtained by adding up.

Agriculture includes "agricultura, gandería y pesca" (farming and fishing) and nonagriculture, all the rest.

products for the years 1960-64.[69] His procedure is different from this one, but the results for the aggregates are similar. His average values for $1 - t_x$ for the period 1960-64 are: wheat, 0.72; corn, 0.79; grain sorghum, 0.54; beef cattle, 0.84; cotton, 0.81; and wool, 0.79. A weighted average of these values gives a value of 0.76. The average for the same period in this study is 0.75.

[69]Reca, *Argentina: Country Case Study of Agricultural Prices and Subsidies.*

Table 20—Gross domestic product at factor cost and current prices, 1939-73

Year	Agriculture	Nonagriculture	Total
		(million pesos)	
1939	24	86	109
1940	24	88	112
1941	27	96	123
1942	30	112	142
1943	30	121	151
1944	35	139	174
1945	35	156	191
1946	55	206	261
1947	62	299	361
1948	71	380	451
1949	71	459	530
1950	89	544	633
1951	142	749	891
1952	154	897	1,051
1953	234	974	1,208
1954	240	1,113	1,353
1955	264	1,339	1,603
1956	334	1,730	2,064
1957	427	2,206	2,634
1958	593	3,230	3,824
1959	1,381	5,849	7,230
1960	1,536	7,713	9,249
1961	1,475	9,392	10,866
1962	2,007	11,737	13,745
1963	2,843	14,358	17,200
1964	4,405	19,797	24,202
1965	5,305	28,329	33,634
1966	5,745	35,749	41,494
1967	7,216	45,790	53,006
1968	7,628	52,987	60,614
1969	9,127	62,704	71,831
1970	11,119	73,504	86,624
1971	16,761	103,402	120,164
1972	30,686	170,081	200,767
1973	50,314	283,833	334,148

Sources and Notes: For the period 1950-73 the series were taken from Banco Central de la República Argentina (BCRA), *Sistema de Cuentas del Producto e Ingreso de la Argentina,* vol. 2 (Buenos Aires: BCRA, 1975).

For the period 1935-49, the basic data were originally published by the Secretaría de Asuntos Económicos and were reproduced in BCRA, *Sistema de Cuentas,* vol. 3.

To match the series, figures from the Secretaría de Asuntos Económicos were transformed into indexes with base 1950 = 100 and applied to the figures for 1950 from the BCRA. The matching was done at the highest level of disaggregation that was available and the aggregates were obtained by adding up.

Agriculture includes "agricultura, gandería y pesca" (farming and fishing) and nonagriculture, all the rest.

Table 21—Exports and imports at constant 1960 prices, 1939-73

Year	Exports	Imports
	(million pesos)	
1939	1,162.9	1,048.1
1940	951.8	910.1
1941	965.2	700.3
1942	887.3	584.0
1943	975.4	399.2
1944	969.3	409.5
1945	967.2	416.3
1946	1,121.9	764.2
1947	1,053.3	1,523.7
1948	887.3	1,551.1
1949	660.9	1,094.9
1950	911.9	937.5
1951	720.3	1,053.8
1952	528.7	776.7
1953	809.4	636.4
1954	866.8	834.9
1955	780.7	1,003.7
1956	895.5	897.6
1957	945.7	1,001.4
1958	974.4	1,044.7
1959	1,018.4	925.0
1960	1,024.6	1,140.5
1961	946.7	1,356.1
1962	1,280.7	1,302.5
1963	1,306.3	1,013.9
1964	1,222.3	1,177.0
1965	1,342.2	1,164.5
1966	1,474.2	1,122.1
1967	1,456.7	1,125.2
1968	1,436.9	1,195.9
1969	1,667.6	1,476.5
1970	1,788.4	1,472.0
1971	1,577.9	1,595.2
1972	1,482.6	1,504.0
1973	1,572.1	1,477.1

Sources and Notes: For the period 1950-73 the series were taken from Banco Central de la República Argentina (BCRA), *Sistema de Cuentas del Producto e Ingreso de la Argentina,* vol. 2 (Buenos Aires: BCRA, 1975).

For the period 1935-49, the basic data were originally published by the Secretaría de Asuntos Económicos and were reproduced in BCRA, *Sistema de Cuentas,* vol. 3.

To match the series, figures from the Secretaría de Asuntos Económicos were transformed into indexes with base 1950 = 100 and applied to the figures for 1950 from the BCRA. The matching was done at the highest level of disaggregation that was available and the aggregates were obtained by adding up.

Agriculture includes "agricultura, gandería y pesca" (farming and fishing) and nonagriculture, all the rest.

Table 22—Exports and imports at current prices, 1939-73

Year	Exports	Imports
	(million pesos)	
1939	18.4	13.6
1940	16.8	14.0
1941	17.5	11.6
1942	22.0	12.6
1943	27.8	9.6
1944	29.7	10.2
1945	31.1	11.3
1946	48.5	22.3
1947	66.2	50.9
1948	65.9	60.3
1949	44.7	49.0
1950	64.1	57.3
1951	82.0	100.7
1952	62.0	95.0
1953	85.7	61.4
1954	82.7	77.3
1955	94.9	114.2
1956	235.6	259.6
1957	270.3	339.9
1958	333.1	401.2
1959	892.0	849.8
1960	1,024.6	1,140.5
1961	935.6	1,324.0
1962	1,549.5	1,770.6
1963	2,066.2	1,650.4
1964	2,162.0	1,969.0
1965	2,777.5	2,316.1
1966	3,719.0	2,738.4
1967	5,541.5	4,319.0
1968	5,920.4	5,134.5
1969	6,912.6	6,691.8
1970	8,011.5	7,533.7
1971	11,330.8	11,597.5
1972	19,833.2	18,452.2
1973	34,908.3	24,189.5

Sources and Notes: For the period 1950-73 the series were taken from Banco Central de la República Argentina (BCRA), *Sistema de Cuentas del Producto e Ingreso de la Argentina,* vol. 2 (Buenos Aires: BCRA, 1975).

For the period 1935-49, the basic data were originally published by the Secretaría de Asuntos Económicos and were reproduced in BCRA, *Sistema de Cuentas,* vol. 3.

To match the series, figures from the Secretaría de Asuntos Económicos were transformed into indexes with base 1950 = 100 and applied to the figures for 1950 from the BCRA. The matching was done at the highest level of disaggregation that was available and the aggregates were obtained by adding up.

Agriculture includes "agricultura, gandería y pesca" (farming and fishing) and nonagriculture, all the rest.

Table 23—Investment and its allocation at current prices, 1939-73

Year	Agricultural Investment: Agricultural Origin	Agricultural Investment: Nonagricultural Origin	Nonagricultural Investment	Gross Domestic Investment
	(million pesos)			
1939	1.9	0.4	10.9	13.2
1940	1.7	0.3	11.5	13.5
1941	1.8	0.0	15.5	17.3
1942	2.6	0.0	13.7	16.3
1943	2.9	0.0	14.5	17.5
1944	3.3	0.0	13.9	17.2
1945	4.7	0.0	16.4	21.1
1946	5.4	0.2	32.8	38.4
1947	5.0	3.2	68.4	76.6
1948	7.7	3.7	97.0	108.4
1949	7.1	1.8	94.5	103.4
1950	9.5	4.0	109.6	123.1
1951	16.2	5.7	182.8	204.7
1952	28.3	7.5	176.3	212.0
1953	43.2	9.5	193.1	245.8
1954	50.1	7.8	196.7	254.6
1955	47.0	12.7	241.4	301.1
1956	43.0	19.7	318.0	380.7
1957	37.1	49.6	450.1	536.7
1958	41.0	66.5	666.7	774.2
1959	150.0	147.8	1,029.4	1,327.2
1960	237.0	265.3	1,673.9	2,176.2
1961	214.0	326.9	2,084.2	2,625.1
1962	157.0	408.3	2,616.2	3,181.5
1963	114.1	445.0	2,588.9	3,148.1
1964	681.3	589.1	3,551.0	4,821.5
1965	867.5	824.9	5,292.2	6,984.6
1966	815.8	884.0	6,290.5	7,990.3
1967	521.1	1,076.7	9,108.5	10,706.4
1968	531.7	1,211.1	11,188.9	12,931.7
1969	852.5	1,319.3	14,283.6	16,455.4
1970	819.4	1,680.4	16,836.6	19,336.4
1971	2,674.7	2,550.4	21,468.9	26,694.0
1972	5,026.6	4,616.5	36,284.3	45,927.4
1973	4,707.9	10,516.0	59,425.5	74,649.5

Sources and Notes: The data for gross domestic investment are decomposed into both investment in fixed capital and investment in inventories. The figures for the period 1950-73 were taken from Banco Central de la República Argentina (BCRA), *Sistema de Cuentas del Producto e Ingreso de la Argentina,* vol. 2 (Buenos Aires: BCRA, 1975). The basic data for the period 1935-49 were originally published by the Secretaría de Asuntos Económicos and were reproduced in BCRA, *Sistema de Cuentas,* vol. 3.

The series of fixed investment was disaggregated by sector (1, agriculture and 2, nonagriculture) using and extending the method of Balboa and Fraccia (M. Balboa and A. Fracchia, "El Capital Fijo Renovable en Argentina en el Período 1935-55," *Desarrollo Económico* 2 [Enero-Mayo 1959]: 17-36). Basically, the approach uses data on current production of agricultural capital goods and on imports and exports.

To complete the series, it was necessary to disaggregate investment in inventories. Such investment was decomposed into changes in the value of livestock and all the rest. Investment in livestock was included in agricultural investment whereas the other component was added to nonagricultural investment.

There is no reported series for the value of livestock. However, there is information on the size of the herd. A series for the number of livestock was constructed by Reca for 1960-71 (Lucio G. Reca, "El Aumento de Existencia de Ganado Vacuno en 1971," in *Estudios sobre la Economía Argentina* [Buenos Aires: Instituto de Investigaciones Económicas y Financieras de la CGE, Enero 1972]). A different series was constructed by Yver (Raul E. Yver, "La Oferta de Ganado Bovino en la Argentina," *Desarrollo Económico* 5 [Abril-Diciembre 1965]: 211-230) for the period 1935-59. This series reports mid-year values. A method developed by Reca was used to transform the series to beginning-of-year values. To add years 1972 and 1973, the Reca method was applied using data from the Junta Nacional de Carnes.

To obtain the value of livestock, a price is needed. Instead of arbitrarily selecting a price for 1960, a detailed study by the Economic Commission for Latin America of agricultural capital in 1950 originally reported, mimeographed, and reproduced in BCRA, *Sistema de Cuentas,* was used. This study contains estimates of fixed capital, to be denoted as ${}^{E}V^{FK}_{50}$ and the value of livestock, ${}^{E}V^{LS}_{50}$. These data were used to derive the ratio ${}^{E}V^{LS}_{50}/{}^{E}V^{FK}_{50} = R_{50}$, which was applied to the series in the table

Table 23—Continued

to derive $V^{LS}_{50} = R_{50} V^{FK}_{50}$, where V^{LS}_{50} and V^{FK}_{50} are the 1950 values of livestock and fixed capital.

Dividing the result by the size of the herd gives a price for 1950. This was then transformed into 1960 pesos, to conform with the other data in fixed prices, by using the agricultural product price deflator. The result was then applied to the size of the herd to generate the livestock series.

Having obtained the values for livestock, annual investment in livestock was obtained as a change in value. The result was added to investment in fixed capital to yield investment in agriculture.

Inventory investment in nonagriculture is obtained by subtracting livestock investment from total inventory investment.

All these computations were done on series at constant prices of 1960. To obtain the disaggregation for the gross domestic investment series at current prices it was assumed that the agricultural investment originating in agriculture experienced the same inflation as did agriculture at large. Similarly, investment goods originating in nonagriculture were inflated by the overall price index of supply (domestic and imported) of nonagricultural products. Small differences between the sum of the disaggregated figures and gross domestic investment were adjusted uniformly for both sectors to keep the total equal to the figures from the Banco Central.

Table 24—Capital stocks and cultivated land, 1939-73

	Capital			
	Agriculture			
Year	Agricultural Origin	Nonagricultural Origin	Nonagriculture	Cultivated Land
		(million 1960 pesos)		(million hectares)
1939	2,069.5	402.0	11,810.4	28,361.0
1940	2,089.9	392.0	11,933.7	27,847.0
1941	2,100.4	373.0	11,922.4	26,888.0
1942	2,102.0	344.0	11,932.7	26,407.0
1943	2,139.9	312.0	11,943.2	27,573.0
1944	2,182.5	287.0	11,869.2	26,711.0
1945	2,256.5	247.0	11,826.7	26,215.0
1946	2,324.0	220.0	11,723.8	27,624.0
1947	2,367.3	206.0	11,739.4	24,986.0
1948	2,392.6	248.0	12,506.6	25,082.0
1949	2,423.2	277.0	13,236.4	23,664.0
1950	2,438.6	273.0	13,558.5	26,063.0
1951	2,487.2	283.0	13,848.2	24,030.0
1952	2,556.6	301.0	14,295.1	27,210.0
1953	2,644.6	322.0	14,735.5	27,039.0
1954	2,771.3	350.0	15,026.7	26,452.0
1955	2,900.0	363.0	15,428.9	26,671.0
1956	3,032.5	396.0	15,892.9	28,793.0
1957	3,129.8	433.0	16,387.3	29,574.0
1958	3,150.4	539.0	16,896.1	29,214.0
1959	3,148.1	639.0	17,446.2	28,169.0
1960	3,210.8	754.0	17,724.3	27,364.0
1961	3,362.9	958.0	18,563.0	28,481.0
1962	3,482.2	1,175.0	19,653.9	27,107.0
1963	3,511.9	1,359.0	20,492.2	28,911.0
1964	3,475.8	1,504.0	21,035.5	28,308.0
1965	3,592.5	1,674.0	21,567.3	27,625.0
1966	3,721.5	1,835.0	22,405.5	28,350.0
1967	3,822.9	1,939.0	23,427.0	29,003.0
1968	3,843.6	2,018.0	24,366.9	30,730.0
1969	3,848.1	2,098.0	25,558.9	30,465.0
1970	3,882.8	2,184.0	27,137.7	28,054.0
1971	3,889.4	2,306.0	28,820.2	26,756.0
1972	4,042.8	2,489.0	30,589.2	28,437.0
1973	4,175.9	2,704.0	32,468.1	26,254.0

Sources and Notes: The series for capital stock at 1960 prices were obtained by extending to 1973 the original estimation of capital stock in M. Balboa and A. Fracchia, "El Capital Fijo Renovable en Argentina en el Período 1935-55," *Desarrollo Económico* 2 (Enero 1959): 17-36. These series are of fixed

Table 24—Continued

capital, not including livestock nor other inventories. The calculation of the value of livestock was explained in the note to Table 23. To obtain the value of inventories it was assumed that the ratio of investment in inventories to investment in fixed capital was the same as the ratio of the two forms of capital in 1935. Applying this ratio to investment in fixed capital generated a series of changes for inventories. The changes were then used to build up inventories using 1935 as a starting point.

To obtain agricultural capital of agricultural origin, the value of improvements was added to the livestock series. Machinery and equipment were considered agricultural capital originated in nonagriculture.

The series of total cultivated land was taken from Bolsa de Cereales de Buenos Aires, *Anuario de la Bolsa de Cereales* (Buenos Aires: Bolsa de Cereales de Buenos Aires, 1975).

Table 25—Population and labor force, 1939-73

Year	Population	Labor Force	
		Agriculture	Nonagriculture
		(1,000)	
1939	13,948	1,773.9	3,025.1
1940	14,169	1,795.0	3,014.1
1941	14,401	1,816.4	3,115.2
1942	14,637	1,838.0	3,368.8
1943	14,877	1,874.4	3,622.3
1944	15,130	1,911.5	3,887.8
1945	15,390	1,949.4	4,134.3
1946	15,654	1,988.0	4,379.3
1947	15,929	2,022.0	4,683.8
1948	16,264	2,016.0	4,866.7
1949	16,668	2,010.0	5,066.1
1950	17,150	2,004.0	5,141.3
1951	17,494	1,998.0	5,543.4
1952	17,850	1,993.0	5,190.1
1953	18,211	1,964.0	5,670.2
1954	18,571	1,935.0	5,545.5
1955	18,928	1,905.0	5,480.8
1956	19,277	1,876.0	5,591.8
1957	19,620	1,847.0	5,797.7
1958	19,956	1,817.0	5,965.8
1959	20,286	1,788.0	5,891.3
1960	20,611	1,758.0	5,941.7
1961	20,930	1,733.0	6,031.8
1962	21,245	1,731.1	5,918.7
1963	21,558	1,721.8	5,827.3
1964	21,868	1,716.4	6,046.8
1965	22,179	1,715.0	6,239.9
1966	22,488	1,717.5	6,392.0
1967	22,800	1,724.0	6,499.9
1968	23,113	1,734.4	6,616.6
1969	23,428	1,748.7	6,874.7
1970	23,748	1,767.1	7,040.3
1971	24,068	1,789.3	7,199.3
1972	24,392	1,815.5	7,425.2
1973	24,719	1,845.7	7,609.6

Sources and Notes: Total population as estimated by the Instituto Nacional de Estadística y Censos and reported in Banco Central de la República Argentina (BCRA), *Sistema de Cuentas del Producto e Ingreso de la Argentina,* vol. 2 (Buenos Aires: BCRA, 1975). The sources for and definitions of the labor force are explained in Chapter 8.

Table 26—Nominal wages and the ratio between imported and domestic nonagricultural prices, 1939-73

Year	Nominal Wages: Agriculture	Nominal Wages: Nonagriculture	Ratio of Imported to Domestic Nonagricultural Prices
	(pesos)		
1939	7.1	17.4	0.696
1940	7.8	17.4	0.886
1941	8.3	18.0	1.144
1942	8.3	18.5	1.537
1943	8.6	18.4	1.715
1944	9.6	20.0	1.330
1945	11.7	21.0	1.342
1946	12.0	28.0	1.142
1947	12.8	39.5	0.887
1948	18.7	51.3	0.868
1949	26.8	65.0	0.810
1950	30.6	78.0	0.758
1951	47.4	96.3	0.844
1952	57.2	126.9	0.795
1953	71.3	135.1	0.756
1954	77.0	157.3	0.718
1955	80.1	176.5	0.729
1956	95.7	213.8	1.009
1957	107.3	258.3	0.894
1958	173.7	363.2	0.840
1959	310.0	585.8	1.049
1960	338.9	755.4	1.000
1961	388.7	975.9	0.879
1962	510.6	1,222.5	0.917
1963	620.6	1,525.0	0.885
1964	914.1	2,007.5	0.800
1965	1,319.0	2,802.6	0.797
1966	1,686.0	3,635.4	0.798
1967	1,991.7	4,761.5	0.906
1968	2,274.3	5,239.8	0.892
1969	2,544.1	5,853.6	0.941
1970	3,093.1	6,819.5	0.969
1971	4,737.0	9,530.5	0.873
1972	7,321.0	14,031.0	1.047
1973	12,396.4	24,717.6	1.112

Sources and Notes: Nominal wages were obtained from Banco Central de la República Argentina (BCRA), *Sistema de Cuentas del Producto e Ingreso de la Argentina,* vol. 2 (Buenos Aires: BCRA, 1975). Several other sources were used to build a series for 1939-50.

The ratio between imported and domestic wholesale prices of nonagricultural goods was computed using the wholesale price index given in Instituto Nacional de Estadística y Censos, *Boletín Estadístico Trimestral,* various issues.

Table 27—Exchange rates, exports, and imports in current dollars, 1939-73

Year	Nominal Exchange Rate	Exports	Imports
	(pesos/U.S. $)	(U.S. $ million)	
1939	0.034	541.2	400.0
1940	0.035	480.0	400.0
1941	0.036	486.1	322.2
1942	0.036	611.1	350.0
1943	0.036	772.0	266.7
1944	0.036	825.0	283.3
1945	0.035	888.6	322.9
1946	0.034	1,426.5	655.9
1947	0.034	1,947.1	1,497.1
1948	0.034	1,938.2	1,773.5
1949	0.036	1,241.7	1,361.1
1950	0.046	1,393.5	1,245.6
1951	0.057	1,438.6	1,766.7
1952	0.064	968.7	1,484.4
1953	0.064	1,339.1	959.4
1954	0.066	1,253.0	1,171.2
1955	0.079	1,201.3	1,445.6
1956	0.192	1,227.1	1,352.1
1957	0.223	1,212.1	1,524.2
1958	0.288	1,156.6	1,393.1
1959	0.795	1,122.0	1,068.9
1960	0.845	1,212.6	1,349.7
1961	0.837	1,117.8	1,581.8
1962	1.135	1,365.2	1,560.0
1963	1.381	1,496.2	1,195.1
1964	1.400	1,544.3	1,406.4
1965	1.721	1,613.9	1,345.8
1966	2.132	1,744.4	1,284.4
1967	3.379	1,639.9	1,278.2
1968	3.477	1,702.7	1,478.4
1969	3,537	1,954.4	1,891.9
1970	3.732	2,146.7	2,018.7
1971	5.274	2,148.4	2,199.0
1972	8.461	2,344.1	2,180.5
1973	9.301	3,753.2	2,600.7

Sources and Notes: The series of exports and imports in current dollars was taken from Banco Central de la República Argentina (BCRA), *Sistema de Cuentas del Producto e Ingreso de la Argentina,* vol. 2 (Buenos Aires: BCRA, 1975) and BCRA, *Memorias del Banco Central,* various issues (Buenos Aires: BCRA, various years).

Exchange rates in nominal pesos per dollar were obtained by dividing exports in current pesos by exports in current dollars.

Table 28—Indirect tax revenues in current prices, 1939-73

Year	Taxes on Agricultural Output	Total Indirect Revenue
	(million pesos)	
1939	7.0	13.5
1940	6.4	14.6
1941	7.4	14.4
1942	10.3	13.9
1943	9.8	13.8
1944	9.7	15.4
1945	10.1	16.7
1946	0.0	22.0
1947	0.0	32.5
1948	0.0	25.1
1949	0.0	32.4
1950	2.0	43.4
1951	2.8	78.3
1952	3.4	70.7
1953	3.9	87.7
1954	4.2	82.7
1955	4.5	93.7
1956	5.7	156.6
1957	6.4	214.2
1958	7.7	195.7
1959	16.2	444.0
1960	22.0	874.6
1961	44.9	1,205.4
1962	46.6	1,184.4
1963	106.5	1,470.5
1964	110.8	1,819.2
1965	190.0	2,759.6
1966	203.6	3,916.6
1967	277.7	6,595.9
1968	293.3	8,113.2
1969	361.6	9,152.6
1970	419.5	10,169.5
1971	548.9	12,503.5
1972	790.6	19,171.4
1973	1,837.0	30,443.6

Sources and Notes: The figures for 1960-73 were taken from Banco Central de la República Argentina (BCRA), *Sistema de Cuentas del Producto e Ingreso de la Argentina,* vol. 2 (Buenos Aires: BCRA, 1975). The basic data for 1935-49 were originally published by the Secretaría de Asuntos Económicos and were reproduced in BCRA, *Sistemas de Cuentas,* vol. 3.

The figures are obtained as a difference between GDP in market prices and factor cost.

Table 29—Exports and imports of agricultural goods at current prices, 1939-73

Year	Exports	Imports
	(million pesos)	
1939	15.0	0.9
1940	13.4	0.9
1941	13.1	0.8
1942	15.3	0.7
1943	17.2	0.7
1944	20.0	1.1
1945	21.3	1.0
1946	35.0	1.5
1947	52.7	2.0
1948	54.1	2.6
1949	36.4	1.5
1950	52.6	2.8
1951	64.6	4.9
1952	42.2	5.5
1953	69.5	5.3
1954	65.6	7.7
1955	69.7	6.3
1956	173.1	13.8
1957	201.5	12.9
1958	276.0	16.8
1959	766.4	20.9
1960	865.8	30.2
1961	761.4	35.4
1962	1,310.4	46.8
1963	1,669.0	48.3
1964	1,645.3	97.6
1965	1,936.5	125.1
1966	2,769.1	172.0
1967	3,974.7	259.4
1968	3,939.3	245.9
1969	3,709.4	400.2
1970	5,313.0	405.5
1971	6,487.5	476.7
1972	11,843.3	1,127.5
1973	22,470.0	2,042.3

Source: Instituto Nacional de Estadístico y Censos, *Boletín de Comercio Enterior,* various issues.

Table 30—Share of agricultural credit, domestic credit, and money supply, 1939-73

Year	Agricultural Credit	Domestic Credit	Money Supply
	(percent)	(million current pesos)	
1939	0.0	0.0	49.8
1940	11.13	35.6	50.6
1941	11.39	38.2	55.0
1942	11.8	43.0	63.3
1943	14.2	43.1	72.0
1944	15	44.4	85.3
1945	16	49.7	100.5
1946	12	67.7	122.3
1947	9	105.7	149.5
1948	9	156.0	183.0
1949	9	210.0	231.6
1950	11	241.4	263.5
1951	14	294.7	319.0
1952	24	351.9	357.9
1953	27	425.0	444.2
1954	29	496.7	526.0
1955	28	593.6	611.0
1956	25	716.5	720.7
1957	26	825.0	848.0
1958	24	1,026.3	1,003.3
1959	26	1,491.6	1,481.0
1960	26	1,799.4	1,992.5
1961	26	2,213.3	2,427.1
1962	24	2,801.0	2,785.1
1963	23	3,373.4	3,396.7
1964	28	4,719.3	4,851.0
1965	30	6,385.6	6,493.2
1966	28	8,277.5	8,312.3
1967	28	10,993.4	11,100.5
1968	21	14,722.9	14,857.6
1969	21	18,689.1	18,833.5
1970	18	19,204.6	21,965.7
1971	18	25,773.8	27,681.4
1972	17	40,755.1	42,526.1
1973	17	68,512.9	73,884.4

Sources and Notes: The figures are from Banco Central de la República Argentina (BCRA), *Boletín Mensual,* various issues.

The money supply includes currency and all kinds of deposits in the financial system (M_3).

Domestic credit is M_3 less the stock of foreign reserves of the financial system at domestic prices.

Table 31—Price indexes of land, livestock, and crops, 1939-73

Year	Land 1935 = 1.00	Livestock 1960 = 1.000	Crops 1960 = 1.000
1939	1.38	0.018	0.020
1940	1.34	0.019	0.018
1941	1.28	0.020	0.016
1942	1.37	0.024	0.017
1943	1.55	0.024	0.021
1944	1.52	0.025	0.021
1945	1.84	0.026	0.027
1946	1.84	0.030	0.052
1947	2.03	0.037	0.046
1948	3.30	0.043	0.051
1949	4.40	0.067	0.057
1950	4.93	0.066	0.061
1951	5.18	0.109	0.102
1952	6.44	0.119	0.109
1953	7.44	0.139	0.136
1954	9.77	0.140	0.137
1955	10.95	0.144	0.147
1956	12.11	0.183	0.226
1957	17.14	0.211	0.317
1958	26.90	0.300	0.384
1959	71.91	0.887	0.841
1960	74.96	1.000	1.000
1961	86.85	0.973	1.086
1962	100.67	1.199	1.608
1963	156.86	1.685	2.117
1964	228.47	2.595	2.326
1965	352.20	3.128	2.290
1966	349.80	3.270	3.252
1967	356.23	4.125	4.072
1968	403.86	4.452	4.487
1969	460.08	4.675	5.009
1970	568.56	6.277	5.019
1971	887.85	10.463	6.414
1972	2,073.85	17.085	15.502
1973	2,675.03	25.957	21.596

Sources and Notes: The price of land was taken from Norberto Ras and Roberto Lewis, *El Precio de la Tierra: La Evolución entre los Años 1916 y 1978* (Buenos Aires: Sociedad Rural Argentina, 1980).

Price indexes for livestock and crops were taken from the wholesale price indexes published monthly by Instituto Nacional de Estadística y Censos, *Boletín de Comercio Enterior,* various issues.

APPENDIX 2:

SUMMARY DATA

Variable	Average	Standard Deviation	Coefficient of Variation	Average Growth Rate	Minimum Value	Minimum Year	Maximum Value	Maximum Year
Per capita output—agriculture (x_1)	79.5	5.5	6.9	−0.4	70.7	1951	91.3	1943
Per capita export—agriculture (x_1^e)	25.6	3.9	15.2	0.3	17.9	1952	34.9	1940
Per capita output of capital goods—agriculture (x_1^i)	9.8	2.5	25.8	0.8	5.2	1940	14.9	1954
Per capita consumption of agricultural products (x_1^c)	44.1	6.5	14.8	−1.1	33.7	1961	59.2	1943
Per capita output—nonagriculture (x_2)	370.9	76.1	20.5	1.9	268.1	1940	556.7	1972
Per capita imports—nonagriculture (x_2^m)	37.7	15.6	41.5	. . .	−1.9	1944	71.3	1948
Per capita output of capital goods—nonagriculture (x_2^i)	74.7	24.7	33.1	3.4	30.0	1944	125.0	1972
Per capita consumption of nonagricultural products (x_2^c)	295.5	48.1	16.3	1.6	216.1	1942	404.3	1972
Foreign price of agricultural exports (p_1^f)	1.68	0.57	34.0	0.6	0.64	1940	3.02	1948
Foreign price of nonagricultural imports (p_2^f)	0.90	0.25	28.3	2.3	0.33	1940	1.30	1952
Implicit price index of domestic nonagricultural products (p_2^d)	1.86	3.06	164.4	20.7	0.02	1940	13.50	1972
Real exchange rate (RE)	0.88	0.34	39.0	−1.3	0.44	1954	1.75	1940
Foreign price of agricultural exports in domestic currency (p_1^e)	1.34	0.31	23.0	−0.7	0.86	1954	2.17	1947
Foreign price of nonagricultural imports in domestic currency (p_2^e)	0.72	0.13	18.1	0.9	0.49	1954	0.96	1958
Price of agricultural goods (p_1)	0.91	0.11	12.3	0.9	0.75	1949	1.28	1972
Price of nonagricultural imports (p_2^{nd})	0.96	0.20	21.2	−0.8	0.73	1954	1.53	1943
Price of nonagricultural goods (p_2)	0.99	0.01	1.3	−0.0	0.97	1949	1.02	1942
Export tax (t_x)	−0.291	0.162	−55.8	. . .	−0.598	1947	0.018	1954
Import tariff (t_m)	0.374	0.334	89.1	. . .	−0.044	1957	1.119	1942
Domestic tax on agricultural goods (t_1)	−0.054	0.118	−219.7	. . .	−0.242	1961	0.254	1940
Domestic tax on nonagricultural goods (t_2)	0.060	0.048	80.1	. . .	−0.059	1948	0.132	1968
Market price of agricultural goods (p_1^*)	0.86	0.13	15.3	0.3	0.64	1950	1.19	1972
Market price of nonagricultural goods (p_2^*)	1.05	0.05	4.3	0.3	0.93	1948	1.12	1968
Price ratio, p_1^*/p_2^* (p^*)	0.82	0.12	14.6	−0.1	0.64	1950	1.09	1972
Price of land (p_A)	1.41	0.52	36.6	3.0	0.85	1952	2.82	1972
Price of livestock (p_{LS})	0.86	0.15	17.5	1.2	0.69	1947	1.32	1972

Price of crops (p_C)	0.86	0.13	15.0	1.0	0.66	1942	1.10	1963
Wage rate—agriculture (w_1)	380.8	79.0	20.7	1.7	269.7	1947	599.4	1972
Wage rate—nonagriculture (w_2)	845.2	150.2	17.8	1.6	628.0	1944	1183.7	1972
Return on capital—agriculture (r_1)	0.078	0.016	20.9	−0.2	0.041	1950	0.115	1947
Return on capital—nonagriculture (r_2)	0.145	0.023	15.9	0.4	0.091	1953	0.174	1946
Land rent (R)	13.61	4.66	34.3	2.6	6.64	1951	24.46	1972
Per capita taxes (y^t)	40.5	14.4	35.6	2.1	23.7	1949	71.2	1969
Per capita income (y)	483.3	92.6	19.2	1.7	386.7	1940	720.2	1972
Per capita investment (i)	87.0	28.7	33.0	3.4	38.9	1944	149.1	1972
Per capita investment—agriculture (i_1)	14.8	6.4	43.1	4.5	5.9	1941	29.9	1972
Per capita investment—nonagriculture (i_2)	72.2	23.6	32.7	3.2	31.4	1944	119.2	1972
Share of agriculture in total investment (θ)	0.168	0.038	22.8	1.0	0.100	1950	0.239	1965
Agricultural investment from agriculture (λ)	0.638	0.229	35.9	−3.4	0.281	1962	1.010	1944
Per capita consumption (c)	389.1	69.9	18.0	1.6	313.1	1944	560.2	1972
Per capita domestic savings (s^d)	94.3	24.4	25.9	2.1	56.8	1940	160.0	1972
Per capita private consumption (c^p)	348.5	58.3	16.7	1.6	277.8	1942	493.6	1972
Population (N)	19.18	3.20	16.7	1.8	14.17	1940	24.39	1972
Labor force—agriculture (L_1)	1.85	0.11	5.7	−0.4	1.72	1965	2.02	1948
Labor force—nonagriculture (L_2)	5.46	1.15	21.1	2.3	3.05	1940	7.41	1972
Total labor force (L)	7.31	1.11	15.2	1.6	4.85	1940	9.23	1972
Outmigration from agriculture (m)	0.016	0.014	87.4	. . .	−0.008	1972	0.035	1953
Unemployment (UN)	0.83	0.51	61.5	. . .	0.00	1950	1.52	1964
Agricultural capital stock from agriculture (K_{11})	2,981	649	21.8	2.3	2,087	1940	4,036	1972
Agricultural capital stock from nonagriculture (K_{12})	884	761	86.1	8.0	224	1946	2,500	1972
Total agricultural capital stock in agricultural prices (K_1)	4,058	1,508	37.2	3.7	2,461	1940	6,697	1968
Total agricultural capital stock in nonagricultural prices (K_1^n)	3,321	1,403	42.3	3.6	1,841	1950	6,897	1972
Capital stock—nonagriculture (K_2)	17,457	5,508	31.6	3.0	11,763	1946	30,626	1972
Cultivated land (A)	27.4	1.4	5.0	0.3	24.6	1948	30.1	1968
Share of agricultural credit (CRED)	19.9	6.9	34.5	2.8	7.5	1940	28.7	1965
Ratio of capital productivities (δ_r)	0.361	0.219	60.6	5.9	0.091	1943	0.765	1970

APPENDIX 3:

EMPIRICAL EQUATIONS FROM ANNUAL DATA

In dealing with the process of growth, it was thought desirable to reduce the transitory variations in the data by working with three-year moving averages. Averaging the data generally improves the fit at a cost of introducing serial correlation. A priori, it may appear that averaging the data affect the empirical analysis and thereby the conclusions of the analysis. Some comparisons were made in the text between results based on annual data and those based on moving-average data. The comparison indicates that the results are qualitatively similar. In what follows the empirical equations of the model are presented as they were obtained from the annual data. The production functions are not included as they were discussed in the text. The estimates are for the period 1946–73. The equation numbers, except for A indicating appendix, are the same as the numbers in the text so that the results can be easily compared.

The expenditure system estimated by FIML yields equations (A4.9), (A4.10), and (A4.12):

Private consumption:

$$c^{p} = \underset{(2.5)}{17.4} + \underset{(2.20)}{0.048}\,(p^{A}A) + \underset{(18.8)}{0.710}\,(x_1 + w_1L_1/N); \tag{A4.9}$$

$$\rho = \underset{(6.2)}{0.66}.$$

Demand:

$$x_2^{c,p} = \underset{(0.2)}{-3.1} + \underset{(14.8)}{0.68}\,c^{p} + \underset{(2.7)}{21.1}\,p^* + \underset{(9.4)}{285.5}\,\omega - \underset{(2.0)}{123.0}(p_1x_1/x)$$

$$+ \underset{(2.8)}{0.136}\,x_2^{c,p}(t-1). \tag{A4.10}$$

Investment:

$$i = \underset{(5.8)}{100.1} - \underset{(5.1)}{38.4}\,(K/X) + \underset{(10.5)}{0.454}\,[x(t) - x(t-1)] + \underset{(22.5)}{0.876}\,i(t-1). \tag{A4.12}$$

The two equations dealing with the allocation of investment were also estimated by FIML:

Intersectoral allocation of investment:

$$\ln\theta = \underset{(5.3)}{2.13} + \underset{(3.9)}{0.71}\ln(K_1^N/K) - \underset{(5.3)}{0.67}\ln\delta_r$$

$$+ \underset{(9.6)}{0.52}\ln \mathrm{CRED} + \underset{(4.5)}{0.31}\ln p_A. \tag{A4.13}$$

Note that lagged dependent variables do not appear in this equation.

Allocation of agricultural investment:

$$\ln \lambda^* = \underset{(0)}{0.007} - \underset{(6.3)}{3.26} \ln (K_{11}/K_1) + \underset{(5.2)}{1.57} \ln p_1(t-1)$$

$$- \underset{(2.3)}{0.60} \ln\lambda(t-1) + \underset{(2.4)}{0.62} \ln\lambda(t-2)$$

$$+ \underset{(10.8)}{1.15} \text{ Dummy } 1962 + \underset{(34.9)}{4.12} \text{ Dummy } 1963; \quad \textbf{(A4.14)}$$

$$\lambda^* = [1/(\lambda - 0.27)] - 1.$$

The remaining equations were estimated by least squares:

$$\ln [m(t-1)+0.01] = \underset{(2.19)}{-1.17} + \underset{(2.24)}{0.89} \ln(w_2/w_1)(t-1)$$

$$- \underset{(3.1)}{0.46} \ln [UN(t-1)+1] + \underset{(9.7)}{0.80} \ln [m(t-2)+0.01]; \quad \textbf{(A4.15)}$$

$R^2 = 0.87$, D.W. $= 1.84$.

Land

$$\ln A = \underset{(1.3)}{0.79} + \underset{(2.0)}{0.36} \ln A(t-1) + \underset{(2.0)}{0.39} \ln A(t-2) + \underset{(2.7)}{0.12} \ln p_A(t-2)$$

$$\underset{(2.2)}{-0.1} \ln p_A(t-6) - \underset{(1.9)}{0.14} \ln p_1(t-1); \quad \textbf{(A4.16)}$$

$R^2 = 0.78$, D.W. $= 1.81$.

Rate of exchange:

$$\ln [(RE)(p^f)] = \underset{(0.2)}{0.01} - \underset{(3.4)}{0.58} \ln(1-t_x) - \underset{(0.6)}{0.10} \ln(1+t_m)$$

$$- \underset{(2.5)}{0.43} \ln (p_1^f/p_2^f)(t-1) - \underset{(2.6)}{0.45} EC + \underset{(1.9)}{0.24} \ln [(RE)(p^f)](t-1); \quad \textbf{(A4.17)}$$

$R^2 = 0.78$, D.W. $= 1.77$

BIBLIOGRAPHY

Argentina, Consejo Nacional de Desarrollo y Naciones Unidas, Comision Económica para America Latina. *Distribución del Ingreso y Cuentas Nacionales en la Argentina.* Buenos Aires: CONADE, 1965.

Balboa, M. and Fracchia, A. "El Capital Fijo Renovable en Argentina en el Período 1935–55." *Desarrollo Económico* 2 (Enero 1959): 17-36.

Banco Central de la República Argentina. *Boletín Mensual,* various issues.

__________. *Memorias del Banco Central.* Buenos Aires: BCRA, 1951–72.

__________. *Sistema de Cuentas del Producto e Ingreso de la Argentina,* vols. 2 and 3. Buenos Aires: BCRA, 1975.

Berlinsky, J. and Schydlowsky, D. M. "Incentives for Industrialization in Argentina." In *Development Strategies in Semi-Industrialized Countries.* Edited by B. Balassa. Washington, D.C.: The World Bank (forthcoming).

Bolsa de Cereales de Buenos Aires. *Anuario de la Bolsa de Cereales.* Buenos Aires: Bolsa de Cereales de Buenos Aires, 1975.

Cavallo, Domingo F. "El Saldo de la Balanza Comercial y el Tipo de Cambio Real." *Ensayos Económicos* 16 (Diciembre 1980).

Chenery, H. B. "Engineering Production Functions." *Quarterly Journal of Economics* 63 (November 1949): 507-531.

Colomé, Rinaldo A. "'Excedente Financiero' del Sector Agropecuario Argentino: Reflexiones en Torno de un Trabajo Anterior y Nueva Estimación." *Desarrollo Económico* 18 (Julio-Septiembre 1978): 275-282.

Danin, Y. and Mundlak, Yair. *Introduction of Techniques and Capital Accumulation.* Working Paper No. 7909. Rehovot: Center for Agricultural Economic Research, 1979.

De Pablo, Juan Carlos. *Politica Antiinflacionaria en la Argentina 1967–1970.* Buenos Aires: Amorrortu Editores, 1972.

Diaz Alejandro, Carlos F. *Essays on the Economic History of the Argentine Republic.* New Haven, Conn.: Yale University Press, 1970.

Ferrer, Aldo. *La Economía Argentina: Las Etapas de su Desarrollo y Problemas Actuales.* Mexico: Fondo de Cultura Económica, 1963.

Fuss, M.; McFadden, D.; and Mundlak, Yair. "Survey of Functional Forms in Economic Analysis of Production." In *Production Economics: A Dual Approach to Theory and Applications.* Edited by M. Fuss and D. McFadden. New York: Elsevier/North Holland, 1978.

Griliches, Zvi. "Hybrid Corn: An Exploration in the Economics of Technological Change." *Econometrica* 25 (October 1957): 501-522.

Heady, Earl O. and Dillon, John. *Agricultural Production Functions.* Ames, Iowa: Iowa State University Press, 1961.

Hilderbrand, W. "Short-Run Production Functions Based on Micro Data." *Econometrica* 49 (September 1981): 1095-1125.

Houthakker, H. S. "The Pareto Distribution and the Cobb-Douglas Production Function in Activity Analysis." *Review of Economic Studies* 23 (No. 1, 1955): 27-31.

Instituto Nacional de Estadística y Censos. *Boletín de Comercio Enterior,* various issues.

————. *Boletín Estadístico Trimestral,* various issues.

Jorgenson, D. W. and Fraumeni, B. M. *Substitution Prices and Technical Change in Production.* Discussion Paper No. 752. Cambridge, Mass.: Harvard Institute of Economic Research, 1980.

Komiya, R. "Non-Traded Goods and the Pure Theory of International Trade." *International Economic Review* 8 (June 1967): 132-152.

Lucas, R. E. Jr. "Econometric Policy Evaluation: A Critique." In *The Phillips Curve and Labour Markets,* a supplement to the *Journal of Monetary Economics.* Edited by K. Brunner and A. H. Meltzer (1976): 19-46.

Magee, S. P. "Factor Market Distortion and Trade: A Survey." *Oxford Economic Papers* 25 (No. 1, 1973).

Mallon, Richard D. and Sourrouille, Juan V. *Economic Policymaking in a Conflict Society.* Cambridge, Mass.: Harvard University Press, 1975.

McKinnon, R. I. "The Exchange Rate and Macroeconomic Policy: Change in Postwar Perceptions." *Journal of Economic Literature* 29 (June 1981): 531-557.

Mundlak, Yair. *Cross-Country Comparison of Agricultural Productivity.* Working Paper No. 8105. Rehovot: Center for Agricultural Economic Research, 1980.

————. "Elements of a Pure Theory of Forecasting and After-Keynesian Macroeconomics." In *Development in an Inflationary World,* pp. 359-373. Edited by M. June Flanders and Assaf Razin. New York: Academic Press, 1981.

————."Functional Forms of Productions: A Survey" and "Estimation of Production Functions: A Survey." Washington, D.C.: Development Research Center of the World Bank, 1973. (Mimeographed.)

————. *Intersectoral Factor Mobility and Agricultural Growth.* Research Report 6. Washington, D.C.: International Food Policy Research Institute, 1979.

————."Long-Run Coefficients and Distributed Lag Analysis: A Reformulation." *Econometrica* 35 (April 1967): 278-293.

————."On the Concept of Non-Significant Functions and its Implications for Regression Analysis." *Journal of Econometrics* (May 1981): 139-149.

Mundlak, Yair and Hellinghausen, R. "Intercountry Comparison of Agricultural Productivity—Another View." *American Journal of Agricultural Economics* 64 (November 1982).

Mundlak, Yair and Mosenson, R. "Two-Sector Model with Generalized Demand." *Metroeconomica* 22 (September-December 1970): 227-258.

Mundlak, Yair and Tropp, Z. "Distortion in the Factor Market and the Short-Run Equilibrium." In *On the Stability of Contemporary Economic Systems,* pp. 130-156. Edited by O. Kyn and W. Schretti. Göttingen: Vanderhoeck and Ruprecht, 1980.

Mundlak, Yair and Volcani, Z. "Correspondence of Efficiency Frontier as a Generalization of the Cost Function." *International Economic Review* 14 (February 1973): 223-233.

Nerlove, Marc. *Distributed Lags and Demand Analysis for Agricultural and Other Commodities.* Washington, D.C.: U.S. Department of Agriculture, 1958.

Nickell, S. J. *The Investment Decisions of Firms.* Cambridge: Cambridge University Press, 1978.

Ras, Norberto and Lewis, Roberto. *El Precio de la Tierra: La Evolución entre los Años 1916 y 1978.* Buenos Aires: Sociedad Rural Argentina, 1980.

Reca, Lucio G. *Argentina: Country Case Study of Agricultural Prices and Subsidies.* World Bank Staff Working Paper No. 386. Washington, D.C.: International Bank for Reconstruction and Development, 1980.

———. "El Aumento de Existencia de Ganado Vacuno en 1971." In *Estudios sobre la Economía Argentina.* Buenos Aires: Instituto de Investigaciones Económicas y Financieras de la CGE, Enero 1972.

Schultz, T. W. *Transforming Traditional Agriculture.* New Haven, Conn.: Yale University Press, 1964.

Solow, Robert M. *Capital Theory and the Rate of Return.* Amsterdam: North Holland Publishing Company, 1963.

———. "Some Recent Developments in the Theory of Production." In *The Theory and Empirical Analysis of Production,* pp. 25-49. Edited by Murray Brown. Studies in Wealth and Income, vol. 31. New York: National Bureau of Economic Research, 1967.

Svensson, L. and Razin. A. *The Terms of Trade, Spending and the Current Account: The Harberger-Larsen-Metzler Effect.* Seminar Paper No. 170. Stockholm: Institute for International Economic Studies, University of Stockholm, 1981.

United Nations Economic Commission for Latin America. *El Desarrollo Económico de la Argentina.* New York: United Nations, June 30, 1958.

Yver, Raúl E. "La Oferta de Ganado Bovino en la Argentina." *Desarrollo Económico* 5 (Abril-Diciembre 1965): 211-230.